The One-Day Marketing Plan

SECOND EDITION

The One-Day Marketing Plan

SECOND EDITION

Organizing and Completing a Plan That Works

Roman G. Hiebing Jr.
& Scott W. Cooper

NTC Business Books
NTC/Contemporary Publishing Group

Library of Congress Cataloging-in-Publication Data

Hiebing, Roman G.
  The one-day marketing plan : organizing and completing the plan
that works / Roman G. Hiebing, Jr., Scott W. Cooper. — 2nd ed.
    p.   cm.
  Earlier ed. published under: The 1-day marketing plan / Roman G.
Hiebing, Jr., Scott W. Cooper. 1992.
    ISBN 0-8442-0247-9 (hardcover)
    ISBN 0-8442-1283-0 (paperback)
  1. Marketing—Management.   2. Strategic planning.   I. Cooper,
Scott W.   II. Hiebing, Roman G.   1-day marketing plan.   III. Title.
HF5415.13.H518   1999
658.8'02—dc21   99-38658
                                                           CIP

Cover design by Jeanette Wojtyla
Cover photograph copyright © PhotoDisc, Inc.

Published by NTC Business Books
A division of NTC/Contemporary Publishing Group, Inc.
4255 West Touhy Avenue, Lincolnwood (Chicago), Illinois 60712-1975 U.S.A.
Printed in the United States of America
International Standard Book Number: 0-8442-0247-9 (hardcover)
International Standard Book Number: 0-8442-1283-0 (paperback)

  4 5 6 7 8 9 0 VLP VLP 0 5 4 3 2

Foreword

Scott and Roman have taken their marketing planning methodology to another level with this new abridged edition, making it not only integrated but interlocking as well. While comprehensive in terms of including all the steps and tasks that must be considered in writing a marketing plan, they have done it in a straightforward, cut-to-the-chase manner that gives you the complete marketing plan with an efficient process that lets you cover all the bases.

They present their methodology without fluff, just a no-nonsense way of, first, doing your homework (what they call a business review) and, then, following the steps from setting the sales objectives to doing an evaluation. And, they found a way to pass on to you their successful planning approach through their ten-step process, which organizes what can be a complicated and sometimes overwhelming task.

Having worked with Scott and Roman for nearly a decade as they give their hands-on, two-day, marketing planning seminar twice a year, I can assure you that they know their stuff and the approach they present here is the way they do it every day with their clients. I can attest that what you are getting is the real thing because seminar attendees from Fortune 500 companies and start-up companies believe the authors' methodology can be successfully applied to their own businesses. Based on my years of consulting, teaching, book authoring, and working with executive marketing programs, I can say that their methodology has and will stand the test of time.

In this fast-paced, rapidly changing business environment that is becoming more competitive every day, this text will be handy for you to use as a template or reference to sort out your business problems and opportunities and to write a successful marketing plan—a plan that you will not only be proud of, but, more important, will also get results.

Sincerely,

Linda Gorchels
Director of Executive Marketing Programs
Executive Education
School of Business
University of Wisconsin—Madison

Brief Table of Contents

Table of Contents

INTRODUCTION

The purpose of this book is to provide you with a practical and proven, step-by-step method for preparing your own marketing plan. This is not a discussion of marketing theory but, rather, a text with real-world answers to help you meet specific marketing challenges head on. The book is organized to keep you focused on addressing the necessary steps in the marketing planning process. It provides a disciplined, integrated, and interlocking approach to marketing planning, a tested approach that will help you develop an effective, target-market-driven marketing plan. You will also find that this book will keep you on track, eliminate wasted effort, and most important, help you implement a planning process that has achieved results for companies both large and small — Fortune 500 companies to entrepreneurial start-ups.

This book focuses primarily on the most important part of any marketing program: the preparation of a marketing plan, not the implementation. It includes helpful planning and research tools; it does not dwell on specific execution.

As marketing practitioners and consultants, we have found that if you take the necessary time and make the required effort to prepare an effective marketing plan, arriving at the actual executional elements is easy, as they flow naturally from the strategic framework of the marketing plan. In our opinion, marketing failures are far too often the result of marketing executions that were *not* rooted in a well-thought-out, disciplined marketing plan.

Disciplined Marketing Planning

The key to writing an effective marketing plan is disciplined marketing planning. However, before defining disciplined marketing planning, it is necessary to first describe what a marketing plan is. A marketing plan is an arranged structure to guide the process of determining the target market for your product or service, detailing the target market's needs and wants, and then fulfilling these needs and wants better than the competition.

Disciplined marketing planning is a comprehensive, sequential, interlocking, step-by-step decision and action process. In using this disciplined approach, you will follow a 10-step, prescribed but logical process that allows you to define issues, answer questions correctly, and make decisions. Each major step (depicted by a box in the chart in Exhibit 1) should be completed before going on to the next. Further, the major steps, such as marketing background and planning, are broken down into individual, ordered steps, providing a clear and efficient road map for preparing an effective marketing plan.

EXHIBIT 1   Ten Steps to Disciplined Marketing Planning

MARKETING BACKGROUND

1 THE BUSINESS REVIEW

Scope
  Company Strengths & Weaknesses • Core Competencies •
  Marketing Capabilities

Product and Market Review
  Company & Product Review • Category & Company Sales •
  Behavior Trends • Pricing • Distribution • Competitive Review

Target Market Effectors
  Consumer/Business-to-Business Targets • Product Awareness &
  Attributes • Trial & Retrial Data

2 PROBLEMS/OPPORTUNITIES

MARKETING PLAN

3 SALES OBJECTIVES

4 TARGET MARKETS AND MARKETING OBJECTIVES

5 PLAN STRATEGIES—Positioning & Marketing

6 COMMUNICATION GOALS

7 TACTICAL MARKETING MIX TOOLS

Product	Distribution	Advertising Media
Branding	Personal Selling/Service	Merchandising
Packaging	Promotion/Events	Publicity
Pricing	Advertising Message	

8 MARKETING PLAN BUDGET AND CALENDAR

9 EXECUTION

10 EVALUATION

The 10-step, disciplined marketing planning method is built on a four-block foundation.

   I. *Marketing background* includes the information base from which the marketing plan is developed.

   II. *Marketing plan* provides direction for the execution in the marketplace.

   III. *Marketing execution* is the actual interaction with the target market and is responsible for generating the projected sales and profits.

   IV. *Marketing evaluation* measures the level of success of the plan's execution and provides learning that is incorporated in the marketing background section developed for the next year's marketing plan.

In this easy-to-use book, each element within the marketing background and plan sections, along with the evaluation process, is discussed in summary fashion. In addition, at the end of each chapter you will find ready-to-use worksheets that will help you organize and present your marketing plan. If you desire a more detailed discussion of the disciplined marketing planning process, along with a unique "Idea Starters by Marketing Situation" grid with over 1,000 different idea combinations, you can refer to the second edition of *The Successful Marketing Plan*, also written by us and published by NTC Business Books.

How to Use This Book in Your Marketing Planning

Before you begin writing your marketing plan, we recommend that you read through the entire book to understand the complete process and all that goes into preparing a comprehensive marketing plan. Next, as you actually prepare your own marketing plan, go through each chapter again and diligently attempt to follow the step-by-step disciplined marketing planning process.

Adapt the Process to Fit Your Business

As you use the disciplined marketing planning process, keep in mind that, while you should understand the basic marketing principles provided throughout this book and follow the recommended methodology, you can adapt the review and planning process to best fit your product or marketing situation. The point to remember is that you want to be open-minded and innovative, but also methodical and consistent as you prepare the marketing background section and write the marketing plan.

Keep Track of Your Ideas

As you go through the whole process, you will come up with all types of ideas for different areas of the marketing plan that might not relate to the specific section of the plan you are currently writing. Don't lose these ideas, because they will be very helpful when you prepare the particular section to which they apply. As you prepare the background section and the marketing plan itself, have separate sheets of paper handy with headings of problems, opportunities, and each step of the marketing plan (including a separate sheet of paper for each marketing mix tool) under which you can jot down relevant ideas as they occur to you. Don't evaluate the worth of each idea as you think of it. Instead, evaluate its application as you actually write the section of the marketing plan to which it pertains.

Apply the Process to Your Own Marketing Situation

Also keep in mind that many of the principles, procedures, and examples provided in this book will have application to your particular marketing situation, even though it has not been written just for your specific product or service. In fact, this book is written for broad application by the marketer of a consumer/package goods product, business-to-business product, service, or retail outlet(s) with a private, public, or nonprofit organization. For simplicity and brevity, however, the word product is usually used throughout this book in generic planning discussions for whatever is to be marketed. When there is specific reference to consumer or business-to-business products, services, or retail, it will be singled out accordingly.

Step 1: The Business Review

MARKETING BACKGROUND

1 THE BUSINESS REVIEW

<u>Scope</u>
Company Strengths & Weaknesses • Core Competencies •
Marketing Capabilities

<u>Product and Market Review</u>
Company & Product Review • Category & Company Sales •
Behavior Trends • Pricing • Distribution • Competitive Review

<u>Target Market Effectors</u>
Consumer/Business-to-Business Targets • Product Awareness &
Attributes • Trial & Retrial Data

2 PROBLEMS/OPPORTUNITIES

MARKETING PLAN

3 SALES OBJECTIVES

4 TARGET MARKETS AND MARKETING OBJECTIVES

5 PLAN STRATEGIES—Positioning & Marketing

6 COMMUNICATION GOALS

7 TACTICAL MARKETING MIX TOOLS

Product	Distribution	Advertising Media
Branding	Personal Selling/Service	Merchandising
Packaging	Promotion/Events	Publicity
Pricing	Advertising Message	

8 MARKETING PLAN BUDGET AND CALENDAR

9 EXECUTION

10 EVALUATION

THE BUSINESS REVIEW: AN OVERVIEW

IN THIS CHAPTER YOU WILL LEARN:

- WHAT TASKS ARE INVOLVED IN ORGANIZING A BUSINESS REVIEW.
- HOW TO DEVELOP AN OUTLINE TO USE AS A ROAD MAP FOR COMPLETING A BUSINESS REVIEW.
- HOW TO USE PRIMARY AND SECONDARY DATA TO COMPLETE A BUSINESS REVIEW, AND WHERE TO FIND THIS INFORMATION.

MARKETING IS A BROAD-BASED DISCIPLINE in which multiple decisions must be made. For each marketing effort, you must determine which potential customer to target, through what specific combination of product features, at what price, through what distribution channels, with what type of product or service, via what type of communication, and at what time of year. Such decisions cannot be made without a systematic review of all known facts. The business review provides these facts so sound decision making can be achieved.

The **business review** is an information decision-making base for the subsequent marketing plan and a rationale for all strategic marketing decisions within the plan. Most important, the business review is a tool that provides for a consumer and customer orientation to your marketing communications.

In this chapter, we present a brief summary of the tasks involved in preparing a business review. These guidelines are intended to help you organize the work you will do to develop your own business review in Chapter 2. We will also discuss the process of conducting the research necessary to develop a thorough business review that will guide your marketing planning efforts.

To save time and help create a more effective database from which to make decisions, follow the suggestions listed here.

- **Make industry category comparisons.** Look not only inward at your company for insights into marketing planning direction, but outside to the industry in which you are competing as well. A business review will help you compare trends within your company to those of your industry category and key competitors. An *industry category* is the overall business in which your organization competes. For example, Sub Zero freezers is in the kitchen appliance industry category, while Hoover vacuums are in the household appliance category.
- **Differentiate between customers and consumers.** To analyze company trends, investigate the behaviors of the company's *customers*—those people who have purchased your company's products. To compare company trends to industry category and key competitor trends, you also need to look at the purchase behavior of

consumers—those people who have purchased the industry category product, whether from your company or a competitor.

- **Complete the business review.** A well-developed business review should be used as a daily reference tool. It also should be updated yearly to reflect the most recent changes in your industry and company. If you are preparing your first business review, don't be overwhelmed. Work now on those sections that most affect your business. Next year, update those sections and work on some of the others for which you don't have time now.

Completing a business review can be more than a one-person job. Request assistance from other people in your organization to help compile the information. The step-by-step process outlined in Chapter 2 allows a marketer to manage the information-gathering process with ease.

Preparing the Business Review

TASK 1
Prepare an Outline

Always start the business review process by developing a written outline that is tailored to your business and industry. It should be as specific as possible, covering each major area of the business review. The outline helps you stay focused and ensures that critical data needed for actionable marketing plans will be obtained in a disciplined and sequential process. It also serves as an overview for more detailed work presented in Chapter 2.

The following is an example of an outline for a business review.

Step 1: Scope
A. Overall strengths and weaknesses of your company
B. Core competencies of your company
C. Marketing capabilities of your company

Step 2: Product and Market Review
A. Corporate philosophy/description of the company
    1. Corporate goals and objectives
    2. General company history
    3. Organizational chart
B. Product analysis
    1. Identification of products sold by both the industry category and by your company
    2. Description of company or product strengths and weaknesses
    3. Competitive strengths and weaknesses
    4. Product trends
C. Category and company sales trends
    1. Sales/transactions/profit analysis
        a) Industry category sales
        b) Company sales
            1) Compared to overall industry
            2) Compared to major competitors
        c) Market share
        d) Store-for-store (for retailers)
        e) Seasonality
        f) Sales by geographic territory

D. Consumer behavior trends
1. Demographic trends
2. Geographic trends
3. Social/consumer trends
4. Technological trends
5. Media viewing trends
E. Distribution
1. Retail
    a) Channel type/trends
    b) Geography
    c) Penetration
2. Packaged goods
    a) Channel types/trends
    b) Market coverage/all commodity volume percentage
    c) Shelf space
    d) Geography
    e) Sales method
3. Business-to-business
    a) Channel type/trends
    b) Geography
    c) Personal selling method
4. Service firms
    a) Type of office
    b) Geography
    c) Penetration
5. Distribution strengths and weaknesses
F. Pricing review
1. Price of your product(s) relative to the industry or competition
2. Distribution of sales by price point relative to the competition
3. Price elasticity of your product
4. Cost structure
5. Company pricing strengths and weaknesses
G. Competitive review
1. Competitive review of your product and the key competition
2. Summary of strengths and weaknesses
    a) Market share
    b) Target market
    c) Marketing objectives/strategies
    d) Positioning
    e) Product/branding/packaging
    f) Pricing
    g) Distribution
    h) Personal selling
    i) Customer service
    j) Promotion
    k) Advertising
    l) Media
    m) Merchandising
    n) Publicity
    o) Testing/marketing research and development
    p) Summary of strengths and weaknesses

Step 3: Target Market Effectors
A. Target market: Consumer
    1. Volume versus concentration
    2. Demographic measures: Industry category versus company target market
    3. Customer tenure segmentation
    4. Demographic segmentation (description and size)
        a) Sex
        b) Age
        c) Income
        d) Education
        e) Occupation
        f) Family/household size
        g) Region/geography
    5. Product usage segmentation
    6. Psychographic/lifestyle segmentation
    7. Attribute segmentation
    8. Heavy-user segmentation
B. Target market: Business-to-business
    1. Standard Industrial Classification (SIC) segmentation
    2. Other methods of segmenting
        a) Dollar size segmentation
        b) Employee size segmentation
        c) Heavy usage segmentation
        d) Product application/use segmentation
        e) Organizational structure segmentation
        f) New versus repeat buyer segmentation
        g) Geographic location segmentation
        h) Decision maker and influencer segmentation
        i) Channel use segmentation
C. Awareness
    1. Unaided awareness (first mention and total awareness)
    2. Aided awareness
    3. Awareness by segments
D. Product attributes
    1. Attribute importance by segment
    2. Attribute ranking by segment
    3. Product life cycle
        a) Introduction
        b) Growth
        c) Maturity
E. Trial behavior
    1. Buying habits
    2. Purchase rates of the industry product category and your company's product
      by geographic markets
        a) Category Development Index (CDI)
        b) Brand Development Index (BDI)
    3. Trading areas
    4. Brand loyalty
F. Retrial behavior
    1. Trial to retrial behavior

TASK 2	List questions that need to be answered for each section of the business
Develop Questions	review outline. The questions will provide direction in determining what specific information you need to accumulate.

TASK 3	Develop data charts with headings to help structure your search for rele-
Develop Data Charts	vant information. When completed, the charts should enable you to answer the major questions pertaining to each section of the business review outline.

Organize the headings and columns of the charts in order to determine what information needs to be found prior to the data search. This forces you to look for data and numbers that will provide meaningful information. Remember, if you look for data before developing your charts, you may tend to construct the charts around what is easy to find, not what should be found.

TASK 4	Always develop charts that have reference points for comparison so that
Develop Reference Points for Comparison	the data are actionable. For example, when you analyze sales growth for your company, compare this against the sales growth for the industry. In this manner, the company's sales growth can be judged against a reference point. A business review should always provide reference points of com-

parison within the company (past year trends), between the company and the industry category, and between the company and its key competitors. Whenever possible, include five-year trend information so that the current year's performance can be judged relative to past years' performance.

The following comparison methods can be used to collect reference point data. They are applicable throughout the business review.

- **Five-year trends.** Review trends when analyzing marketing data. This allows you to determine not only increases and decreases from year to year, but also to see shifts in the marketplace over time. For example, while any given product or target market segment may account for the greatest sales volume in one year, a review of five years' worth of data might show that the leader has had flat sales and that another product or target segment will soon dominate the category if the trends continue.
- **Trends within your company.** What customer segment accounts for the most volume? Has this same segment grown, flattened, or declined in volume over the past five years? Is there another company segment that is growing faster and will be in the dominant target market in the future? If your organization is large, it is also insightful to compare geographic regions or segments of the company to the overall company system. This regional review is helpful when determining different local target markets or marketing objectives versus company system target markets or marketing objectives.
- **Company-to-company comparisons.** It is also important to compare the company to the industry category. Are the target markets responsible for the most company product volume the same target markets responsible for the most industry category volume? Is your company's sales trending comparable, above, or below the industry category across products with the highest sales volume, transaction volume, or profit potential? What are your company's market share trends (share of sales or transaction volume relative to the industry) overall and among various target market segments?
- **Competitive comparisons.** Take into consideration the competitive environment and any changes and/or trends that will make it harder or easier to capture market

share against identified target market segments. For example, has there been an increase in the total number of competitors? Has a competitor developed a product or manufacturing innovation resulting in a price or product attribute advantage?

- **Benchmarking.** Although the concept of *benchmarking*, that is, comparing relative points of data, started in the retail industry, its principles can be applied to all business types—retail, package goods, service, and business-to-business. Benchmarking is particularly successful in businesses that have multiple locations or geographic markets. The idea is to find departments, product lines, stores, or markets with similar characteristics, such as product mix and sales potential, and then compare results. This way, sales by store, sales by product, sales by target market, customer counts, sales per transaction, purchase ratios, profits, and expenses can be compared. With this benchmark across a marketer's system, strong and weak performances can be identified and management can take necessary actions based upon exceptions to the average.

In summary, providing comparisons within your company and comparing your company to the industry category allows you to:

1. Identify products and/or target markets that are performing below or above the company average, thus providing insight to further exploit strengths or solve weaknesses.
2. Identify shifts in target market and product trends within the industry.
3. Compare, or benchmark, your firm to your industry, thus providing insight into how your company is actually performing compared with the competition.

| **TASK 5**
Conduct Data Search | Institute a disciplined data search using the source provided later in this chapter. Stay focused on what needs to be found by constantly reviewing your outline. This will allow you to feel confident that you have compiled all of the existing data necessary to complete your charts. |

| **TASK 6**
Write Summary Statements | After the charts have been completed, write brief statements summarizing the major findings and answering the questions you developed in Task 2. Include a summary rationale when needed. Keep the summary objective by strictly reporting the findings; don't provide solutions at this point. |

The business review is not for developing objectives and strategies; it is for providing facts from which to develop a marketing plan and the supporting rationale. However, as mentioned in the introduction, as you prepare your business review, jot down your thoughts and ideas for potential use later when writing your marketing plan.

| **TASK 7**
Organize the Business Review | The sections of the final written business review should follow the same sequence as the steps developed in your outline. Each section should include summary statements followed by completed, detailed data charts. |

| **TASK 8**
Write the Business Review | Finally, write the marketing background and plan in the third person, being as objective as possible. Do not interject personal feelings that cannot be documented by fact. Write in a very clear, concise manner so there can be no misinterpretation of what is presented. Also, don't assume that everyone who reads the plan will have the same base of information as |

the writer. Include all available information pertinent to the issues being discussed so everyone reading the plan will have the same frame of reference.

Conducting Research

Data for your business review can be obtained through primary and/or secondary research. **Primary research** is original research gathered specifically to answer the question at hand. **Secondary research**, on the other hand, is existing information, usually gathered by an outside source. If you employ a research firm or marketing communications firm that conducts research, or have an in-house research department, then primary research specific to your needs can be obtained fairly easily. If you do not have access to a professional researcher, however, secondary research will be sufficient in preparing a marketing database and business review.

PRIMARY RESEARCH

Original research compiled to meet your specific data requirements is broken down into two categories, quantitative research and qualitative research.

Quantitative Research

Quantitative data and information are usually obtained through surveys, with results gathered from a representative random sample of a given universe. The samples are large enough to make inferences that are statistically significant. We refer to two types of quantitative research methods most often throughout this book. One is *customer-based research*, which provides information about a company's own customers. The other is *market-wide research*, which is used to provide information about the overall industry category user/purchaser base. The most common types of quantitative research are tracking studies where the awareness, attitudes, and behavior of both customers and noncustomers are analyzed on a yearly or semiyearly basis.

Qualitative Research

Research methods that do not statistically represent the target market universe provide qualitative data. Qualitative research typically involves small groups of consumers, such as focus groups, who are asked to provide insights into their likes and dislikes of a particular product, and why and how they purchase or use one type of product versus another. Qualitative research also is used to gain insights into the strengths and weaknesses of advertising and other forms of communication.

Qualitative research often is used to add depth and richness to quantitative findings. For example, quantitative research may determine that a company has a perceived customer service problem relative to the competition. Qualitative research can be used to help further explain what consumers feel customer service entails in the company's particular industry and what specifically is lacking in the company's customer service as compared to that of other companies.

Qualitative research commonly is used in what is referred to as "exploratory research," in which the facts and implications of a particular situation or marketing problem are explored. Such exploration is useful prior to quantitative research, as it can help determine the key issues to include in the study. Particularly if there has been no previous research, a company may want to utilize a focus group to provide added insights into consumer thinking prior to formulating a quantitative study. The information and insights gained from initial qualitative research can then be verified through quantitative, statistical research. Qualitative exploratory research also can be used following a quantitative study to further explore issues brought up in the quantitative research.

Finally, a word of caution: Used by itself, qualitative research can be very misleading because it is not statistically based; a roomful of 10 people is often a poor representation of what the marketplace really thinks. Qualitative research is most valuable when used to enrich quantitatively defined observations.

SECONDARY RESEARCH

Secondary research, which may also be quantitative or qualitative, is not specifically compiled for your company; it is existing information that is available through outside sources. An example of a secondary research source is census information. Just as with primary research, combining this type of secondary research information with your company's data will allow you to develop insights into your customers, your market, and the problems and opportunities facing your company. The only difference is that primary research is conducted to answer specific questions a company might have. To answer these questions with secondary research you may have to dig a little more and be willing to analyze multiple studies to find your answers. Even then, you may not be able to answer all of your questions, so you will have to rely on judgment. Of course, secondary research is also typically less expensive than primary research. In most cases, a mix of both primary and secondary research is appropriate. A secondary search should be completed first, with primary research conducted to fill the voids of the existing data where possible.

Common Sources of Secondary Information

The following are commonly used sources of information available to most any marketer. They will help you obtain the necessary data to complete the business review portion of your marketing plan. Many of these sources can be found in your local library or on-line, can be obtained for free, or can be purchased at a reasonable cost. This is by no means an exhaustive list, but it will help you get started.

A.C. Nielsen Company
media and retail measurement, consumer panels, test market profiles
212/707-7500
http://www.acnielsen.com

Claritas, Inc.
PRIZM market segmentation system
800/234-5973
http://www.claritas.com

Gale Research Company
myriad research directories
248/699-4253
http://www.gale.com

IPSOS-ASI
advertising research, copy testing, brand equity
203/328-7000
http://www.advertisingresearch.com

Mediamark Research, Inc. (MRI)
demographics, market size, and product user characteristics
212/599-0444
http://www.mediamark.com

continued

Nielsen Media Research

television ratings and audience research
212/708-7795
http://www.nielsenmedia.com

Scarborough

local market demographics/product usage profiles and media usage reports
212/789-3560
http://www.scarborough.com

Standard Rate and Data Service (SRDS)

media buying and print production information
800/851-7737
http://www.srds.com

SRI International

VALS and VALS II lifestyle measurement programs
415/859-3032
http://www.sri.com

U.S. Census Bureau

http://www.census.gov

To find additional information sources that pertain to your specific industry, we recommend the following methodology:

1. Go through the Standard Rate and Data Service directory and write down all trade and consumer publications pertaining to your industry.
2. Contact each trade publication, talk to the research department, and ask what information is available. Many times publications' research departments are aware of other studies that may help you.
3. Ask your university or local library to do a subject search for you, pulling all available reference material.
4. Dig, dig, and dig some more.

INDEXING

Indexing, used extensively in the business review, is a process that presents a number or group of numbers in relation to an average, or base. It is a method of showing a relationship between two sets of numbers or percentages. Indexing is based upon an average of 100. Anything over 100 means the index represents something greater than the average; anything below 100 is less than the average.

When indexing, a base number is established and all other numbers are compared to it. For example, assume 60 percent of the population owns a home, and home ownership is further broken down by age category, as shown in Exhibit 1.1. Because 60 percent is the average percentage of home ownership, it becomes the base number from which to measure any subset of the population. For example, among 18–24-year-olds, only 20 percent own homes, so 20/60 = 0.33. (For purposes of clarity and easier communications, the decimal is then

EXHIBIT 1.1	Indexing Example	
Age Category	**Home Ownership***	**Index**
18–24	20%	33
25–34	48	80
35–44	60	100
45–54	74	123
55–64	70	117
65–74	50	83
Average—all ages	60	100

*These numbers are used only for example. They do not reflect current home ownership rates.

multiplied by 100 to give a round number—0.33×100 = an index of 33. From this point on in the book we will not explicitly show the multiplication by 100.) Thirty-three is substantially below 100; thus, 18–24-year-olds own homes at one-third the average across all ages.

In another example, 30 percent of a national company's consumers live in Chicago. With that, you would expect them to consume 30 percent of the product (30/3 = an index of 100, or average). But if Chicago consumers consume 60 percent of the company's product, they are consuming at a rate of 60 percent, divided by the base of 30 percent, for an index of 200. Thus, the Chicago market would compare at twice the national average, or 100 points above the expected consumption pattern.

We usually consider an index meaningful if it is 100 ± 10. In other words, we look for number 110 and above or 90 and below. If all age groups index between 95 and 105 in terms of consumption, we determine that our target market is flat across all age groups. However, if the 25–34 and 35–44 age groups indexed at 115 and 180, respectively, and all other age groups were at or below average (or below 100), then we would determine that those two age groups consumed at significantly higher levels.

Step 1: The Business Review

MARKETING BACKGROUND

1 THE BUSINESS REVIEW

Scope
Company Strengths & Weaknesses • Core Competencies •
Marketing Capabilities

Product and Market Review
Company & Product Review • Category & Company Sales •
Behavior Trends • Pricing • Distribution • Competitive Review

Target Market Effectors
Consumer/Business-to-Business Targets • Product Awareness &
Attributes • Trial & Retrial Data

2 PROBLEMS/OPPORTUNITIES

MARKETING PLAN

3 SALES OBJECTIVES

4 TARGET MARKETS AND MARKETING OBJECTIVES

5 PLAN STRATEGIES—Positioning & Marketing

6 COMMUNICATION GOALS

7 TACTICAL MARKETING MIX TOOLS

Product	Distribution	Advertising Media
Branding	Personal Selling/Service	Merchandising
Packaging	Promotion/Events	Publicity
Pricing	Advertising Message	

8 MARKETING PLAN BUDGET AND CALENDAR

9 EXECUTION

10 EVALUATION

PREPARING A BUSINESS REVIEW

2

IN THIS CHAPTER YOU WILL LEARN:

- THE DATA REQUIREMENTS AND THE MATERIALS THAT NEED TO BE ANALYZED IN EACH OF THE THREE BUSINESS REVIEW STEPS.
- THE KEY MARKETING ISSUES AND QUESTIONS THAT NEED TO BE ANSWERED IN EACH STEP OF THE BUSINESS REVIEW.
- HOW TO ORGANIZE YOUR OWN COMPANY'S INFORMATION IN A LOGICAL MANNER.

THE BUSINESS REVIEW IS FUNDAMENTAL to the success of your marketing plan. Good data, organized in a meaningful and disciplined manner, will provide you with tremendous insights into your target customers and their purchase behavior. As outlined in this chapter, the business review process provides for direct links from the data you organize here to the decisions made later in the marketing plan.

The preparation of a business review involves three broad steps: scope, product and market review, and target market effectors. In this chapter, we will provide the following information for each step:

1. General *background discussions* that detail each area covered in the step.
2. *Marketing questions* that must be answered in order to provide an adequate quantitative database for each step.
3. *Charts and worksheets* to help you organize your information in a disciplined, efficient manner, so you will be able to answer the marketing questions accurately. Example charts are presented in the text, and worksheets are provided at the end of this chapter to help you organize your own data search.

Step 1: Scope

The first step in developing a business review is to determine the overall scope of your organization. The purpose of the scope section is to:

- Define what business your organization is in and the strategic leverage it will use to compete.
- Define product areas in which the organization will grow and concentrate its business efforts.
- Help shape the positioning, marketing strategies, and communications sections you develop later in the marketing plan.
- Drive where the organization seeks growth and where it does not. In other words, it determines the boundaries of the business review.

A word of warning: The business scope is different from the communication positioning you will develop later in the plan. Scope answers the question, "What business are we in?" *Communication positioning*, on the other hand, defines the overriding benefit that makes your organization's product desirable to the marketplace. That benefit might be the best value, some service attribute, business relationships, product availability, a strong local sales force, or a superior product attribute such as softness, value, or quality. Once you have determined your business's scope, you will have a greater degree of focus in terms of developing the rest of your business review. Without answering this question, a business review can become unnecessarily broad, unfocused, and inefficient in terms of gathering data. Don't make the mistake of thinking your business scope is defined by your communication positioning.

As a case in point, the American Automobile Association told us their business was peace of mind. But peace of mind is a communication positioning, not a business scope, and can pertain to any number of combinations of businesses—insurance, securities, moving companies, travel agencies, automobile clubs, and many more. Going through the scope process in the business review, AAA was able to define their business as a membership travel organization.

TASK 1 *Provide an Overview of Company Strengths and Weaknesses*	First, you need to identify your company's strengths and weaknesses across target market needs, product, operations, distribution, pricing, and communication programs. A *strength* is any capability or resource the organization has that could be used to improve its competitive position (share of market or size of market) or financial performance. A *weakness* is any capability or resource that may cause the organization to have a weaker competitive position or poorer financial performance.

Worksheets designed to help you determine your company's strengths and weaknesses are provided at the end of this chapter.

Questions to Be Addressed

List your organization's strengths and weaknesses across the following categories:
- What are your company's advantages as they relate to *target market needs, wants, and consumption trends?*
- What are its advantages due to the *value* the organization brings the target markets?
- What are its *product and technological advantages* relative to target market needs?
- What are its advantages due to *operational efficiencies* that make dealing with the organization a superior experience for the customer?
- What are the *distribution efficiencies* or advantages that make the organization unique?
- What *pricing advantages* can the organization offer the customer?
- What are your company's *promotion/marketing communication advantages* over the competition?

TASK 2 *Identify the Organization's Core Competencies*	*Core competencies* represent the consolidation of firm-wide technologies and skills into a coherent thrust. Core competencies must: (1) make a significant contribution to the perceived customer benefit of the product and (2) be difficult for competitors to imitate. They are the firm's core reason for being. A core competency becomes the focus of an organization relative to both the target market and the competition, enabled by underlying strengths of

the organization in functional areas. The key to strategic management can be the management of core competencies rather than business units. These are found by grouping together similar strengths or by identifying underlying reasons for a particular strength.

Examples of AAA's core competencies were the organization's full-service travel-related services under one roof—from travel packages, to travel information, to travel insurance—and the extensive branch system across the country. The branches provide *access* to millions of AAA members, and the size of the membership provides travel purchasing clout for AAA.

A worksheet designed to help you determine your company's core competencies is provided at the end of this chapter.

QUESTIONS TO BE ADDRESSED

- Which of your company's strengths or underlying reason for a particular strength make a significant contribution to the perceived customer benefit of the end product and which of those are difficult for competitors to imitate?

TASK 3

Identify the Organization's Marketing Capabilities

Marketing capabilities are a second tier of scope factors below the core competencies. Marketing capabilities are those characteristics that specifically link your business to the consumer, such as high awareness, strong distribution capabilities, superior customer service ability, or a large customer base. Some businesses do not have a core competency and must therefore focus on marketing capabilities when developing scope. For example, a company may have high awareness for a specific category of products. While this is not an advantage that can't be duplicated (a competitor with a significantly larger communications budget could, over time, dominate awareness), such a marketing capability is a significant factor in choosing the business focus or scope.

A worksheet designed to help you identify your company's marketing capabilities is provided at the end of this chapter.

QUESTIONS TO BE ADDRESSED

- What are your firm's marketing capabilities?

    Examples:

    — Highly regarded brand name.
    — Large membership.
    — National organization with local presence.
    — Ability to relate one-on-one with members via branches, the Internet, or the sales organization.
    — Strong retention.
    — Regularly published magazine for customers.

TASK 4

Develop Potential Business Scope Options

Based upon your work so far, develop alternative scope options. For example, after reviewing strengths and weaknesses, core competencies, and marketing capabilities, a lighting manufacturer we worked with considered the scope options for their business as an ambient lighting firm, a direct lighting firm, or an indirect lighting firm. Each of the three scopes had a different competitive set and different product ramifications, along with different channel and distribution structures. Until we could come to a conclusion as to this firm's scope, we could not proceed, as we really could not define which business the firm was in and thus which *business category* to review.

A worksheet designed to help you develop your business scope options is provided at the end of this chapter.

TASK 5

Analyze Your Options

To complete the analysis of the scope options you developed in Task 4, the following steps need to be accomplished:

1. For each scope positioning option, list what is needed for your organization to succeed.
2. Determine whether each need fits a strength or is a weakness of your organization.
3. Identify the core competency needed to succeed with each scope option. Then determine if the core competency needed matches your organization's core competency.

4. Identify the market capabilities needed to succeed with each scope option. Then determine if the marketing capabilities needed match your organization's marketing capabilities.
5. Analyze the competitive set with each scope option. List the strengths and weaknesses of each competitor as they pertain to the core competencies and marketing capabilities needed to succeed. Compare the competitors to your company.
6. Determine the risks and opportunities for each strategic positioning. Each strategic positioning will have upsides and downsides to it, as positioning by its very nature is the art of sacrifice. Your job here is to look at both the risks (downsides) and the opportunities (upsides) of each potential positioning.

Worksheets designed to help your scope options are provided at the end of this chapter.

QUESTIONS TO BE ADDRESSED

- What are the business scope options for your firm?
- What would be needed for your organization to succeed with each scope option?
- Is what is needed a strength or weakness of your organization?
- What is the core competency needed to succeed with each strategic scope option?
- Does the core competency needed for each option's success match your core competencies?
- What are the marketing capabilities needed to succeed with each scope option?
- Do your company's marketing capabilities match those needed to succeed for any of the options?
- What is the competitive set with each scope option? What are the strengths and weaknesses of your competitors as they pertain to the core competencies and marketing capabilities needed to succeed?
- What are the risks and opportunities for each scope option?

Step 2: Product and Market Review

The second step in the business review process is the *product and market review*. This provides the first level of insight into your customers' and prospective customers' behaviors, needs, and wants. The focus of this section is on determining these customer and consumer insights by reviewing what products are being consumed, through which distribution channels, and at what prices, both in terms of your company and for the wider competitive category. A review of consumer behavior trends affecting consumption and sales is also performed. Before you get to specifics, however, you must first look at your company's overall philosophy, goals, and objectives; history; and organizational structure.

TASK 1

Describe Corporate Philosophy/ Description of the Company

Different companies are unique in the ways they do business, their historical backgrounds, and their organizational structures—all of which have some level of impact on the development of a marketing plan. Before you begin your product and market review, it is important to describe briefly predetermined corporate and company-wide objectives, pertinent company history, and current organizational parameters. By considering the culture and aspirations of the organization prior to writing the marketing plan, you stand a better chance of developing a plan that will be implemented effectively throughout the organization.

Corporate Goals and Objectives

The first step in this task is to describe your organization's long- and short-term goals, missions, and objectives. Also consider the company's budget and profit contributions, as well as its overriding philosophy.

A worksheet designed to help you describe your company and its philosophy is located at the end of this chapter.

Questions to Be Addressed

- What are the long-term and short-term goals, mission, and objectives of the company? Are there existing sales goals, profit goals, and marketing expectations? If so, what are they?
- What is the operating budget for the company? What are the margins and planned profit contributions of each product?
- Is there a corporate philosophy on how to do business? What are the principles of the business in regard to working with customers, developing and selling product, and addressing internal management?

General Company History

This section can provide many insights into the inherent drama of your industry and company. Include a historical and evolutionary perspective of your company, and summarize your company's results to date. Understanding the history of the company helps in understanding why certain strategies have evolved. More important, this knowledge can be used later in the positioning and communications portions of the plan.

Along with a review of the company from a historical perspective, an analysis of future trends also serves to establish guidelines. It helps to understand both where a company has been and what its potential may be before you develop plans for its future. This trend analysis can provide insight as to what the future may hold in terms of marketing, operations, and technological innovation for your company and the total industry or product category.

Questions to Be Addressed

- What is the history of your industry? Why was it started, how did it grow, and why is it successful?
- How did the company get into the market for the particular product around which this plan is based? What has the company's approach to this business been historically? How has the company marketed previously?
- What have been the most significant changes to your company and/or the industry in which your company competes over the past five, 10, or 20 years?
- What are the critical strategies that have driven your company?
- What have been your company's biggest mistakes?
- What does your company want to be known for? What are you best at? Why do consumers purchase from you?
- Where has your company succeeded and failed? Why?
- What future trends (marketing, product, technological, operations, distribution) will affect your company's performance?

Organizational Structure

Organizational structure tells a great deal about a company and its chance for successful marketing. Study your company's organizational chart, specifically as relates to the marketing department. Is the marketing department set up to develop and implement marketing plans efficiently? Where does your marketing department fit in relation to the rest of the business? Who makes the final decisions regarding marketing direction or the company's marketing policies?

It is extremely important that you understand how the marketing department interfaces with the rest of the organization. Our feeling is that all areas of the marketing mix should be the direct responsibility of the VP marketing director, brand manager, or target market director, and that this person should report directly to the president of the company. This means that the marketing director has decision-making impact on the sales, product, pricing, distribution, advertising, media, promotion, publicity, and merchandising functions. If that is not the case, there is less chance for cohesive implementation of the marketing plan; marketing strategies that should affect sales, product, pricing, and advertising might be interpreted and executed differently. This diminishes the synergistic effect of the marketing tools working together to achieve the company-wide sales and marketing objectives established in the marketing plan.

QUESTIONS TO BE ADDRESSED

- Is your marketing department sufficiently organized to develop and execute a disciplined marketing plan? Do you have enough resources to plan, implement, and analyze results?
- To what degree is the company committed to marketing? Where does marketing fit in your overall organizational structure? Do you have a marketing director? Does she or he report directly to the president?
- Does your marketing department have the ability to communicate with and have a positive impact on other departments within the company?
- Does your marketing department have influence over all the marketing tools and the decisions made regarding sales, product, pricing, distribution, advertising, media, promotion, publicity, and merchandising?
- Is the company driven by operations, finance, merchandise, product, sales, or marketing? In other words, what area of the company is most responsible for the company's success? Will that be true in the future? How does the marketing department fit in? How will this affect your ability to develop and implement effective marketing plans?

TASK 2
Analyze the Product

An analysis of the product is important at this time, as it will be the first key in determining consumer behavior. In this Product and Market Review, we'll look at product sales as an initial measure of customer and consumer demand. Later, in the Target Market Effectors step, we will further analyze customer and consumer segments of products with the greatest sales or most significant potential for sales growth in the future. A worksheet designed to help you analyze your product is located at the end of this chapter.

Products Within Determined Scope of Business

In Step 1, you determined or reviewed the scope of your business. Now list the products sold in the industry category and the products sold by your company under the determined scope. For example, if you determined that the scope of your business is insurance, you would list the different insurance products sold in the industry (life, auto, home, etc.). You would then list the insurance products your company currently sells. This activity prevents you from defining the market by your company's experience; rather, you analyze the whole range of competitive product offerings from a sales standpoint, including the subset that is your company's products.

QUESTIONS TO BE ADDRESSED

- What are the products sold in the industry category(ies) within the scope of your business?

- What products does your company sell under each industry category within the scope of your business?

Company Products: History, Strengths, and Weaknesses

Now that the products that fit within the scope of your marketing plan have been identified—both from an industry and company standpoint—list those products and determine their strengths and weaknesses relative to the competition. This step is sometimes a difficult one to communicate because many companies, particularly service firms, don't think in terms of products but rather in terms of the whole company. For example, accounting firms think they offer accounting—but in reality their customers are buying audits, year-end reviews, estate planning, business compensation consulting, etc. No one buys "accounting"; they buy accounting products or individual services. It is important to break the business down into these tangible products so you can start to determine what customers are really buying.

QUESTIONS TO BE ADDRESSED
- How would you describe your company's products or services? What benefit do they provide your customer?
- Does your company provide groupings of products or services that are used together, in the same manner or at the same time, by your customer or their end customer?
- Do the products your company manufactures or sells have any potential manufacturing or service/operational problems? Are specialized parts, labor, or manufacturing processes necessary? Are the products vulnerable to shortages or other consumer, environmental, technological, or economic factors? If so, how?
- What are your products' strengths?
- What are your products' weaknesses?
- What is the history of your products? Have they always been successful? Why were they first marketed? Over the years, how have your products changed?
- What are the plans for growth and expansion among new product categories?

Competitive Product Strengths and Weaknesses

Now describe your competitors' strengths and weaknesses as they relate to your products. Describe the history of your competitors' products. Identify any plans you are aware of for growth and expansion among current lines or for growth plans into new product categories.

QUESTIONS TO BE ADDRESSED
- Describe your competitors' products or services. What benefit do they provide your customer?
- What are your competitors' products' strengths?
- What are your competitors' products' weaknesses?
- Do your competitors' products have any potential manufacturing, environmental, technological, or economic constraints that your product does not have?
- What are the growth and expansion plans for your competitors' products?

Product Trends

Highlight trends within your product category in terms of innovation, technological advantages, manufacturing process, appearance, how the product is used by the consumer, distribution, pricing, and marketing. For example, the trend toward convenience and time-saving measures will affect banks and the way they market to their customers. Instant cash machines, banking by Internet, the use of check and debit cards, extended lobby hours, instant loan programs, and many more innovations have been developed and widely used based upon consumers' needs for convenience or time-saving measures.

QUESTIONS TO BE ADDRESSED

- How has your product category done in terms of growth?
- What are the trends over the past five years in terms of product innovation, marketing, distribution, pricing, and merchandising?
- What are the product trends in terms of appearance and technological and manufacturing capabilities?
- Are there product usage or consumer trends that might drive changes in the future?

TASK 3

Analyze Category and Company Sales Trends

Having looked at the big picture, you can now begin to focus in on your products and markets. We start with an analysis of sales data.

The sales analysis gives you a broad indicator of consumer demand. It allows you to establish a clear picture of the sales trends for the industry, your company and its products, and competitors and their products. By comparing these data, you may find that the industry category is doing well yet the company is doing poorly. Conversely, you may find that the company is doing well even though industry category growth is minimal or declining. Each situation would mean taking vastly different directions in the development of a marketing plan.

As a case in point, we once looked at the paper napkin industry for Fort James. We found that while the company dominated the printed lunch napkin category (with its Mardi Gras brand), it had little presence in luncheon white or dinner napkins. In looking at sales trends, we learned that luncheon napkins sales led the category in terms of both units and dollar volume. This data matched Fort James's strengths; however, dinner napkins, though not the dominant category, had shown double-digit increases in sales over a five-year period. Although this information by itself does not necessarily drive any one decision, we recognized it as an area worth investigating for future consideration as a growth category.

Exhibits 2.1 through 2.4 are provided to acquaint you with how sales analysis data can relate with each other and to point out general and specific trends. Duplicate worksheets that can be customized for your own use are provided at the end of the chapter.

QUESTIONS TO BE ADDRESSED

INDUSTRY CATEGORY SALES

- Review the industry category products listed earlier in Task 2. Which products have the highest industry category
    - —sales?
    - —growth rates?
    - —profit margins and/or total contributions to profits?
    - —total number of transactions or highest purchase rates?
- If your industry category is made up of multiple products, what is the sales percentage of the total industry category of each product?
- Is the overall industry product category strong? Is it growing or declining? What are industry sales, transactions, and profit margins for the past five years? What is the percent increase over that period?

COMPANY SALES

- Review the company products listed earlier in Task 2. Which products have the highest company

EXHIBIT 2.1   Industry Sales Compared to Company Sales

Year	Total Industry Sales (M)	Change	Total Company Sales (M)	Change	Your Company's Market Share
1995	$100,000	—%	$4,500	—%	4.5%
1996	110,000	10*	5,500	22*	5.0*
1997	120,000	9	7,000	27	5.8
1998	130,000	8	8,000	14	6.2
1999	150,000	15	9,000	13	6.0

Estimated Sales by Competitor	Sales 1999 (M)	Market Share	Sales 1998 (M)	Market Share	Sales 1997 (M)	Market Share	Sales 1996 (M)	Market Share	Sales 1995 (M)	Market Share
Competitor A	$6,500	6.5%	$7,500	6.8%	$9,500	7.9%	$11,000	8.5%	$12,000	8.0%
Competitor B	3,000	3.0	4,000	3.6	7,000	5.8	8,000	6.2	9,000	6.0
Competitor C	7,500	7.5	8,000	7.3	9,000	7.5	10,000	7.7	10,000	6.7
Total Market Sales		100.0%		100.0%		100.0%		100.0%		100.0%

*Note that company performance is over twice that of the industry and thus market share is increasing.

EXHIBIT 2.2   Store-for-Store Sales

Market	Sales Volume (M)	Change from Previous Year	Number of Stores	Per Store Average (M)	Change from Previous Year	Per Store Average Indexed to System Average ($569.2M)
Tulsa	$2,202.7	+12%	2	$1,001.4	+12%	$176
Minneapolis	6,147.5	+54*	8	768.4	+35*	135†
Milwaukee						
Atlanta						
Tampa						

*The percent change for total sales volume is higher than per store average volume due to a decrease in per store averages and an addition of stores. For example, this would be evident if there were a chart showing seven stores versus eight in the Minneapolis market the previous year.
†Minneapolis stores do 35 points better on a per store basis than the system average, which is $569.2M.
Break-even per store average for total system: $500,000. (Include this figure as another comparison point to be utilized when analyzing market performance.)
Note: Make sure your year-to-year analysis of per store averages includes comparable stores that have been open for the full year.

    —sales?
    —growth rates?
    —profit margins and/or total contributions to profits?
    —total number of transactions or highest purchase rates?
- What are the total company sales, transactions, and profit levels for the past five years? What has been the growth rate over the past five years?
- Do your high-volume products correlate to the industry's high-volume products? If not, why not?

EXHIBIT 2.3   Sales Seasonality by Month

Month	Company Percent of Sales	Company Index to Average (8.33)	Industry Percent of Sales	Industry Index to Average (8.33)
January	10%*	120*	8%*	96*
February	7	84	7	100
March	5	60	9	56
April				
May				
June				
July				
August				
September				
October				
November				
December				

*10 percent of the company's sales occur in January. If sales are equal each month, 8.33 percent of the sales would occur in January (10/8.33 = 120); January was above average for sales. The industry index of 96 was slightly below average, demonstrating that company sales for the month of January are substantially above the norm when compared to industry sales. Another way to do this would be to take *total* sales and divide by 12 to get an average. Use this average as the base and divide each month's sales by the base to get an index.

EXHIBIT 2.4   Brand Seasonality by Month

| | Base* | November | | December | | Etc. |
		Percent of Total Dollars	Index to Total Year	Percent of Total Dollars	Index to Total Year	
Company Brand X	38.2%*	41.9%*	110*			
Company Brand Y	18.5	22.8	123			
Company Brand Z	6.2	11.2	181			

Base equals total figures for the year. Brand X accounts for 38.2 percent of the total company business.
*Brand X accounts for 38.2 percent of the sales volume during the year. During November, Brand X accounts for 41.9 percent (41.9 percent/38.2 percent = 110). This means that Brand X does better than it normally does throughout the year during the month of November, while accounting for 41.9 percent of the company's total business.

- What is the market share for your total company sales within your industry category? Have you been gaining or losing share over the past five years?
- What is the market share for your company's high-volume, high-profit-margin, and high-growth products? Are you gaining or losing market share? Why?
- Are market sales likely to expand or shrink in the next two, five, or 10 years? Why? How will this affect your company?
- What competitors have gained or lost market share? Why?

STORE-FOR-STORE SALES FOR RETAILERS
- What are store-for-store sales over the past five years? Have they been increasing or decreasing? How do they compare to total sales?

- Is there a certain per-store sales average that must be met to break even?
- Which markets are above the break-even point and which are below?
- Which stores/markets are above or below budgeted sales and profits?

SEASONALITY OF SALES

- Which products sell during certain times of the year? Does demand vary by season, business conditions, location, or weather?
- How does the seasonality of your company sales differ from that of the total industry category? Is there a time of the year in which you don't do as well or in which you outperform the industry as a whole? What is the seasonality of your company's product and the product category as a whole?
- Do specific products have strong seasonal selling periods that differ from the category nationally?
- For retailers, what are the weekly and daily seasonality trends of your product? Which days of the week are strong in sales relative to others? Which weeks are strong in sales relative to others?

SALES BY GEOGRAPHIC TERRITORY

- Are there areas of the country that provide more total sales and profits and/or sales per capita than others? Why? Consider the following:
    - Total sales.
    - Sales by product line.
    - Average sales per transaction or per customer.
    - Average sales per store for retailers.

TASK 4

Analyze Behavior Trends

Consumer behavior is the process and activities people are involved in as they move through the purchase decision-making process. Consumers and consumer segments behave in certain ways and change their behavior over time due to many social, personal, geographic, and psychographic trends. Because the business review's purpose is to collect actionable data on the industry, company, overall industry category consumer, and company consumer, the consumer behavior trends are an important part of the process. It is important to review both the consumer behavior situation as it currently exists and to note trends that will affect its change into the future.

We analyze the following aspects of consumer behavior because we feel they are the most actionable in terms of determining target markets and developing strategies later in the marketing plan; however, you need use only those sections applicable to your business. While most examples of behavior trends pertain to consumer products and services, behavior trends can also apply to business marketing as well, such as the trends toward downsizing and outsourcing. The trends we look at here are:

- Demographic, that is, population, income, household size, employment.
- Geographic, that is, population growth, geographic differences in demographic.
- Societal/consumer, that is, how we use products in the future based on changes in society.
- Technological, that is, the impact of technology on your company or products.
- Media-viewing trends, that is, how your customers will receive their information.

Worksheets to help you gather and organize information related to each of the above trends are provided at the end of this chapter.

Questions to Be Addressed

For each of the following, delineation of national averages and product category averages is useful for comparison purposes.

Demographic

- What are the age trends in terms of usage, and how will they affect your business?
    - Median age of usage.
    - Shifts in total product usage accountable by each age segment.
- What percent of the consumers are in the labor force, and how will this affect your business?
- What are the educational levels for the different age segments, and how will this affect your business?
- What are the income trends for the different age segments, and how will this affect your business?
- What are the trends in terms of composition of the family, and how will this affect your business?
- What are the minority trends in terms of population as a whole and for your product category, and how will this affect your business?
- What are the trends in business buying, such as downsizing and outsourcing?
- What growth changes are affecting key segments? Describe the segments by SIC code, industry type, firm make-up, etc.

Geographic

- What are the population growth trends by geographic region, and how will they affect your business?
- What are the geographic differences in the percentage of the population in each age segment, and how will they affect your business?
- What are the geographic differences in education levels, and how will they affect your business?
- What are the geographic differences in income levels, and how will they affect your business?
- What are the geographic differences in family composition, and how will they affect your business?
- What are the geographic differences in ethnic minorities, and how will they affect your business?
- Are there geographic differences in terms of how the product is used or how much the product is used?

Social/Consumer

- What are the social trends affecting the population as a whole and specifically those in your product category, and how will they affect your business? Consider the following trends:
    - Home.
    - Activity.
    - Purchase.
    - Economic.
    - Attitudes toward aging and youth.
    - Health.
    - Consumerism.
    - Time pressures.
    - Environmental concerns.
    - New generational trends.

—Clothing.

—Spending power.

—Activities.

TECHNOLOGICAL

- What are the major trends in information gathering, and how will they affect your business?
- What are the new product developments and capabilities in your industry, and how will they affect your business?
- How will new technologies (just introduced or on the future horizon) affect consumer behavior?

MEDIA

- For business-to-business firms, what are the trends in trade publication readership? Are certain publications or formats gaining greater acceptance or dominance among certain target audiences?
- What are the consumer trends of traditional media (TV, radio, newspaper, magazines, and outdoor)? Which medium is increasing in terms of viewership and which is decreasing? How do these trends affect your business?
- What are the consumer trends within each of the traditional media? How do these trends affect your business? Consider the following trends:
    - Radio listenership by day part.
    - Radio listenership by program format.
    - TV programming.
    - Cable penetration.
    - Cable viewership versus network viewership.
    - Type of cable programming that is most popular.
    - Viewership profiles to different programming alternatives.
    - Most popular magazine formats.
    - Most popular newspaper formats.
    - Most innovative direct mail applications.
- What are the trends in nontraditional media? How do these trends affect your business? Consider the following:
    - Interactive.
    - PC services.
    - Home shopping alternatives.
    - Other.

TASK 5
Analyze Distribution Methods

Distribution is the method of delivering the product to the consumer. At this point in the business review, your job is to determine which method of distribution is used most successfully by the industry, your company, and your competitors. The concept of distribution varies depending upon the type of business category. Let's look at each business type separately.

Retail

Retailers need to be aware of how and where their product is sold in relation to the industry. There are many unique ways to distribute the product to the consumer, and retailers should be aware of which distribution methods are increasing or decreasing in their industry and the advantages and disadvantages of the different methods.

Channel Type/Trends. Retailers have to determine and review the optimum outlet category or categories for the product being sold and the consumer who is purchasing. Common retail distribution outlet types include mass merchandise, discount, off-price, department stores, specialty shops, chain stores, and direct mail. Each is a unique distribution method that a retailer can use to sell the product to the consumer. To determine your company's optimum outlet category, analyze the current channel trends. The business review may determine that the two fastest-growing methods of distribution for your product category are smaller, single-line specialty shops and direct mail. If you were not currently using these channels, you would need to address in your marketing plan the industry's shift in emphasis toward these alternative methods of distribution. This could be done by adapting some of the strengths of specialty store retailing to your channel environment or by experimenting with direct mail. A worksheet designed to help you detail dollar sales and unit sales by outlet type is provided at the end of this chapter.

Geography. The geographical distribution of outlets also should be studied. Try to grade the location of your stores relative to your competitors. Is your firm located in the optimal trading areas of the market? Are they easy to get to and do they have good access? Are they on or near thoroughfares with high traffic counts and other thriving retail locations? Are there markets or specific trading areas within markets that have large numbers of purchases per person and/or household and low levels of competition where you should be doing business?

Penetration. Optimum *penetration levels* (number of stores per market) should be calculated to determine if more distribution outlets are needed. Note that in the broadest sense we define markets as Designated Market Areas (DMAs) or Television Coverage Areas, but markets can be defined in terms of a DMA, Standard Metropolitan Statistical Area (SMSA), county, or city/metro trading area. Penetration levels are evaluated on three issues:

1. The total number of competing outlets a market can support.
2. The number of your stores a market can support before cannibalization (stealing of customers from one of your stores by another) occurs.
3. The number of stores that are required in order for mass media such as newspapers, television, and radio to be efficiently leveraged, making the media affordable for your company from a percent-of-market sales or sales-per-store standpoint.

Two worksheets designed to help you determine optimum store penetration levels for each market are provided at the end of this chapter.

Questions to Be Addressed

- Where do consumers shop for products in your category? Where do they shop for your company's product? What channel or outlet type do consumers use most when purchasing?
- What is the importance of department stores, supermarkets, specialty stores, chain stores, independents, direct mail, discount stores, or other types of outlets that sell your product category or product? What are the five-year sales trends of each outlet type used by your product category?
- What channels or methods of distribution are receiving increased use by the industry? Are new channels emerging? What trends are noticeable in the stores that dominate the sales for your product category?
- What channels or methods of distribution does your competition use? If they use different channels from you, why?
- Do you have adequate penetration of outlets to maximize sales in any given market?
- Does expansion into new territories make sense? Are there additional areas of the country (states, regions) or of the world in which you should be doing business?
- Does your product require mass, selective, or exclusive distribution? Why? Does it require a combination of distribution methods? Who can best provide this type of distribution? Do your competitors' products require mass, selective, or exclusive distribution?

Package Goods

A package or consumer goods company views distribution differently from a retailer. Package goods companies sell to outlets, which in turn sell to consumers (e.g., a cereal company sells to grocery stores, which in turn sell to consumers). Unlike retailers, package goods companies don't own the channel of distribution; thus, more emphasis is placed on making sure the package goods product is accepted and sold into the channel and that it receives proper shelf space and merchandising support relative to competitors' products.

Channel Type/Trends. As a package goods marketer, you must determine the type of channel(s) best suited for the product. For example, it may be chain grocery stores, independent grocery stores, mass merchandisers, specialty stores, or convenience stores.

Market Coverage. As with retailing, you need to determine the number of outlets required to cover a trading area efficiently. However, because the package goods firm doesn't own the outlets, there is less concern with over-penetration. In some cases, the goal is to reach 100 percent market coverage of grocery store outlets in a given market. At the other extreme, some manufacturers offer exclusive distribution to a chain in return for greater sales and merchandising support. In still other situations, the product is distributed on a more limited basis to outlets that are consistent with the image of the product.

In most cases, package goods marketers do not refer to distribution coverage in terms of total stores. Instead, distribution refers to the percent of total grocery store dollar volume that the stores carrying the marketer's product account for in all grocery commodities, or all commodity volume (ACV). Thus, the term *65 percent ACV* means that the marketer's brand is carried by grocery stores accounting for 65 percent of all commodity grocery store volume. A worksheet designed to help you detail market coverage for your product(s) is provided at the end of this chapter.

Shelf Space. The amount of shelf space a product receives is critical to how well the product will do from a sales standpoint. Limited shelf space, or facings, and poor positioning on the shelf are both reasons for concern and need to be corrected. An average shelf space figure for your company could be calculated and included in your market coverage chart. The percent shelf space number can be compared to the shelf space percentages of your major competitors and can help you establish future shelf space goals.

Geography. As with retail, the package goods marketer should analyze the geographic territories of the firm's distribution to determine if there are markets that should be further penetrated or new markets that should be entered.

Personal Selling Method. An integral part of package goods distribution is the personal selling method. Some companies choose to use an in-house sales force, others use independent sales representatives and brokers, and still others use distributors or wholesalers. Analyze your current method as well as what your competitors use and then decide the best method or combination of methods for your company.

Another issue that needs to be explored is the selling programs your company has in place to sell to the trade. The following questions are designed to establish the importance of trade deals, co-op advertising, and other allowances in your marketplace.

QUESTIONS TO BE ADDRESSED

- Where do consumers shop for products in your category? Where do they shop for your company's product? What channel or outlet type do consumers use most when purchasing?
- What is the importance of department stores, supermarkets, specialty stores, chain stores, independents, direct mail, discount stores, or other types of outlets that sell your product category or product? What are the five-year sales trends of each outlet type used by your product category?
- What channels or methods of distribution are receiving increased use by the industry? Are new channels emerging? What trends are noticeable in the stores that dominate the sales of your product category?

- What channels or methods of distribution does your competition use? If they use different channels from you, why?
- Do you have enough market coverage to maximize sales in any given market?
- What is the ACV in each of your company's markets? What is the ACV for each of your major competitors in those same markets?
- Is the percent of shelf space your product receives in major outlets greater than, the same as, or lower than your competitors?
- Does expansion into new territories make sense? Are there additional areas of the country (states, regions) or of the world where you should be doing business?
- Does your product require mass, selective, or exclusive distribution? Why? Does it require a combination of distribution methods? Who can best provide this type of distribution? Do your competitors' products require mass, selective, or exclusive distribution?
- How many potential dealers, wholesalers, distributors, brokers, or retail outlets are there in your category? What are their distribution trading areas geographically?
- How do you sell your product to the retail trade or other businesses? Do you use in-house sales staff, independent reps, wholesalers, or distributors? What is the most efficient method of selling to distributors, wholesalers, or the retail trade?
- What is the importance of your product to the retail stores and/or distribution channel that sell it? Do you need the channel's services more than they need your product? Who has the channel power? How important is your product to the channel in terms of profit and volume (units and dollars)? Does your product help build or sustain traffic? Is it prestigious? Does it help sell other goods? How do these points differ from your competition?
- How do retailers or other distributors sell or market your product? Does your product receive aggressive sales support, or does your product have to sell itself? Does your product receive prominent display relative to the competition? Does your product get promoted in-store or to the ultimate purchaser by the distribution channel? Does your product receive the same merchandising and promotion support (more or less) relative to the competition? Does your product receive other promotion, advertising, or merchandising support?
- How established is your product with the trade? How well is it known and accepted by the trade? Is it important to them? Do you receive cooperation from the channels to which you sell? How does your competition rate in these areas?
- What is the minimum order size you require of your customers/channels? Is this standard in your industry? What are the payment terms? How often is restocking needed?
- Do storage, price marking, packaging, or accounting practices help sell to the trade or create problems?
- Do quantity discounts, cooperative advertising, promotion allowances, price discounts, trade promotions, or other deals play a large role in the selling of your product category to the trade? How? Does your company have the same programs as your competitors?
- What is the customary markup of your product by the trade? Does this affect your marketing to the trade or the acceptance of your product by the end consumer?
- Are retail sales or sales to the trade subject to taxes or legal restrictions?

- What are the stocking requirements of the trade? How does your company make allocation decisions? Who gets the best fill rates and why? How are out-of-stock situations handled?
- When, how often, and by whom are the orders placed?

Business to Business

Business-to-business firms sell directly to other businesses and/or sell through channels such as wholesalers or distributors. As such, the emphasis here is placed on business segments and the decision makers and influencers within each business.

Channel Types/Trends. Business-to-business firms must decide the most efficient and effective channel method for their companies. We did a business review for a national manufacturer of sinks and disposals that clearly demonstrated the growing trend of "do-it-yourselfers" who install their own sinks and disposals. Further study demonstrated that a shift in purchasing patterns had accompanied the strength of do-it-yourselfers in the marketplace; home centers and lumberyards were now selling more of this type of product than traditional plumbing channels. Thus, because of the channel trend section of the business review, selling emphasis was placed against home centers and lumberyards, establishing a new channel of distribution for the manufacturer.

Geography. Again, business-to-business marketers should look at the geographic territories of distribution to determine if there are markets that should be further penetrated or new markets that should be entered.

Personal Selling Method. As with package goods firms, business-to-business companies must decide how to sell the product through distribution channels. Company sales representatives, independent sales representatives, or wholesalers/distributors all have advantages and disadvantages. These are detailed in the Personal Selling/Service chapter later in this text. Remember: In the business review your job is to analyze which method is used most successfully within the industry, as well as by your company and your competitors.

As with the package goods section, the business-to-business firm must also address the issues of sales programs to the channels. The importance of deals, allowances, co-op advertising, and other sales program issues are detailed in the questions outlined below.

Questions to Be Addressed
- What channels or methods of distribution are receiving increased use by the industry? Are new channels emerging? What trends are noticeable?
- What channels or methods of distribution does your competition use? If they use different channels from you, why?
- Do you have enough market coverage to maximize sales in any given market?
- Does expansion into new territories make sense? Are there additional areas of the country (states, regions) or of the world where you should be doing business?
- Does your product require mass, selective, or exclusive distribution? Why? Does it require a combination of distribution methods? Who can best provide this type of distribution? Do your competitors' products require mass, selective, or exclusive distribution?
- How many potential dealers, wholesalers, distributors, or retail outlets are there? What are their distribution trading areas geographically?
- How do you sell your product to the retail trade or other businesses? Do you use in-house sales staff, independent reps, wholesalers, or distributors? What is the most efficient method of selling to distributors, wholesalers, or the retail trade?
- What is the importance of your product to the retail stores and/or distribution channel that sell it? Do you need the channel's services more than they need your product? Who has the channel power? How important is your product

to the channel in terms of profit, volume (units and dollars)? Does your product help build or sustain traffic? Is it prestigious? Does it help sell other goods? How do these points differ from your competition?

- How do retailers or other distributors sell or market your product? Does your product receive aggressive sales support, or does your product have to sell itself? Does your product get promoted to the ultimate purchaser by the distribution channel? Does your product receive the same merchandising and promotion support (less or more) relative to the competition? Does your product receive other promotion, advertising, or merchandising support?
- How established is your product with the trade? How well is it known and accepted by the trade? Is it important to them? Do you receive cooperation from the channels to which you sell? How does your competition rate in these areas?
- What is the minimum order size you require of your customers/channels? Is this standard in your industry? What are the payment terms? How often is restocking needed?
- Do storage, price marking, packaging, or accounting practices help sell the trade or create problems?
- Do quantity discounts, cooperative advertising, promotion allowances, price discounts, trade promotions, or other deals play a large role in the selling of your product category to the trade? How? Does your company have the same programs as your competitors?
- What is the customary markup of your product by the trade? Does this affect your marketing to the trade or the acceptance of your product by the end consumer? Are sales subject to taxes or legal restrictions?
- What are the stocking requirements of the trade? How does your company make allocation decisions? Who gets the best fill rates and why? How are out-of-stock situations handled?
- When, how often, and by whom are the orders placed? Are there many decision makers? What is the decision criteria and sequence?

Service

The service industry's method of distribution is much like the retailer's. It encompasses the business's office and how the service is sold to customers.

Type of Office. Of consideration for the service business is the type of office used to sell the service. For a service company, one of the only tangible things associated with the company is the actual office. Therefore, the office becomes an important representation of the more intangible service being sold. For many services, the service itself is sold or delivered out of the office. In this case, how and where the service is sold and delivered must be closely analyzed.

Geography. An important decision is where to locate an office or offices within a given market. When The Hiebing Group first began operation, we wanted to be close to Capitol Square in Madison, Wisconsin, because of the positive image associated with being downtown, adjacent to the center of state government, and close to the University of Wisconsin. When we outgrew our first location, we decided to stay close to downtown and the university, while maintaining a positive creative image. We found an historic old mansion overlooking Lake Mendota, and then later, as we continued to grow, converted an old Christian Science Church close to downtown, achieving our goals and creating an office environment and image consistent with that of the agency.

Another issue that must be addressed by service firms is the number of markets in which you do business. What markets seem ripe for geographic expansion, and which ones are not currently profitable and may need to be abandoned?

Penetration. As with retailers, proximity is also important to firms providing service. Accordingly, service companies have to decide how many locations and sales and/or service people are needed to cover any given market effectively and efficiently.

QUESTIONS TO BE ADDRESSED

- Where do consumers of services in your category shop?
- What are the current methods of delivery used for services in your category? Are new methods of delivery emerging? Are there noticeable trends among the firms that dominate your service category?
- How does your competition deliver its services? If the competition uses different delivery methods than you, why?
- Does expansion into new territories make sense? Are there additional areas of the country (states, regions) or of the world where you should be doing business?
- Does your product require mass, selective, or exclusive distribution? Why? Does it require a combination of delivery methods? Who can best provide this new method of delivery? Do your competitors require different methods of delivery?
- Is there a best way to deliver your service through company-owned offices, franchises, or dealerships?
- As with retail, what is the physical exposure of the office and its signage to passing potential customers? This exposure can have a dramatic effect on the awareness of the company's name.
- What type of office is most consistent with your company's image? Describe the office interiors/exteriors of your competitors; are they similar to or different from yours? Where, when, and how is your service best sold to consumers?

Overall Distribution Strengths and Weaknesses

Once you have considered all of the relevant questions to be addressed, analyze your company's strengths and weaknesses and compare them to your competitors'.

TASK 6
Analyze Pricing Structures

Price is a prominent part of the marketing decision-making process. A price that is too high may discourage purchase of the product and encourage competition in the form of lower price and more entries into the product category. Alternatively, a price that is too low may be a deterrent to reaching profit and sales goals.

The business review section on pricing is designed to provide pricing data regarding the competition, changes in the marketplace price structure, and strengths of consumer demand. This information will provide a reference and help guide your pricing objectives and strategies in the subsequent marketing plan.

The business review should provide you with the following four major insights on pricing:

1. Price of your product/brands relative to the competition.
2. Distribution of sales by price point relative to the competition.
3. Price elasticity of demand for your product.
4. Cost structure of the product category.

Price of Your Product. Changes in a competitor's price structure often cause reactive price strategies in the marketplace. Frequent competitive price checks should be made in order to track historical pricing patterns of the competition. To a large degree, competitive pricing information allows you to determine market supply and demand and provides accurate yardsticks from which to make timely pricing decisions of your own.

The pricing worksheet at the end of this chapter helps you analyze your company's prices relative to the competition during key selling periods of the year. It also allows you to determine the pricing policies of the competition. Use this knowledge when developing competitive pricing and promotion strategies later in the marketing planning process.

Distribution of Sales by Price Point. In figuring the distribution of sales by price range relative to the competition, first determine what percent of the product category purchases are at each price level (low, medium, and high), then compare your product's price category to the distribution of category sales by price point. You might be surprised to find that your major price category accounts for a small percentage of industry category sales or that there has been increased sales growth in your product's price category. This information will allow you to judge the potential impact of your pricing decisions later in the marketing plan. A worksheet designed to help you develop information specific to your company is provided at the end of this chapter.

Price Elasticity. Consumer purchase behavior responds directly to price changes. The effect and extent of price changes on consumer demand for a product is measurable in terms of price elasticity. Demand for a product is considered to be *price elastic* if sales go down when the price is raised and sales go up if the price is lowered. Demand for a product is considered to be *price inelastic* if demand is not significantly affected by changes in price.

Actual price elasticity can be determined in two ways. One method is through simulation research; the other method is through actual price changes in test markets. However, the way many marketers determine or estimate price elasticity is by monitoring competitive price changes and price changes on their own products and then noting the resulting effects on sales. This can be done by obtaining market share figures through secondary sources; by talking to consumers, sales representatives, buyers, and wholesalers of your product; or by shopping your competitors to determine the results of various price changes.

Cost Structure. The cost structure of your product relative to the selling price should be reviewed. This information will need to be available when you establish your pricing segment later in the plan. The following should be included:

- Fixed and variable costs associated with the selling of your product.
- Cost of goods sold.
- Margin and profit.
- Gross price or gross sales figure.

QUESTIONS TO BE ADDRESSED
PRICE OF YOUR PRODUCT

- What is the pricing structure for the product category? Are there price point products, brands, or stores that sell for more or less than yours? Is there a range from premium to off-price/discount pricing in your industry?
- What is the pricing structure for your product relative to the competition? Does the relationship of your product's price to that of the competition change during different selling seasons? Has it changed over a period of years?
- In addition to pure price, are discounts, credit, promotional allowances, return policies, restocking charges, shipping policies, and the like, important to the ultimate sale of your product?

DISTRIBUTION OF SALES BY PRICE POINT

- What is the distribution of sales by price point for your industry and your company (five-year trend)? Do the majority of sales fall in one price category, or can consumers or businesses be segmented by price point?
- What has been the trend in pricing (five-year trend)? Are there price segments that are growing or shrinking?

PRICE ELASTICITY

- How price elastic is your product category? When you raise and/or lower the price, how does it affect demand? Are consumers price sensitive to your product category?
- Where is your product priced in relation to your major competitors? Why is it priced where it is?

Overall Pricing Strengths and Weaknesses. Once you have considered all the questions to be addressed, analyze your company's strengths and weaknesses as compared to your competitors.

TASK 7
Competitive Review

The final task in the Product and Market Review section is a competitive analysis. The competitive analysis section is designed to provide you with a summary of how your company is performing in comparison to the competition across key marketing and communication variables. This task forces you to consider strategic and tactical differences and similarities in product marketing between your company and the competition. An analysis of your company's marketing activities in relation to the competition can provide benchmark information necessary to prepare your marketing plan. This knowledge will provide insights into potential defensive or offensive strategies that you can include in the marketing plan to curtail or exploit a major competitor's strength or weakness. In addition, by thoroughly studying your past marketing efforts and those of the competition, you may look at successes and failures in a new light—there might be ways to modify some of your competitors' more successful programs and make them your own, or there might be changes that can be made to successful programs that will make them even better.

Review your company and your competitors in terms of sales, target market, positioning, marketing objectives and strategies, positioning, product/branding/packaging, pricing, distribution, personal selling techniques, promotion strategies and expenditures, customer service, merchandising, and publicity. Make sure to review the previous two years; past years' successes and failures for both your company and your competitors can be great learning tools. Also, if possible project competitive activity into the future.

In addition, consider the results of your marketing testing and research and development program. Did you introduce any new products, line extensions, services, merchandise, or store concepts? Did you test different approaches in your advertising message? Did you test the use of new and/or investment spending? Did you test various promotional offers? What can you learn from past tests that can be translated into future success? If you have been doing the same things year after year, you should explore new uses of your marketing tools to ensure a competitive edge that will help guarantee increased sales and profits year after year.

Competitive analyses are not easy to complete because it is often difficult to apply the findings to obtain specific information about competitors. However, you can use secondary sources and the worksheets at the end of this chapter. We also encourage you to attend trade shows and shop your competition by purchasing your competitors' products. In addition, there is a lot to be learned from media representatives regarding the media expenditures of your competitors. Finally, one of the best ways to obtain competitive information is through awareness, attitude, and behavior primary research. If your company uses market tracking surveys, you can determine trends of the following:

- Awareness levels of competitors relative to your company.
- Ranking of product attributes and consumers' rating of key product attributes for your company relative to the competition.
- Market share estimates for competitors relative to your company.
- Purchase ratios/trial and repeat purchases for your product relative to the competition.
- Shopping habits for your product versus the competition (normally shop first, etc.).

QUESTIONS TO BE ADDRESSED

MARKET SHARE
- What is the trend in your company's market share and sales relative to key competitors?
- What is the market share growth/decline for your company or product over the past five years?
- What is the competitive set and relative market share overall, in your primary geographic area, and from market to market?

TARGET MARKET
- What is your primary target market? What percent of sales does it account for? How does this compare to the industry and your key competition?
- Is the description of your heavy users the same as that of the industry's or your key competitors'?

MARKETING OBJECTIVES/STRATEGIES
- What are your company's marketing objectives and strategies? How do they appear to differ from your key competitors? (Whenever possible, develop answers for the past two years and project activity for the upcoming year.)

POSITIONING
- What is the positioning of your company and your competitors? Is your positioning preemptive? Do you have a strong positioning relative to your competitors?
- Is your positioning dominating a strong attribute that is important to your target market?

PRODUCT
- What are your product's strengths and weaknesses relative to the competition?

PRICING
- Are your prices the same, lower, or higher than the competition?

DISTRIBUTION/STORE PENETRATION/ MARKET COVERAGE STRATEGY
- How does your distribution strategy differ from that of your competitors?

PERSONAL SELLING
- What was your sales performance last year? Did you meet your goals?
- How does your company's selling philosophy differ from that of your competitors? Are there different methods that you may want to consider in the future? If so, why?

CUSTOMER SERVICE POLICIES
- What are your company's customer service policies? Do they differ from the competition's? If so, how?

PROMOTION

- Do you rely more, the same, or less on promotion as compared to your competition?
- What were the results of your company's promotions and those of your competitors last year? What was successful or unsuccessful? Why? How do your company's promotions differ from those of your competitors?
- What promotions does your competition execute that are particularly successful?

ADVERTISING MESSAGE

- How does your advertising compare to that of your competitors? Is it similar or different? What is the message of your advertising as compared to your major competitors?
- How successful has your advertising been relative to your competitors' advertising? Based not just on your judgment but on objective research, what are the strengths and weaknesses of your advertising and that of your competitors?

MEDIA STRATEGY AND EXPENDITURES

- Where, when, and how do you and your competitors use the media?
- What is the media spending both overall and by medium for your company and your competitors? Do you dominate any one medium? Where are your competitors the strongest? How does this situation compare from market to market?

MERCHANDISING

- What is the merchandising philosophy of your competitors? Is your merchandising similar or different to that of the competition? Why? Does your merchandising help to communicate your positioning? Which specific merchandising executions by your company and the competition appear to be most effective?

PUBLICITY

- Do you have an active publicity and press relations program? Does your competition? How much publicity did your product receive versus competitive products? What was effective?

TESTING/MARKETING DEVELOPMENT

- What tests did your company and the competition execute in the past year? Were they successful? What did you learn from the tests?

SUMMARY OF STRENGTHS AND WEAKNESSES

- Based on the information above, what are the strengths and weaknesses of your company as compared to each major competitor?

Step 3: Target Market Effectors

In the Product and Market Review, you analyzed a first level of target market behavior as measured by product performance-company and product sales, use of distribution channels, and purchases by price points. The final step in the business review, Target Market Effectors, moves your analysis to the next level: identifying customer and noncustomer segments and their awareness, perceptions, and behavior toward your product(s). Specifically, we will look at segmentation, or the breaking of the aggregate consumer or customer of products identified in the Product and Market Review into groups of consumers or customers with similar needs, wants, or purchase patterns. This information or segments will serve as the bridge to developing marketing objectives and strategies later in the marketing plan.

The target market effectors are based upon the premise in order to market to a specific target market segment, that segment has to be aware of your company or product. Once aware, there needs to be a positive attitude toward your product or company among the target segment before purchase or trial takes place. If the customer likes the product, the product is repurchased. This is what the hierarchy of effectors is all about—defining target market segments and then determining the segment's awareness, attitudes, trial or purchase rates and retrial or repurchase rates. In summary, the target market effectors help you analyze your business in the following manner:

Target Market
Determine for the industry and for your company the market segments that purchase the product. Provide the following:
> —Description of segment.
> —Size of segment/number of potential purchasers.
> —What dollar volume sales segment accounts for.
> —Profit attributed to segment.
> —Trend of the target segment in terms of users and dollar volume.

Awareness
For each of the above segments, measure the awareness for your product and industry products (competitive products).

Attributes
For each of the defined segments, determine the most important purchase attributes (e.g., product quality, after-sale service, selection, security, price, etc.). Then rank your product's performance against that of the industry and/or specific competitors.

Trial
Determine the percent of the target market universe that has tried your product. Also, determine other key behavior variables relevant to your product category, such as the average number of purchases a customer makes, the dollars spent per purchase, and the decision-making process.

> *Example:* In the target market section you might have determined that one segment of purchasers was research and development (R&D) staff positions at food companies. You determined how many there were in the industry and how many customers you had in this segment. You then determined the volume from the R&D food company sales. Now, be specific as to how many R&D staff people from food companies have ordered from you within the past year. Determine the average order amount and the average order dollars, among other behavior data.

Retrial
What percent of the customers initially try your product and then make a repeat purchase?

By breaking the target market effectors into the steps consumers take when purchasing (awareness of product, the formation of attitudes, trial, and retrial) we can identify areas of concentration later in the marketing plan.

> *Example:* A product is competing in a large market segment, yet only a small percentage of the target market is aware of the product. Of those who are aware of the product, there are strong, positive attitudes, trial, and retrial.

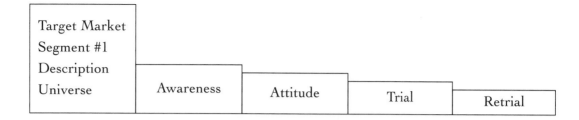

In this situation, there is an adequate target market universe, but the volume of actual customers is small. (See the small trial level relative to the potential target market box.) The problem is a low awareness level. One potential solution here would be to increase awareness, with the assumption that a percentage of those who are aware will try and retry the product.

Example: A product is competing in a large target market segment; a significant percentage of the target market is aware of the product, but their positive attitudes are small in comparison.

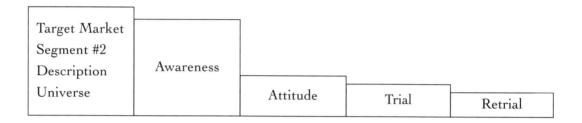

Here the problem is poor attitudes. In this situation, the target market is large enough and awareness is high, but there is a big drop in positive attitudes and relatively small trial and retrial percentages. The solution here would involve product changes and communication addressing the attitude problems.

There are many additional scenarios that can unfold in your plan. The above examples should provide a good start in understanding how we use this section of the business review later in the plan.

Each step of the hierarchy is used in specific sections of the marketing plan. The target market section helps define the target market and its size later in the plan. The middle two sequences, awareness and attribute, provide information needed to establish communication objectives and strategies. The behavior sequence is used to develop marketing objectives, because marketing objectives affect target market behavior quantitatively, translating to sales.

TASK 1

Review Consumer and Business-to-Business Target Market Segments

The business review provides for a format that sorts current and potential customers into segments. Segmentation places customers and consumers into groups according to common purchasing characteristics. This, in turn, allows you to analyze which customer group is currently most profitable and which noncustomer group has the most potential for your company. As a result, you are able to focus your company's marketing resources (messages, product, and other marketing mix elements) on an ultimate target market that has some common characteristics. Instead of trying to be all things to all people, the company can direct its energies toward satisfying essentially one person, as characterized by the target market segment or segments. Such directed efforts are considerably more effective and efficient.

Target Market Effectors: What's Needed and How to Use Them

Target Market	Awareness	Attitude	Behavior (Trial and Retrial)
		Work to Do in Business Review	
• Determine category and company product segments • Define number of potential consumers and customers in each segment • Determine sales volume accountable to each segment	• Determine awareness by segments— company product versus competition	• Determine attribute importance by segment • Determine company/ product ranking	• Average purchase amount, frequency purchase for each industry consumer and company segment • Trial and retrial per industry and company segment • Decision-making process for each industry and company/product segment
		Use in Marketing Plan	
• Defining target markets	• Communication Awareness Goals (Example: increase unaided awareness from 10% to 14%) • Communication strategies • Spending strategies	• Communication Attitude Goals (Example: shift attitude rating from 40% to 60%) • Communication strategies • Product strategies	• Establish marketing objectives (Example: increase purchase frequency from 1.5 times per year at $38 to 2.0 times per year at $45)

CONSUMER SEGMENTATION METHODS

The following five segmentation methods are commonly used by businesses to segment their customers and potential customers.

Demographics. The marketer's traditional method of defining and segmenting markets is by utilizing demographic factors, including sex, age, income, education, occupation, family/household size, and region/geography.

The key to determining segments is identifying whether a specific demographic or combination of demographic variables predicts a significant volume or concentration of usage or purchases. *Volume* is the total number of purchases or percent of total purchases attributable to any given demographic target market segment. For example, if total sales in a category equal $1MM and 18–24-year-olds account for $150M, then that segment's volume equals 15 percent of the total purchases. *Concentration* is the percent of a given demographic target market segment that purchases the product. For example, if 80 percent of all 18–24-year-olds purchase the product, then 80 percent equals the concentration in that segment.

Worksheets designed to help you determine demographic profiles by volume and concentration are provided at the end of this chapter.

Product Usage. For some products, demographics aren't as important as the reason the product is purchased or how it is used. Many times purchasers with similar demographics purchase the product for different reasons. This offers the opportunity to segment based on usage of the product. For example, baking soda is purchased by women who bake from scratch and use the product in the baking process. It is also purchased by women who use it as a refrigerator deodorizer. Many of the people who purchase baking soda as a deodorizer do not bake on a regular basis, so they do not purchase the product for baking. Thus, usage of this product helps define customer segments, and knowledge of the customer's usage is critical to determining how this product would be marketed to each of the two customer groups.

Psychographics/Lifestyle. Marketers effectively use *psychographics*, or lifestyle factors, to help identify target markets. Lifestyle descriptors attempt to define a customer segment in terms of the attitudes, interests, and activities of the consumer. They are usually combined with demographics to form a more precise definition of the target market.

Attribute. Some products are purchased because of the specific product attributes. For example, in the roasted coffee business, the whole bean coffee customer segment is defined primarily by the desire for quality coffee (an attribute) rather than by age, income, or education (demographics).

Heavy Use. Most product categories have a group of heavy users—consumers who purchase or use the product at far greater rates than that of the average consumer. Heavy users are important because they offer the potential of marketing to a smaller, more defined group of people who account for the majority of purchases. By our definition, a category has a meaningful heavy-user segment if approximately one-third or less of the consumers account for approximately two-thirds or more of the purchases. For example, in the shoe business one-third of purchasers buy more than 63 percent of the shoes.

A worksheet designed to help you compare heavy-user demographics to all users is provided at the end of this chapter.

QUESTIONS TO BE ADDRESSED
DEMOGRAPHIC SEGMENTATION

- Do the different user groups have differing demographics? What is their size in terms of volume of purchases and number of consumers?
- What is the industry category (consumer) demographic profile of the product category nationally? What is the profile of the individuals who consume or purchase the most from a volume standpoint? Do some demographic categories have a higher concentration of purchasers?
- Do new customers purchase at different rates than older established customers?
- Which consumer profile or segments are growing the fastest in terms of volume?
- What is your customer's demographic profile? How would you describe your customers in terms of age, sex, income, occupation, education, number of children, marital status, geographic residence, and ownership of home?
- Do your dominant customer segments differ from the dominant industry category segments?
- What company customer segments are growing the fastest in terms of volume?
- How many customers purchase your product? How many potential industry consumers exist in your product category? Has the number of consumers been growing or shrinking over the past five years?
- Are there geographic areas where the product category is purchased at greater rates? How many industry consumers and customers are there in each geographic area?

PRODUCT USAGE SEGMENTATION
- How is the product used in terms of the overall product category? Is the industry product used in the same manner as your company's product?
- If there are multiple uses of your product, are there consumers who use the product for one type of use or benefit but not another? Are there multiple, independent user groups? How many consumers and customers are there for each of the uses?
- Are there products purchased by a specific target market that might be used as a foundation to cross-sell the target to other company products?

PSYCHOGRAPHIC/LIFESTYLE SEGMENTATION
- What are your customer's personality descriptors, activities, and interests?
- Do religious, political, or other social economic factors make a difference in the purchase of your product or service?
- Can you further break a demographic segment into subsegments based upon different lifestyle characteristics?
- How many industry consumers and company customers are there for each psychographic segment?

ATTRIBUTE SEGMENTATION
- Is there a key attribute that defines how products in the industry category are purchased? Are there different purchasing segments based upon a desire for a different attribute?
- Is there a key attribute that determines purchases for your company products?
- How many industry consumers and company customers are there in each of the attribute segments?

HEAVY USE
- Is there a group of heavy purchasers of your product? What percent of the purchasers do they constitute and for what percent of the purchases are they responsible?
- What is the difference between the demographic and lifestyle profile of the heavy user and that of the overall user?
- How many heavy users are there in terms of the industry and in terms of your company customers?

BUSINESS-TO-BUSINESS SEGMENTATION METHODS

Business-to-business firms typically have far fewer potential customers than consumer companies. In addition, each business-to-business customer usually generates larger sales than the typical consumer customer does. As with consumer target markets, it is important to segment so that you can determine which type of business is most profitable and has the most potential for your company.

Standard Industrial Classification (SIC) Categories
One of the best ways to segment businesses is with SIC codes. Businesses are classified into 10 broad, two-digit SIC categories: Agriculture/Forestry/Fishing, Mining, Manufacturing, Construction, Transportation/Communication/Public Utilities, Wholesale Trade, Retail Trade, Finance/Insurance/Real Estate, Services, and Public Administration. Within each two-digit SIC category there are further breakouts into four- and eight-digit classifications. For example, within the Retail SIC there is category 56, Apparel and Accessory stores; within category 56 there is 5611, Men's and Boys' Clothing. Firms such as Dun's Marketing Services specialize in providing mailing lists and other market information for businesses according to any SIC classification.

Worksheets designed to help you determine market segments by SIC category are presented at the end of this chapter.

QUESTIONS TO BE ADDRESSED

- To what SIC segments or other user segments do customers who purchase your product belong?
- What is the demand potential for your product?
- What is the penetration of your company in each SIC category?
- How many businesses that are in SIC categories that purchase product in your category are not purchasing from you? Why aren't they?

Other Business-to-Business Segmentation Methods

Dollar Size. Using SIC categories as your base, you can determine total company sales volume per category, and then calculate the average dollar size of each client in the category(ies) by dividing the total company volume in each SIC by the number of clients you have in that SIC. When combined with the penetration information developed earlier, these data can tell you a lot about the current and future potential of the different categories. If one SIC classification averages substantially above other SIC classifications in terms of average dollar per client and your company has not fully penetrated that classification (your company's clients represent a small percentage of the total businesses in the SIC), then that classification should be targeted for further expansion.

Employee Size. Another way to segment business is by the number of employees in the firm. Employee size often is an indicator of the company's volume and how they do business. For example, large companies tend to be more centralized and have formalized organizational structures, while smaller companies tend to be less formalized. Pricing, product, and service requirements often differ between large and small companies. Thus, the marketing approach may differ due to a function of the size of the business customer.

Heavy-Use Rates. Are there categories of heavy or light users? Determine the reasons for this. Maybe a category of light users would become heavier users if you were to modify your product, service, or pricing. Or perhaps you should consider narrowing your firm's focus to concentrate on just the heavy-user categories, especially if the earlier analysis determined that there was potential growth in these categories.

Product Application. How do businesses use your product? If you find that there are different uses for your product, you can segment target markets by usage type and begin to provide more focused service and expertise to each segment.

Organizational Structure. Different companies have different organizational structures. Find out if your company sells better to one type of company than another. You might find you get more business from centralized organizations with formalized bidding procedures and thus want to target these types of businesses within the SICs you currently service. You also might analyze why you don't do as well with decentralized entrepreneurial firms and then make changes to increase your success with them. Subsequently, you may do well when targeting headquarters but perform poorly in generating sales from branches. In summary, you may need to develop independent marketing strategies and executions for different target groups as defined by their organization structure, purchasing habits, and purchasing requirements.

New versus Repeat Buyers. Some companies are good at getting new business and poor at developing long-term relationships. For others, it's just the opposite. Determine the percentage of your business that comes from new buyers versus repeat buyers. Analyze your ability to keep repeat customers. Correct your weaknesses if it becomes evident that you either aren't getting new business or can't develop long-term clients.

This area is a good client satisfaction check and should be analyzed yearly. It also allows you to develop alternative marketing strategies depending upon the type of customer (new versus repeat) you are targeting.

Geographic Location. In analyzing sales, you may determine that you are strong in one part of the country but weak in another. It could be the result of your distribution system, it might be caused by a competitive situation, or you may find that demand is higher in some geographical areas than others. In addition, you might discover that you do very well against a particular SIC category in one region of the country but that you haven't marketed to that SIC category elsewhere. By analyzing where your current business exists and where you have potential to expand, you can segment your target market by geographic location.

Decision Makers and Influencers. Finally, you need to determine who actually decides to purchase your product and who influences the purchase of your product. Remember, *companies* don't buy products, *people* do. Analyze the purchase decision-making process. Describe who is the entry person at a company for your product. Also decide who makes the ultimate purchasing decision, how they arrive at the purchasing decision, what the purchasing criteria are, and to what degree people influence the purchaser. The purchaser may be a committee, which means you will need to target many individuals if all have an equal role in the decision process. Typically, the decision maker or purchaser becomes your primary target market, and those individuals influencing the decision become the secondary target market.

QUESTIONS TO BE ADDRESSED

- What is the revenue distribution for the industry category and your company by SIC or other applicable segments?
- How many industry category consumers and company customers are there for each SIC or other applicable segment?
- Based upon the above two questions, you can now calculate the average dollar revenue per industry category consumer and company customer. What are they?
- What is your company's penetration in each SIC segment? Do any of the segments with high average dollar per customer have low company penetration rates?
- What size are the companies that purchase from you? Do large companies respond differently than small ones? If so, why?
- Are there heavy users within SIC categories? Are some SIC categories heavier users than others?
- Do different SIC category businesses use your product for different purposes? Why do SIC categories use your product? Is your product used more by some industries than by others? Can you expand use to others?
- Are purchasers of your product original equipment manufacturers (OEMs) who utilize your product in the manufacturing of another product? Do they sell to another business or directly to the consumer? How exactly does your product fit into the OEM's manufacturing structure? Why is your product important? How is it used?
- What is the organizational structure of your customers' companies? Do you have more success with centralized companies than with decentralized? Why? Do purchasing procedures differ among customers? Do you get more business from companies with a single purchasing agent versus those with a purchasing committee that requires more formalized bidding?
- Are the majority of your customers new or repeat buyers? Why?
- Where are your customers located? Are there areas of the country that have businesses from SIC categories with which you are successful but which you currently are not covering? Are there potential customers that match your customer profile that you are not reaching? Do some parts of the country provide more business for you than others? If so, why? Is it due to servicing, distribution, sales efforts, or competitive factors? Or do some parts of the country use more product than other parts for other reasons?

- Who are the decision makers and influencers in the purchase of your product? What is the decision maker's function and role in the purchase decision? What is the decision sequence? What are the purchase criteria?

<table>
<tr><td>

TASK 2

Analyze Product Awareness, Attributes, and Life Cycle

</td><td>

We have documented in case after case that an increase in awareness of a quality product leads to increases in purchase rates or, in the terminology of our firm, *increased share of mind leads to increased share of market.* Therefore, awareness of your product or service is an important barometer of its future success.

</td></tr>
</table>

PRODUCT AWARENESS

Awareness is typically measured through primary research on two levels, unaided and aided. *Unaided awareness* is generally considered a more accurate measure because it involves consumers recalling specific product names without any assistance. *Aided awareness* is the awareness generated by asking individuals which product they are familiar with after reading or reviewing with them a list of competing products. Worksheets regarding product attributes and product awareness are provided at the end of this chapter.

When analyzing awareness, we typically review the following levels in order of importance.

Unaided Awareness. Two levels of unaided awareness are measured. The first is known as *first mention, top of mind.* This is the awareness level that will most closely parallel with market share. It is obtained through telephone research in which the interviewer asks the respondent which products or companies come to mind in a specific product category—shoes, propellers, spray-dried ingredients, banking services, etc. The respondent mentions the companies, firms, or products with which he or she is familiar, the first one mentioned being the first mention or top of mind. Typically, the first mentioned company or product is the first choice or one most recently purchased—a direct correlation to shopping intent.

The second unaided awareness measure is *total unaided.* All companies or products mentioned without prompting are part of what is known as the *evoked purchase set*—considerations when the respondent purchases. In situations where more companies or products are mentioned than less, it is an indication that the category exhibits less loyalty from its purchasers and that there is more shopping around either before purchase or between purchase situations. This fact should be noted and used strategically later in the marketing plan. For example, in nonloyal categories, promotions are often heavily used to steal market share and customers with strong after-purchase retention programs.

Aided Awareness. Once the respondent has provided unaided responses, the interviewer can say, "Have you ever heard of _____?" If the respondent says yes, it is considered aided awareness. We feel this is a very weak measure of association or familiarity with a company or product; however, it does serve as a disaster check. If, after prompting, the respondent has not heard of your product or company, there is little chance they will be a purchaser or customer.

Awareness by Segments. The awareness measures need to be broken out by the segments developed in the target market section. For example, let's say you determine there are three main segments for your high volume banking products as determined by age and product use.

Age	Banking Product Use
18–34	Checking, auto cash machine, credit card
35–54	Credit (home loan, home equity, car loan)
55+	Savings (CD, money market, trust management)

Now you need to determine awareness levels for all three age segments. You may find vastly different degrees of awareness of your firm and products from one segment to the next, signifying a need for different communication strategies and spending levels.

Awareness measures allow the marketing manager to fine-tune the advertising message and media strategies. Some examples of how awareness is used to help formulate subsequent marketing strategies are:

- *Low awareness* levels signal the need for a more aggressive or effective advertising and promotional plan. Often, the primary problem is that the product has low awareness among consumers, not that the product necessarily needs a repositioning. This is especially true if the product has positive attribute ratings from current users and it has a high trial/repeat usage ratio.
- Markets with *high awareness* levels often don't need as much media weight to sustain existing sales levels as those markets that have low awareness. It often requires less media weight to generate successful promotions in established markets with high awareness than in newer markets, where a customer base is not yet established and only a minimal number of potential consumers have heard of your product or company. As an example, markets in which a product has low awareness often require larger print ads than markets with higher awareness levels. Our experience has shown that small newspaper ads are more likely to be seen by current users and that it takes larger ads to attract the attention of infrequent users or individuals who are not aware of your product.
- Markets with *falling awareness* levels often indicate isolated, market-specific problems such as increased competitive activity. These problems may require an individual market plan tailored to the specific market situation, along with investment spending over the short-term to stabilize and increase awareness levels.

QUESTIONS TO BE ADDRESSED

- What is the unaided and aided awareness of your product among the various target market segments in your industry and among customers of your company?
- How do those awareness levels compare to those of your competition?
- Have awareness levels been increasing or decreasing over the past five years?
- What is the first mention level of awareness (first product mentioned) within each target market segment?

PRODUCT ATTRIBUTES

Product attributes, or benefits, are derived from consumers' perceptions of the product. This step of the business review allows the marketing manager to define the strengths and weaknesses of the company's products relative to the competition. It is necessary to identify which attributes are important to the purchasing segments and users of your product and then to determine how your company or product compares to the competition on these attributes. There may be attributes that you need to improve for certain segments, or you may find there are certain needs that no one in the marketplace is fulfilling, providing your company the opportunity to dominate an important niche or purchasing segment. The repositioning of a menswear chain we worked with was brought about because the research determined that the most important attributes to the heavy-user target market segment (businessmen) were quality and value, not low purchase price, which was being emphasized. The repositioning emphasized value (a good price on perceived quality brands). The theme line became "Pecks Businessmenswear," which denoted a special quality and expertise and labeled a specific group of people identified with quality men's clothing (heavy-user purchasing segment).

There are two types of product attributes: rational attributes and emotional attributes. A worksheet designed to help you determine product attributes is presented at the end of this chapter.

Rational Attributes. The first step is to determine which attributes are most important for each target market segment you are analyzing. In the shoe retail category, quality, comfort, and value are of primary importance to women with children. Price is middle of the pack. In the highly technical computer diagnostic business, product reliability, service response time, software, and ease of use were the top required attributes for the research and development target segment, with price, state-of-the-art design, supplier reputation, upgradability, and application support being more important to the purchasing agents.

Emotional Attributes. In addition to ranking the rationale attributes, we also develop a list of the most important emotional reasons customer segments purchase. For example, the women customers of a large HMO desired "partnership." When we explored what that meant, it translated into the willingness to accept the fact that the patient has to do his or her share to stay healthy in today's medical climate. But the doctor has to be willing to listen and should not treat the patient simply as a number or as a disease. In this case, partnership meant two-way communication, an emotional attribute.

Attribute Ranking by Segment. Next, your company is ranked against the most important rational and/or emotional attributes relative to the competition. Again, this is typically done through survey research. You are then able to say that quality is the number-one desired attribute and that your company either does or does not perform well on this variable. This type of analysis, based upon the realities of the marketplace, puts the consumer in the position of guiding the direction the company takes.

QUESTIONS TO BE ADDRESSED

The information needed to answer these questions is normally obtained through primary research. If your company cannot afford to undertake primary research to answer these questions, then you should use available secondary research and attempt to answer the questions yourself in as much detail as possible. Also, have other individuals in your organization answer them to see if your perceptions match those of your coworkers. You might even get individuals outside of your company to answer the questions in order to compare their answers with those from people within your organization.

- How is your product used? What is the product's primary benefit to the industry category consumer segments?
- What are the important product attributes of your product's industry category against each segment? What are the important attributes of your competitors' products? How do your company's products rank on those attributes versus the competition on a segment-by-segment basis?
- What does each purchaser and user segment like and dislike about your product?
- Are there differences between heavy users' likes and dislikes as compared to the other user segments of your product category?
- Are there substitutes that can be used in place of your company's product or the product category?
- Is there anything unusual about how your product is manufactured or designed that would be of interest or benefit to consumers? Is there anything about your product that can help differentiate it from the competition? For example, how is it manufactured? Does it have a unique color, shape, or texture? Does your product last longer than others like it? What about guarantees? Are there unique performance attributes that make it superior to the competition? Is there unique packaging? Is your product more convenient to use than the competitor's? Is your product of better quality? What about the competitors' products?

- Are there any inherent product qualities that have not been communicated but that are important to the buyer segments? (Same for your competition.)
- For each segment, what are the rational attributes and emotional attributes that are important predictors of purchasing in your product category and/or for your company's products?
- If you have many competitors, how does your product rank in terms of overall quality? How does your product rank in terms of value (the combination of quality and price)? Where does your product rank in terms of performance, durability, serviceability, and aesthetic appearance when compared to the competition? How does your product rank, relative to the competitive products, across other key purchasing attributes by each target market segment?
- What is the history of your product? When was it first marketed? What changes have been made to the product and why? (Same for your competition.)
- Is your product accepted by a broad consumer base or a narrow segment? Why?
- Does your product have any patents that are active? Does your unique advantage depend upon a specific design, formula, or manufacturing capability that could be readily copied? Or is your product unique due to patent protection or some manufacturing process that is difficult or costly to duplicate?
- What are the new developments in your product category? What will be the next big innovation? What product improvements do consumers desire?

PRODUCT LIFE CYCLE

Most products go through a product life cycle. Understanding your product's stage in the product life cycle will help predict anticipated target markets, competition, pricing, distribution, and advertising strategies. The following is a brief outline of how we view the product life cycle and how each stage affects these five areas.

Introduction Phase

Target Market. Usually innovators try new products. The goal is to get opinion-leader types of people to try and use the product. It is usually more difficult to sell a new product or concept to a mass audience during the introduction period.

Competition. Typically, there are few competitors in the introduction stage, as the technology and start-up costs for a new product or product category are high.

Pricing. Usually the company that first introduces a product has the freedom to set prices as desired. Companies can "cream the price," setting it high for maximum profits on each unit, or set a low price in an attempt to obtain as many customers as possible. The pricing decision is often a function of the company's ability to produce the product, product availability, and the amount of anticipated competition.

Distribution. During the introduction stage, distribution is usually through specialized channels rather than mass distribution channels. This is because a good deal of attention needs to be paid to educating consumers about the product and how to use it.

Advertising. Advertising of a new product is usually educational in nature, convincing people to try the product and explaining how the product will provide benefits not currently found in the marketplace.

Growth Phase

Target Market. The market is still growing, with new users purchasing the product for the first time. The product is becoming accepted by a wider profile of consumers.

Competition. As product acceptance grows, the number of competitors increases.

Pricing. While competition is focused primarily on product attributes, pricing variations are introduced along with diversification and differentiation of the product. Price cutting occurs, and discounters try to steal market share and broaden the customer base by making the product or service more affordable. Higher-priced, higher-quality products are also introduced and marketed.

Distribution. Distribution expands from specialty stores to more mass distribution channels, such as chains.

Advertising. The communication focus moves away from selling the product category and educating consumers. As a result of product differentiation and increased competitive levels, advertising takes on the role of positioning particular products with specific attributes or benefits against the competition.

Maturity Phase

Target Market. The product is now accepted by all or most consumers. When bank automated teller machines were first introduced, only young innovators used them, with older adults preferring to go into a bank for transactions. Now, after a prolonged introduction period, people of all ages more readily use the machines.

Competition. The market is very competitive at this stage.

Pricing. In this stage, pricing becomes very important. Products are often standardized, with fewer product innovations and fewer discernible differences. Thus, the selling emphasis is not as much on product attributes as it is on price and customer service.

Distribution. All channels now have access to the product.

Advertising. The communication strategy shifts toward keeping and improving brand-name awareness and differentiating your product from the competition's. By this time, share of mind equals share of market. The company needs to communicate its brand name and have it included in the "evoke set" of brands that comes to mind when a customer is thinking of purchasing.

QUESTIONS TO BE ADDRESSED

- Where is your product in the product life cycle? How will this affect your marketing decisions?

TASK 3

Analyze Trial and Retrial Behavior

TRIAL BEHAVIOR

Analyze purchase rates and buying habits of the consumer and customer segments to further determine where, how, and why consumers and customers are purchasing. Buying habit information can provide invaluable insight into the target market and provide impact for marketing objectives and strategies during the writing of the marketing plan. These decisions revolve around taking advantage of consumption patterns, changing current consumption patterns (which is most difficult), or recognizing the patterns and modifying the product and the way in which the product is sold to better meet the needs of the target market.

Buying Habits. Analysis of the following factors should yield a picture of the target segment's buying habits. Most of this information can be quantified, and forms the basis of marketing objectives later in the plan.

The first task is to quantify the number of purchases and the average dollar amount per purchase per industry category and company target segments. Next, determine the average time between purchases. Knowing this, you can decide how frequently to advertise the product or provide purchase incentives. The next task is to analyze the number of items purchased per customer. If there are multiple items purchased per customer, this would significantly add to the average value of each customer. It also provides insights into cross-selling strategies (moving customers to multiple product purchases) for later in the plan. In addition, the marketer should determine if the purchase is made spontaneously or is a planned purchase.

Finally, in looking at buying habits, everything about the purchasing environment and buyer actions should be detailed. These include some of the following:

- The buying decision process of the customer. Are there other key influences that need to be addressed (spouse/child influence, point of sale merchandising, ego gratification, etc.)?
- The average purchase ratio (the percentage of store visits that result in a purchase, or the percentage of sales calls resulting in a closed sale).
- The seasonality of purchases for each of the segments analyzed.

QUESTIONS TO BE ADDRESSED

- What factors are important to the purchase decision-making process? What is the purchase decision sequence each segment makes when purchasing your product? How can you positively affect this?
- What is the average purchase amount (number of times per year and dollar amount per year) for consumer segments in your product category and for your customer segments? Do these vary? Is there an opportunity to narrow the purchase amount between the industry average and your company if you are below the average? Specifically, what is the average number of purchases per year, dollar size, and quantity of each purchase for the industry consumer segments and for your customer segments? (One, two, three bars of soap per trip/large, medium, or small package sizes?) Do consumers and customer segments purchase in bulk, stock up, or purchase your product one at a time?
- How frequently are purchases made? What is the purchase cycle for your product or service in the industry compared to your company? What is the frequency of purchase for heavy users versus other segments?
- What is the purchase ratio among industry consumer and customer segments? What percent of consumers and customers purchase when they visit the store/office or receive a sales call?
- How important is customer service, personal selling, and salesperson advice/consultation to each of the segments?
- Is the buying decision spontaneous or planned? What percent of the buying decisions are made at the point of purchase versus at home or over a longer period of time?
- Do the heavy users have different buying habits than the overall users?
- Do different target segments display unique or strong seasonality purchases? How do seasonality purchases differ among target segments?

Purchase Rates of the Industry Product Category and Your Company's Product by Geographic Markets. Geographic markets should be analyzed for their importance in sales for the category and sales for your company's product. These figures are derived using the Category Development Index and Brand Development Index, respectively. Worksheets designed to help you determine sales by category and by product are presented at the end of this chapter.

The *Category Development Index (CDI)* determines the product category's strength on a market-by-market basis. It provides a quick index of whether the geographical area or any given market's purchases are at, above, or below the average, given the size of its population in relation to the total country's population. CDI information allows the marketer to determine markets that have strong per capita sales potential. This information can be used in recommending expansion markets, predicting sales, or as rationale for investment-spending decisions.

The formula for calculating the CDI is:

$$\text{CDI} = \frac{\text{Percentage of product category's national dollar volume in a given market}}{\text{Percentage of U.S. population in a given market}}$$

EXHIBIT 2.5　National Category Development Index (CDI)

DMA*	Percent of U.S. Population	Percent of Product Dollar Volume	Category Development Index: CDI (Volume/Population)	Population Number (000)	Dollar Volume of Product Category Nationally (000)	Per Capita Consumption
Chicago	3.5%†	4.5%†	129†	8,493‡	$827,548‡	$97.4‡
Madison						
Philadelphia						
Minneapolis						
Atlanta						

*DMA = Designated marketing area defined by television viewing audience.
†3.5 percent of the U.S. population lives in Chicago; 4.5 percent of the category's national sales volume (for example, all shoes sold nationally) is from the Chicago DMA. The Chicago DMA does better in category business than the average DMA as is indicated by the CDI of 129 (4.5/3.5 = 129).
‡Further, 8,493,000 people live in the Chicago DMA. The Chicago population consumes $827,548,000 worth of the product for a per capita consumption of $97.4.

Exhibit 2.5 presents a chart that can be used to develop this information.

The *Brand Development Index (BDI)* provides an index that determines whether a geographical market purchases your company's product at, above, or below average rates, given its population in relation to your company's national market population. For example, if your company did business in only three cities, those three cities and their surrounding trading area population would define your company's national market population. BDI information is used to help formulate geographic spending strategies. Strong company markets can be protected, and weak markets can be targeted for growth.

The formula for calculating the BDI is:

$$\text{BDI} = \frac{\text{Percentage company's dollar volume in any given market}}{\text{Percentage of company's national market population that lives in any given market}}$$

Exhibit 2.6 presents a chart that can be used to develop this information.

CDI and BDI numbers are often used together. High CDI markets mean the potential exists for good sales, as the product category as a whole does well. If these same markets have low company BDI indexes with adequate product distribution and store penetration/market coverage, the markets are often targeted for aggressive marketing plans. Thus, strong category sales (high CDI) and low company sales (low BDI) can mean potential for your company's growth.

QUESTIONS TO BE ADDRESSED

- Where exactly do your customers reside? Where does the research segment reside? Do they live nationwide or are they limited to certain regions? Are they living in large cities, suburbs, or rural areas?
- Where are sales for product category strongest and weakest nationally (CDI)? Where are your company's sales strongest and weakest (BDI)?
- What markets have above- or below-average consumption per household or per person (CDI)? Does your company have different geographical distribution from that of the category in general?

EXHIBIT 2.6   Company Brand Development Index (BDI)

DMA	Percent of Company's National Market Population	Percent of Dollar Volume	Brand Development Index: BDI (Volume/Population)	Population Number (000)	Dollar Volume Company (000)	Per Capita Consumption
Chicago	11.2%*	10.0*	89*	8,493†	$200,000†	$23.55†
Madison						
Philadelphia						
Minneapolis						
Atlanta						
Etc.						

*11.2 percent of the company's total market population lives in the Chicago DMA; 10 percent of the company's sales are from the Chicago DMA. The BDI for Chicago is 89 (10/11.2 = 89) which means the DMA has a below average BDI as compared to other DMAs in the system.
†Further, 8,493,000 people live in the Chicago DMA. Company sales in Chicago are $200,000 or $23.55 per person.

EXHIBIT 2.7   Trading Areas by Store

Zip Codes Surrounding Store	Percent of Customers Over 1 Week Period
53704	20%
53705	30
53703	20
53702	10
53711	10
53708	5
53709	1
Other	4

- What are the markets at, above, or below average purchase rates on a household or per person basis (BDI)?
- Are national sales increasing at greater or lesser rates than the population growth? Are there specific markets where this is different?

Trading Areas. In addition to CDI and BDI information, the retail/service marketer should determine the trading area for the product. A *trading area* is the geographical territory where consumers and customers live. This is important from a media purchasing standpoint and also for determining future store locations, as discussed in the Distribution chapter.

Through a simple in-store customer survey, as shown in Exhibit 2.7, you can determine where your customers come from. Or, if you keep accurate customer mailing lists, they can allow you to construct trading areas.

QUESTIONS TO BE ADDRESSED

- What is the trading area for your product category? How far do consumers in the category typically travel in miles and time to purchase the product?
- How far do consumers travel to purchase your product?

RETRIAL BEHAVIOR

After trial of the first purchase of your product, it is critical to generate a second purchase, or *repeat*. If you don't generate a repeat purchase you will never get the purchaser to become an ongoing customer. If you continually generate trial but poor repeat, chances are your product is inferior to the competition, and it requires your attention for improvement. Two ways to measure retrial behavior are through brand loyalty and trial-to-retrial behavior.

Brand Loyalty. While repeat sales are more immediate, *brand loyalty* is a measure of how loyal your consumers and customers are over a period of time. If your customers primarily use only your company's product, they are brand loyal. If they use your product a majority of the time but occasionally use your competitors' products, they are moderately brand loyal. Low brand loyalty exists if brand or product switching occurs regularly in your category or with your products.

Brand loyalty is analyzed to provide insights into the following types of issues:
- How difficult it will be to keep your own customers.
- How difficult it will be to steal market share from competitors.
- The degree of promotional offers that will be needed to induce trial.
- How much media weight will be necessary to increase trial, retrial, and sales.
- Whether a true product difference or innovation is needed to compete.

A product category with extremely high brand loyalty will require more media weight, larger promotional offers or inducements, and perhaps even a product innovation in order to steal market share from existing competitors. With a low brand loyalty product category it is extremely difficult to keep your own customers, but it is also easier to steal market share.

QUESTIONS TO BE ADDRESSED
- Is buying by brand name important to consumers in your category? What percent of the consumers in the category are brand loyal most of the time, all of the time, and never?
- How brand loyal are your customers? Is brand switching common? Do heavy users have different loyalty than the overall users?

Trial-to-Retrial Ratio. Another important area of investigation is trial and retrial by consumer and customer segment. This is calculated by simply figuring the percentage of customers who purchase a second, third, or more times from you. The Hiebing Group did work for a national facial tissue manufacturer that had a specialty line of consumer package good products. The product sold was basically the same, but each was packaged for specific uses — packages of facial tissue for the car, the teenager's bedroom, dad's work area, and the woman's purse. The initial thinking was that we would expand usage categories for the products; in other words, find other places besides the car for consumers to use the product geared to the car (kids taking it to school). However, after studying the buying habit findings in the situation analysis, we discovered two things:
1. Overall trial of the family of products was very low.
2. Of those people who tried the products, retrial was very high.

In summary, the challenge was not to find more uses for the family of products, but to promote trial. Once consumers tried one of the products, the chances were good they would continue to purchase them. However, if we had found that the retrial rate was in fact very poor, we would have had another set of product-related problems on which to focus, thus taking our marketing emphasis in the direction of finding out why customers weren't satisfied with the product.

Questions to Be Addressed

- What is the trial and retrial ratio of industry consumer segments? What is the ratio for your customer segments?
- What percent of the consumer segments have tried the product category?
- What percent of your customer segment have tried your products?
- How common is retrial? What percent repeat? What percent become regular or loyal users?
- Do heavy users have different trial and retrial rates than the overall users?

Business Review Writing Style

Once you have answered the questions in each section and completed the charts, we recommend that you summarize the important findings from each section. This is helpful for two reasons. First, it is much easier to develop problems and opportunities (as you'll be doing in Chapter 3) if the business review has been condensed and summarized. Second, the summary statements provide a good management summary and support during presentations.

We've found there is no way to shortcut the length of a business review. Marketing is a broad discipline, and the marketer needs to look at relationships between many numbers in order to reach sound conclusions regarding his or her company, the marketplace, the competition, and the needs and wants of the consumer.

We recommend developing summary statements for each section of the business review. These summaries should precede each section, serving as a management summary when the final business review is ready for presentation. Your summary statements should be objective; this is no place for developing strategy. Keep the statements concise and focused on reporting the facts. Include summary rationale when needed. Here are some examples of summary statements, in this case reporting on the major findings for a canning company:

Target Market. Canned vegetable consumption is dominated by medium and heavy users. Thirty-seven percent of canned-good purchasers account for over 65 percent of the canned vegetables used per month.

Trial and Retrial. Canned vegetables are used by a high percentage (80 percent) of households. Canned vegetables are a relatively high-usage category. Fifty-nine percent of homemakers use four or more cans per month. Twenty-nine percent use 10 or more cans per month. Thirteen percent use 16 or more cans per month.

Sales. While the canned tomato category has increased dramatically (140 percent) for the industry over the past five years, Company X has experienced only moderate growth (20 percent). This is far below the industry growth pattern.

WORKSHEET

Company Strengths

- Target market needs, wants, and consumption trends

- Value the organization brings to the target market

- Product and technological

- Operational

- Distribution

- Pricing

- Promotion/marketing communications

Definition of strength:
Any capability or resource the organization has that could be used to improve its competitive position (share of market or size of market) or financial performance.

Where to find this information:
Internal company data.
Surveys of employees and management.

WORKSHEET

Company Weaknesses

- Target market needs, wants, and consumption trends

- Value the company brings to the target market

- Product and technological

- Operational

- Distribution

- Pricing

- Promotion/marketing communications

Definition of weakness:
Any capability or resource that may cause the organization to have a weaker competitive position or poorer financial performance.

Where to find this information:
Internal company data.
Surveys of employees and management.

WORKSHEET

Core Competencies

1.

2.

3.

4.

Core competencies must meet the following criteria:
- Make a significant contribution to the perceived customer's benefit of the end product.
- Are difficult for competitors to imitate.

Where to find this information:
Internal company data.
Surveys of employees and management.

WORKSHEET

Marketing Capabilities

1.

2.

3.

4.

A marketing capability must meet the following criterion:
- A unique ability to provide access to target markets versus the competition.

Where to find this information:
Internal company data.
Surveys of employees and management.

WORKSHEET

Alternative Scope Options

1.

2.

3.

4.

Where to find this information:
Internal company data.
Surveys of employees and management.

WORKSHEET

Scope Options—Strengths Needed to Succeed

Option 1 _____

Organization Rating

What's needed to succeed for the above option

	Strength	Weakness
1.		
2.		
3.		
4.		
5.		
6.		
7.		
8.		
9.		
10.		

Option 2 _____

Organization Rating

What's needed to succeed for the above option

	Strength	Weakness
1.		
2.		
3.		
4.		
5.		
6.		
7.		
8.		
9.		
10.		

Option 3 _____

Organization Rating

What's needed to succeed for the above option

	Strength	Weakness
1.		
2.		
3.		
4.		
5.		
6.		
7.		
8.		
9.		
10.		

Where to find this information:
Internal company data.
Surveys of employees and management.

Scope Options—Core Competencies Needed to Succeed

Correlation to your
organization's core competencies?

Option 1 _____

	Yes	No

1.

2.

3.

4.

Correlation to your
organization's core competencies?

Option 2 _____

	Yes	No

1.

2.

3.

4.

Correlation to your
organization's core competencies?

Option 3 _____

	Yes	No

1.

2.

3.

4.

Where to find this information:
Internal company data.
Surveys of employees and management.

WORKSHEET

Scope Options — Marketing Capabilities Needed to Succeed

Correlation to your
organization's capabilities?

Option 1 _____

Yes	No

1.

2.

3.

4.

Correlation to your
organization's capabilities?

Option 2 _____

Yes	No

1.

2.

3.

4.

Correlation to your
organization's capabilities?

Option 3 _____

Yes	No

1.

2.

3.

4.

Where to find this information:
Internal company data.
Surveys of employees and management.

WORKSHEET

Scope Options—Risks and Opportunities

OPTION 1
_____

RISKS

    1.

    2.

    3.

    4.

    5.

OPPORTUNITIES

    1.

    2.

    3.

    4.

    5.

OPTION 2
_____

RISKS

    1.

    2.

    3.

    4.

    5.

OPPORTUNITIES

    1.

    2.

    3.

    4.

    5.

OPTION 3
_____

RISKS

    1.

    2.

    3.

    4.

    5.

OPPORTUNITIES

    1.

    2.

    3.

    4.

    5.

Where to find this information:
Internal company data.
Surveys of employees and management.

WORKSHEET

Corporate Philosophy/Description of the Company

- Corporate goals and objectives

- General company history, future trends

- Organizational structure

Where to find this information:
Internal company data.

WORKSHEET

Product Analysis

- Identify products sold in the industry category and within the scope of your business.

    Industry   Company

    1.   1.

    2.   2.

    3.   3.

    4.   4.

    5.   5.

- Describe your products' history. What developments over the past years make them special today?

- Describe company and product strengths and weaknesses.

- Describe competitive product strengths and weaknesses.

- Highlight product trends within your product category(ies) from both an industry and company perspective.

Where to find this information:
Internal company data.

Sales Growth Analysis of Company Product Categories Relative to Industry Trends

	1999 Units $	1998 Units $	1997 Units $	1996 Units $	1995 Units $	% Change 1995–1999 Units $
Industry sales						
Product category						
Product category						
Product category						
Company sales						
Product/brand						
Product/brand						
Product/brand						

Where to find this information:
U.S. Bureau of the Census, current industrial reports.
Fairchild Fact Files.
Trade research.
Trade publications.
Sales and Marketing Management Survey of Buying Power.
Internal company data.
Annual reports/10-K reports from public companies.

Industry Category Sales Compared to Company Sales Resulting in Market Share Estimates

Year	Total Industry Sales M	Change	Total Company Sales M	Change	Your Company's Market Share
	$	%	$	%	%
1995					
1996					
1997					
1998					
1999					

Estimated Sales by Competitor	Sales 1999	Market Share	Sales 1998	Market Share	Sales 1997	Market Share	Sales 1996	Market Share	Sales 1995	Market Share
		%		%		%		%		%
Competitor A										
Competitor B										
Competitor C										
Total market sales										

Where to find this information:
Industry research reports.
Trade publications.
Fairchild Fact Files.
U.S. Bureau of the Census reports.
Annual reports/10-K reports from public companies.
Internal company data.
Similar chart for transactions and profits (margins).

Company Sales Trends — Store-for-Store Sales

Market	Sales Volume (M)	Change from Previous Year	Number of Stores	Per Store Average (M)	Change from Previous Year	Per Store Average Indexed to System Average ($)	(M)
City A							
City B							
City C							
City D							
City E							

(M = $000)

Note: Make sure your year-to-year analysis of per store averages includes comparable stores that have been open for the full year.

Where to find this information:
Company data.

WORKSHEET

Company Sales Trends—Sales Seasonality by Month for Industry Category and Company

Month	Company Percentage of Sales	Company Index to Average ( )	Industry Category Percentage of Sales	Industry Index to Average ( )
January				
February				
March				
April				
May				
June				
July				
August				
September				
October				
November				
December				

Where to find this information:
Fairchild Fact Files.
Company data.

WORKSHEET

Company Sales Trends—Product Brand Seasonality by Month for Industry Category and Company

	Base*	November		December		Etc.
		Percent of Total Dollars	Index to Total Year	Percent of Total Dollars	Index to Total Year	
		%		%		
Industry category sales						
Company product/brand sales						
Major competitor product/brand sales						
Company brand						

*Base equals total figures for the year.

Where to find this information:
Company data.

WORKSHEET

Behavior Trends

- Demographic trends

- Geographic trends

- Social/consumer trends

- Technological trends

- Media viewing trends

Where to find this information:
U.S. Bureau of the Census data—current population projections.
The Popcorn Report.
Yankelovich Monitor Study.
American Demographics Magazine.

WORKSHEET

Distribution Options—Purchases by Outlet Type (5-Year Trend)

	Total Sales					
	1999		**1995**		**Points Change (1999–1995)**	
Distribution Outlet Type	**Units**	**Dollars**	**Units**	**Dollars**	**Units**	**Dollars**
	%	$	%	$	%	$

Where to find this information:
Fairchild Fact Files.
Trade publications.

Distribution Methods—Store Penetration Analysis I

| | Number of Stores | Sales Last Year (M) | Estimated Number of TV HHs (M) | Current Advertising Plans | | | Future Advertising Plans | | | |
				Sales per HH	( )%* of Sales (M)	Target Market Media Weight Level	Average Sales per HH	Number of Stores Needed	( )%* of Sales (M)	Target Market Media Weight Level
Group 1 Markets (Weaker Markets)										
A										
B										
C										
D										
E										
F										
Subtotal										
Group 2 Markets (Stronger Markets)										
G										
H										
I										
J										
K										
L										
Subtotal										
Totals/Averages Groups 1 and 2										

Average per store sales Groups 1 and 2 $_____.
(M = 000)
(HH = Household)

*Fill in current percent of advertising spending and future spending based upon company records.

Where to find this information:
In-house sources/company data.
Standard Rate and Data Service publications.
Nielsen Test Markets Profiles.

WORKSHEET

Distribution Methods—Store Penetration Analysis II

	Number of Stores	Existing Stores per 100M* HHs	Total Sales Last Year (M)	Advertising Budget: Percent of Sales
A				
B				
C				
D				
E				
F				
G				
H				
I				
J				
K				
L				
All Stores				

*Or whatever you determine to be the optimum.

			Penetration of 1 Store per 100M HHs		
	Estimated 1 Week Cost	Estimated Number Weeks	Minimum 1/100M HHs	$	New Estimated Number Weeks
A					
B					
C					
D					
E					
F					
G					
H					
I					
J					
K					
L					
All Stores					

(M = 000 or $000)

(HH = Household)

Where to find this information:

In-house sources/company data.

Standard Rate and Data Service publications.

Nielsen Test Markets Profiles.

WORKSHEET

Distribution—Market Coverage Chart

	Coverage for Your Product % ACV	Percent of Shelf Space Given Your Product in Store	Percent Shelf Space for Main Competitors in Product Category	
			Competitor 1	Competitor 2
Outlet A				
Outlet B				
Outlet C				
Outlet D				
Outlet E				
Outlet F				
Outlet G				
Outlet H				
Outlet I				

Note: An identical chart would be created for each key market.

Where to find this information:
Store checks/interviews with store managers.
Nielsen.
SAMI.

Pricing—Price of Your Company's Product Relative to the Competition During Key Selling Periods

	Price 1st Quarter	Price 2nd Quarter	Price 3rd Quarter	Price 4th Quarter
Your Company				
Competitor A				
Competitor B				
Competitor C				
Competitor D				

Where to find this information:
Company data.

WORKSHEET

Pricing—Distribution of Sales by Price Point (5-Year Trend)

	Price Range Industry Product Category		Price Range Company's Product	
	Percent of Sale	Percent of Items	Percent of Sale	Percent of Items
1999				
$____ to $____				
$____ to $____				
$____ to $____				
$____ to $____				
$____ to $____				
$____ to $____				
1998				
$____ to $____				
$____ to $____				
$____ to $____				
$____ to $____				
$____ to $____				
$____ to $____				
1997				
$____ to $____				
$____ to $____				
$____ to $____				
$____ to $____				
$____ to $____				
$____ to $____				
1996, etc.				
1995, etc.				

Where to find this information:
Fairchild Fact Files
Company data.
Trade publications.

Competitive Analysis—Marketing Communications Review

Company	Total Dollar Expenditures	Share of Spending—Total Expenditures	Change from Last Year	Television			Newspaper		
				Total Dollar Expenditures	Percent	Change from Last Year	Total Dollar Expenditures	Percent	Change from Last Year
	$	%	%	$	%	%	$	%	%

Competitor	Magazine			Radio			Outdoor		
	Total Dollar Expenditures	Percent	Change from Last Year	Total Dollar Expenditures	Percent	Change from Last Year	Total Dollar Expenditures	Percent	Change from Last Year
	$	%	%	$	%	%	$	%	%

Note: The above information should also be obtained on a quarterly basis to track seasonality of spending. If available, total dollars for each category should also be obtained.

Where to find this information:
Media representatives from television stations, newspapers, radio stations, outdoor companies.
LNA (Leading National Advertisers) for national companies.
PIB.
RADAR.
Media records.
BAR.

WORKSHEET

Competitive Analysis—Marketing Review

	Your Company	Competitor A	Competitor B	Competitor C	Competitor D
Market Share/Sales					
Current					
Growth/Decline Past 5 Years					
Target Market					
Primary					
Secondary					
Marketing Objectives/Strategies					
Positioning					
Product/Branding/Packaging					
Strengths					
Weaknesses					
Pricing Strategies/Pricing Structure					
Higher/Lower/Parity					
Distribution/Store Penetration/Market Coverage Strategy					
Geographic Sales Territory					
Store/Outlet locations and descriptions of locations (e.g., for retailers strip center, mall, etc.)					
Personal Selling Strategies					
Promotion Strategies					
Advertising Message					
Media Strategies and Expenditures					
TV					
Radio					
Newspaper					
Direct Mail					
Other					
Customer Service Policies					
Merchandising Strategies					
Publicity Strategies					
Testing/Marketing R&D Strategies					
Summary of Strengths and Weaknesses					

Where to find this information:
Your company's past experiences.
Primary research.
Fairchild Fact File.
Trade publications.
Industry 10-K reports.
Media representatives.
Field sales reps.
Radio/TV reports.

WORKSHEET

Industry and Company Review of the Consumer Target Market — Demographic Profile by Volume

Demographic Descriptor	Industry Category			Company		
	Total Number of Customers	% of Total Customers	% of Total Purchases	Total Number of Customers	% of Total Customers	% of Total Purchases
Age						
Under 18						
18–24						
25–34						
35–44						
45–54						
55+						
Sex						
Male						
Female						
Household Income						
$15,000 and Under						
$15,001–$24,000						
$24,001–$30,000						
$30,001–$40,000						
$40,001–$50,000						
$50,001+						
Education						
Did not graduate high school						
Graduated high school						
Some college						
Graduated college						
Occupation						
White-collar						
Blue-collar						
Farmer						
Employment						
Full-time						
Part-time						
Unemployed						
Family Size						
1						
2						
3–4						
5–6						
7+						
Geography						
Urban						
Suburban						
Rural						
Home						
Own home						
Rent						

Where to find this information:
SMRB (Simmons Market Research Bureau).
MRI (Mediamark Research, Inc.).
Fairchild Fact Files.
Census data/county business patterns.
Industry trade publications/research departments.
Industry research studies (supplied through trade associations).

WORKSHEET

Industry and Company Review of the Consumer Target Market — Demographic Profile by Concentration

Demographic Descriptor	Percent of Industry Total Category that Purchases Product Nationally	Concentration Index*	Percent of Company Customer Who Purchases
Age			
Under 18			
18–24			
25–34			
35–44			
45–54			
55+			
Sex			
Male			
Female			
Household Income			
$15,000 and Under			
$15,001–$24,000			
$24,001–$30,000			
$30,001–$40,000			
$40,001–$50,000			
$50,001+			
Education			
Did not graduate high school			
Graduated high school			
Some college			
Graduated college			
Occupation			
White-collar			
Blue-collar			
Farmer			
Employment			
Full-time			
Part-time			
Unemployed			
Family Size			
1			
2			
3–4			
5–6			
7+			
Geography			
Urban			
Suburban			
Rural			
Home			
Own home			
Rent			

*% of industry category that purchases/% of the total population that purchases (e.g., 10% of all people purchase, but 30% of the 18–24-year-olds purchase, or a 300 index — 30 + 10)

Where to find this information:
SMRB (Simmons Market Research Bureau).
MRI (Mediamark Research, Inc.).
Fairchild Fact Files.
Census data/county business patterns.
Industry trade publications/research surveys from trade publications.
Your company records.

WORKSHEET

Review of the Consumer Target Market — Demographic Description of Company Purchasers Compared to Industry Category Purchasers

Demographic Descriptor	Percent Purchasers of Industry Category Nationally ( )*	Percent Purchasers of Company Product ( )*	Index: % Company/% Industry
Age			
Under 18			
18–24			
25–34			
35–44			
45–54			
55+			
Sex			
Male			
Female			
Household Income			
$15,000 and Under			
$15,001–$24,000			
$24,001–$30,000			
$30,001–$40,000			
$40,001–$50,000			
$50,001+			
Education			
Did not graduate high school			
Graduated high school			
Some college			
Graduated college			
Occupation			
White-collar			
Blue-collar			
Farmer			
Employment			
Full-time			
Part-time			
Unemployed			
Family Size			
1			
2			
3–4			
5–6			
7+			
Geography			
Urban			
Suburban			
Rural			
Home			
Own home			
Rent			

*Provide total dollar volume in parentheses.

Where to find this information:
SMRB (Simmons Market Research Bureau).
MRI (Mediamark Research, Inc.).
Your company records.
Primary research.

WORKSHEET

Review of the Consumer Target Market—Heavy-User Demographic Descriptors Compared to All User Demographics Descriptors

Heavy User Demographic Profile	% of Purchases
Age	
Sex	
Household income	
Education	
Employment	
Family Size	
Geography	
Home ownership	

Lifestyle description of the heavy user compared to the average user

Attribute preference

Geographic location

Where to find this information:
SMRB (Simmons Market Research Bureau).
MRI (Mediamark Research, Inc.).
Your company records.
Primary research.

WORKSHEET

Business-to-Business Target Market—National Distribution of Businesses by Size Within SIC Category

SIC	Total Businesses		Percent of Businesses by Employment Size Class						Percent of Businesses by Dollar Volume					
	Number	% of Total Census	1 to 4	5 to 9	10 to 19	20 to 49	50 to 99	100+	$000– $1MM	$1MM– $10MM	$10MM– $50MM	$50MM– $100MM	$100MM– $500MM	$500MM+
Agriculture/ Forestry/ Fisheries														
Mining														
Construction														
Manufacturing														
Transportation														
Public Utilities														
Wholesale Trade														
Retail Trade														
Finance/ Insurance/ Real Estate Services														
Public Administration														
Percent														
Total Census (M = $000)														

Where to find this information:
County business patterns.
U.S. Department of Commerce.
U.S. Bureau of the Census.
Dun's Marketing Service, a company of the Dun & Bradstreet Corporation.

Business-to-Business Target Market—Company Distribution of Customers by Size Within SIC Category

This chart demonstrates the total number of customers a firm has and categorizes those businesses by SIC category. The SIC categories could be further broken out if necessary (e.g., sporting good retailers versus the overall category of retailers.) It also delineates the number of businesses by SIC within the size parameters of number of employees and dollar volume of the business. This chart can then be compared with the previous one to determine company penetration of each SIC category.

SIC	Company Customers % of Total Number	Customers	Percent of Businesses by Employment Size Class 1–4	5–9	10–19	20–49	50–99	100+	Percent of Businesses by Dollar Volume $000–$1MM	$1MM–$10MM	$10MM–$50MM	$50MM–$100MM	$100MM–$500MM	$500MM+
Agriculture/ Forestry/ Fisheries														
Mining														
Construction														
Manufacturing														
Transportation														
Public Utilities														
Wholesale Trade														
Retail Trade														
Finance/ Insurance/ Real Estate														
Services														
Public Administration														
Percent														
Total Census (M = $000)														

Where to find this information:
Company data.

Business-to-Business Target Market — Revenue Distribution of Customers by SIC Category

SIC	Number of Customers	Total Company Sales per SIC Category	Average $ per Customer ($M)	Index to Average (Average $ per Customer/ Average all Categories)
Agriculture/ Forestry/ Fisheries				
Mining				
Construction				
Manufacturing				
Transportation				
Public Utilities				
Wholesale Trade				
Retail Trade				
Finance/ Insurance/Real Estate Services				
Administration				
Total				
Average All Categories (M = $000)				

Where to find this information:
Trade publications.
Company records.

WORKSHEET

Business-to-Business Target Market — Product Category Purchases by Outlet Type

Outlet Type	Where Consumers Purchase	Percent of Total Outlets

Where to find this information:
Trade publications.
Industry sources.

Product Awareness

- First mention/top of mind awareness relative to competition by target market segment

    Segment 1:

    Segment 2:

    Segment 3:

- Unaided awareness relative to competition by target market segment

    Segment 1:

    Segment 2:

    Segment 3:

- Aided awareness relative to competition by target market segment

    Segment 1:

    Segment 2:

    Segment 3:

Where to find this information:
Primary research data—telephone survey.

WORKSHEET

Product Attributes

- Attribute importance by target market segments

<u>Segment</u>   <u>Attribute Importance</u>

1.

2.

3.

4.

- Competitive ranking of attributes by target market segments
  (Your company's rank for each attribute relative to the competitors')

<u>Segment</u>   <u>Attribute Ranking</u>

1.

2.

3.

4.

Where to find this information:
Primary research data—telephone survey.

WORKSHEET

Behavior — National Category Development Index (CDI)

DMA	Percent of U.S. Population	Percent of Industry Category Dollar Volume	Category Development Index: CDI (Volume/ Population)	Population Number (000)	Dollar Volume of Industry Category Nationally ($000)	Per Capita Consumption
City 1	%	%			$	$
City 2						
City 3						
City 4						

Where to find this information:
Sales & Marketing Management Survey of Buying Power.

WORKSHEET

Behavior — Company Brand Development Index (BDI)

DMA	Percent of Company Population	Percent of Company Dollar Volume	Brand Development Index: BDI (Volume/ Population)	Population Number (000)	Dollar Volume of Company ($000)	Per Capita Consumption
City 1	%	%			$	$
City 2						
City 3						
City 4						

Where to find this information:
Company data.

WORKSHEET

Behavior — Trading Areas by Store

Zip Codes Surrounding Store	Percent of Customers over 1 Week Period
	%
_____	_____
_____	_____
_____	_____
_____	_____

Where to find this information:
Company store survey.
Company mailing lists.

WORKSHEET

Behavior — Brand Loyalty

Brand	All	Sole	Loyalty Index	Sole and Primary	Loyalty Index	All Users
	%	%		%		%

Where to find this information:
SMRB (Simmons Market Research Bureau).
MRI (Mediamark Research, Inc.).
Primary research.

WORKSHEET

Behavior — Purchase Rates/Buying Habits

- Average # of purchases per <u>customer</u> in industry　　　　　　_____

- Average # purchases per <u>company</u> customer　　　　　　_____

- Average industry: $ per <u>consumer</u> purchase　　　　　　_____

- Average company: $ per <u>customer</u> purchase　　　　　　_____

- Average industry: number of items purchased per
  consumer purchase　　　　　　_____

- Average company: number of items purchased for
  customer purchase　　　　　　_____

- Company market share　　　　　　_____

  $ market share　　　　　　_____

  % of target market penetration
  (Percent of target market universe which is a customer)　　_____

Note: The above should be completed for the aggregate consumer/customer and for each significant segment.

Note: A similar chart should be developed for the heavy user segment contrasting heavy users to all users.

WORKSHEET

Purchasing Rates/Buying Habits for Retail

This chart provides examples of how to monitor heavy user purchase behavior through primary research. A "heavy purchasers" and "all purchasers" category is provided for each question.

Number of _____ (whatever the product category) purchased in one year.
        Heavy purchasers _____.
        All purchasers _____.

Number of stores usually visited to find what you want per purchaser.
        Heavy purchasers _____.
        All purchasers _____.

Amount purchased per visit (dollars and units).
        Heavy purchasers _____.
        All purchasers _____.

Visits to your store per month/year.
        Heavy purchasers _____.
        All purchasers _____.

Visits to all stores per month/year.
        Heavy purchasers _____.
        All purchasers _____.

Purchases at your store per month/year.
        Heavy purchasers _____.
        All purchasers _____.

Purchases at all stores per month/year.
        Heavy purchasers _____.
        All purchasers _____.

Average purchase ratio in percent or people who purchase versus those who do not with each visit to the store.
        Heavy purchasers _____.
        All purchasers _____.

Note: The above should be completed for the aggregate consumer/customer and for each significant segment.

Where to find this information:
In-store survey.

WORKSHEET

Behavior—Trial/Retrial

	Percent Ever Used	Percent Used Last 6 Months	Loyalty Measure: Percent Used Past 6 Months/ Percent Ever Used
Company			
1. Segment			
Product			
Product			
Product			
2. Segment			
Product			
Product			
Product			
Competition			
1. Segment			
Product			
Product			
Product			
2. Segment			
Product			
Product			
Product			

Where to find this information:
Market survey.

Step 2: Problems/Opportunities

MARKETING BACKGROUND

1 THE BUSINESS REVIEW

Scope
Company Strengths & Weaknesses • Core Competencies •
Marketing Capabilities

Product and Market Review
Company & Product Review • Category & Company Sales •
Behavior Trends • Pricing • Distribution • Competitive Review

Target Market Effectors
Consumer/Business-to-Business Targets • Product Awareness &
Attributes • Trial & Retrial Data

2 PROBLEMS/OPPORTUNITIES

MARKETING PLAN

3 SALES OBJECTIVES

4 TARGET MARKETS AND MARKETING OBJECTIVES

5 PLAN STRATEGIES—Positioning & Marketing

6 COMMUNICATION GOALS

7 TACTICAL MARKETING MIX TOOLS

Product	Distribution	Advertising Media
Branding	Personal Selling/Service	Merchandising
Packaging	Promotion/Events	Publicity
Pricing	Advertising Message	

8 MARKETING PLAN BUDGET AND CALENDAR

9 EXECUTION

10 EVALUATION

PROBLEMS AND OPPORTUNITIES 3

FROM THIS CHAPTER YOU WILL LEARN:

- HOW TO IDENTIFY PROBLEMS AND OPPORTUNITIES FROM THE MATERIAL YOU DEVELOPED IN YOUR BUSINESS REVIEW.
- HOW TO EXPRESS ACTIONABLE PROBLEMS AND OPPORTUNITIES IN A SUCCINCT WRITTEN FORMAT THAT ALLOWS AN ORGANIZED TRANSITION INTO WRITING THE MARKETING PLAN.

NOW THAT YOU HAVE DEVELOPED A THOROUGH, OBJECTIVE BUSINESS REVIEW, you can use this material to begin preparing your marketing plan. The first task is to categorize your business review's major conclusions into either problems that need to be solved or opportunities that can be exploited. When you write your marketing plan, your objectives and strategies will come directly from the problems and opportunities you identify here. The next task is to record your identified problems and opportunities as concise, actionable statements.

TASK 1

Identify Problems and Opportunities

To begin, list headings that correspond to the steps and sections of your business review (e.g., Product and Market Review—Behavior Trends or Product and Market Review—Distribution) on pieces of paper. Under each heading, create separate categories for problems and opportunities. A worksheet showing the format for this task is provided at the end of this chapter.

Next, carefully read each section of the business review to identify as many meaningful problems and opportunities as possible. Ask yourself whether this information is actionable? Is it a current problem that needs to be solved, or an opportunity that can be exploited?

What Is a Problem?

A *problem* is derived from situations of weakness. The common denominator among problems is that they are defensive in nature; as a result, you will be correcting a negative. A problem statement is an actionable statement that can be derived from a single finding or a set of findings that make for a potentially negative situation. A problem statement also addresses market conditions that can result in a disadvantage for your company or the industry as a whole.

As a case in point, in reviewing the target market section in the business review for a retail client, we discovered that there was a heavy-purchaser group—30 percent of the customers purchased 68 percent of the product. When we looked more closely at this heavy-purchaser group, the heaviest concentration was in the segment composed of females aged 35–49 with children. Our client was strongest in attracting younger purchasers, and while the heavy purchaser shopped at our client's stores, the majority of her purchases were made elsewhere. This information led to the following problems under the target market effectors section:

- The company's purchaser tends to be younger, with fewer 35–49 purchasers (the single strongest purchasing segment for heavy users) when compared to the profile of the heavy purchaser.

- The heavy purchaser is shopping the stores but is making a majority of her purchases elsewhere.

Subsequently in the marketing plan, the retailer put effort into developing a program to more fully satisfy the heavy purchaser's needs through the merchandise selection, and also doing a better job of selling the customer in-store on the full line of products.

What Is an Opportunity?

Opportunities are developed from strengths or positive circumstances. They are statements that point out strengths of the firm. They also identify areas where your company can exploit a weakness of the competition. In short, they address market conditions that can result in an advantage to your company if positive action is taken. Often, a combination of circumstances makes for a potentially positive situation, creating an opportunity. When we reviewed the competitive situation for a statewide accounting firm, we determined that there were very few accounting firms with aggressive, disciplined marketing programs. Even fewer of these firms actually advertised through mass communication vehicles. Also, we found that, of the firms advertising, none were targeting small- to medium-sized businesses. An earlier demand analysis had shown that the greatest potential for our client was in providing a full range of accounting services to small- to medium-sized businesses in the retail, service, and financial SIC categories. This combination of information provided the following opportunities:

- While there is fairly heavy competition in the trading areas of the CPA firm, there is limited advertising of CPA services; no single CPA firm dominates either consumer or business awareness of accounting firms.
- No CPA firm is directly communicating to the small- to medium-sized business target market, yet this market represents the majority of potential business in terms of actual numbers of clients.

These opportunities meant two things: First, because of the limited advertising clutter pertaining to accounting firms, an aggressive, targeted campaign could dominate the accounting advertising and build high awareness levels. Second, if the messages were strategic and meaningful to the target audience, then the increased share of mind or awareness level should be translated into increases in share of business or share of market.

Is It a Problem or an Opportunity?

Many times, what appears to be a problem can also be an opportunity. An example is the following sales analysis problem:

> While Heartland Men's Apparel sales are strong during the holiday period of November and December, sales are below that of the men's apparel category nationally. This situation occurs because Heartland Apparel stores are not located in malls that generate heavy traffic during these periods.
>
> While this is a problem for the company, it is also an opportunity. If national sales are at a peak during the November and December periods, then the opportunity exists to capture a larger percentage of these sales. However, because of the stores' locations, it is difficult to do as well as the average store nationally during this period. Thus, this statement is both a problem and an opportunity.

As a general rule, try to determine if the statement is more of a problem or an opportunity. In this example, it is very difficult to change locations in retail, so this overriding factor would make the above statement a problem. In either case, however, the marketer would probably choose to address the problem or the opportunity by attempting to increase sales in the months of November and December.

Problem and opportunity statements are concise, one-sentence statements that draw conclusions. If necessary, there can be a brief follow-up using supporting data or rationale. The rationale should utilize key factual data or findings from the business review. This will enable you to quickly support your problem and opportunity statements during a presentation.

Writing Style Examples

The following examples demonstrate the writing style to use when formulating problem and opportunity statements.

Product and Market Review — Sales

Problems

- *The men's suit and sport coat market constitutes a relatively limited market.* Total purchases of suits and sport coats by males in a given year are low in the absolute, and the category has lower purchase rates when compared to most other nondurable consumer goods. In addition, while small percentages of males purchase any suit or sport coat in a given year, the majority of those purchasers buy only one suit or sport coat per year.
- *The Reed Company has experienced a market share decline over the past five years.* This loss in market share has been primarily to the market leaders, Birkenshire and Cale Corporation, which increased share during the last five years. The remainder of the market has remained fairly stable during this time period.

	Market Share	Percentage Change Last 5 Years
The Reed Company	10	–12%
Birkenshire	25	+15
Cale Corporation	20	+7

Opportunity

- *Sales data show that a small number of distributors account for a majority of sales dollars.* Forty accounts provide nearly 70 percent of the distributor's sales, yet these 40 accounts make up only 12 percent of the distributors who purchase from Seth Cooper & Sons Office Supplies.

Target Market Effectors — Target Market

Problems

- *Multiple target markets exist.* Each target market has different demographics, needs, and wants. No single dominating customer group can be targeted.
- *The facial tissue's customers skew very old, with a small to nonexistent percentage of users coming from teens and young adults.* The brand is developing virtually no new users from which to regenerate the consumer franchise.

Target Market Effectors — Awareness

Problem

- *Unaided awareness for the Philo company is fourth.* This continues its trend downward relative to the top three competitors over the past three years.

Opportunity

- The Brennan Company dominates unaided awareness among the most influential target market of purchasing agents at snack food companies.

Target Market Effectors — Trial and Retrial Behavior

Problem

- *While the Southwest consumes more of the product on a per capita basis than any other part of the country, The Torger Company has relatively poor sales in this region.* This is because it has yet to fully expand distribution to this portion of the country.

Opportunity

- *Although total trial of the company's brands is very low, retrial is above the category average.* Thus, greater rates of consumers become regular users than is normal for the category, meaning product acceptance is very high.

It is important that your problem and opportunity section stay factual by summarizing findings from the business review. Problems and opportunities do not show what is to be done, but rather point out areas that need attention. They describe the current market environment. Leave the solutions to the marketing plan.

The following is not an opportunity statement because it demonstrates what should be done:

Advertise during the strong seasonal times of the year that exist during August, September, December, and April.

The correct opportunity statement relating to the above would be:

The industry is extremely seasonal, with strong purchasing months of August, September, December, and April.

FORMAT

Problems and Opportunities

Scope

Problems   Opportunities

Product and Market Review

Corporate Philosophy/Description of the Company

Problems   Opportunities

Product Analysis

Problems   Opportunities

Category and Company Sales

Problems   Opportunities

Behavior Trends

Problems   Opportunities

Distribution

Problems   Opportunities

Pricing

Problems   Opportunities

Competitive Review

Target Market Effectors

Target Market

Problems   Opportunities

Awareness

Problems   Opportunities

Attitudes

Problems   Opportunities

Trial

Problems   Opportunities

Retrial

Problems   Opportunities

Step 3: Sales Objectives

MARKETING BACKGROUND

1 THE BUSINESS REVIEW

Scope
- Company Strengths & Weaknesses • Core Competencies • Marketing Capabilities

Product and Market Review
- Company & Product Review • Category & Company Sales • Behavior Trends • Pricing • Distribution • Competitive Review

Target Market Effectors
- Consumer/Business-to-Business Targets • Product Awareness & Attributes • Trial & Retrial Data

2 PROBLEMS/OPPORTUNITIES

MARKETING PLAN

3 SALES OBJECTIVES

4 TARGET MARKETS AND MARKETING OBJECTIVES

5 PLAN STRATEGIES—Positioning & Marketing

6 COMMUNICATION GOALS

7 TACTICAL MARKETING MIX TOOLS

Product	Distribution	Advertising Media
Branding	Personal Selling/Service	Merchandising
Packaging	Promotion/Events	Publicity
Pricing	Advertising Message	

8 MARKETING PLAN BUDGET AND CALENDAR

9 EXECUTION

10 EVALUATION

SALES OBJECTIVES

- WHAT SALES OBJECTIVES ARE, AND WHY THEY ARE IMPORTANT.
- THE QUANTITATIVE AND QUALITATIVE FACTORS THAT AFFECT THE SETTING OF SALES OBJECTIVES.
- HOW TO SET YOUR OWN SALES OBJECTIVES USING A THREE-STEP PROCESS.

NOW THAT YOU HAVE COMPLETED THE BACKGROUND SECTION of the planning process—the business review and problems/opportunities—you are ready to prepare the actual marketing plan.

Your first task is to set sales objectives. *Sales objectives* are self-defining in that they represent projected levels of goods or services to be sold. Everything that follows in the marketing plan is designed to meet the sales objectives—from confirming the size of the target market and establishing realistic marketing objectives all the way through to setting the amount of product produced or inventoried. Further, because this step sets the tone for the entire plan, establishing sales objectives is one of the most important and demanding steps in the process.

As you read through this chapter and begin setting your own sales objectives, keep the following guidelines in mind:

1. Because sales objectives have substantial impact on a business, they must be simultaneously challenging and attainable. Accordingly, sales objectives should be based on an accurate estimate of the market opportunity and the capacity of the organization to realize those opportunities.

2. You must set time-specific sales objectives in order to provide a start and end date for your marketing program. It is also important to set both short-term and long-term sales objectives. Short-term sales objectives are generally for time periods of one year or less, while long-term ones usually include sales objectives for a minimum of three years.

3. Setting measurable sales objectives provides the means for determining what must be included in your marketing plan and for evaluating its success. Accordingly, sales objectives are quantified in terms of dollars and units for manufacturing firms, dollars and transactions (and occasionally units) for retail firms, and dollars and persons served for service firms.

4. Projected profits, a direct result of sales, should also be included in the sales objective section of your plan. As the author of this plan, you must understand the profit expectations to effectively prepare and evaluate the marketing plan. Further, if you are not operating in a pure business environment, keep in mind that sales objectives can be defined in terms other than dollars or units. As an example, for a nonprofit organization with programs dedicated to the prevention of child abuse, the goal might be a specific number of phone calls asking for help or reporting cases of abuse.

5. Both quantitative and qualitative factors must be taken into consideration in the development of sales objectives. Quantitative factors are used first and can help to numerically calculate specific sales objectives, such as (1) the trending

of the market and your company's share of the market, (2) sales history of your company, and (3) historical and projected company operating budgets along with profit expectations.

Qualitative factors are more subjective because of nonavailability and difficulty in quantifying certain types of information, such as the future economy and competition and where your product is relative to its life cycle. Therefore, interpretation of these additional subjective factors leads to an adjustment of the quantitatively based sales objectives.

How to Set Sales Objectives

The methodology we recommend for setting sales objectives involves three tasks, as depicted in Exhibit 4.1:

1. Setting individual sales objectives using three different quantitative methods.
2. Reconciling these different quantitative goals into composite sales objectives.
3. Adjusting the composite objectives through the interpolation of relative qualitative factors.

Because this methodology is both quantitative and qualitative, your sales objectives will be a composite of data-based estimates and educated guesses. If you use a disciplined process in setting sales objectives, these goals will be based more on realistic estimates and less on guessing.

Worksheets designed to help you set sales objectives and a marketing plan format for writing sales objectives are provided at the end of this chapter.

TASK 1
Set Quantitative Sales Objectives

If the data are available, we suggest you use the following three quantitative methods for setting sales objectives: outside macro, inside micro, and expenses plus. Each method helps you develop a sales objective estimate, and each estimate will provide one of three parameters from which to make realistic judgments in arriving at a final sales objective(s). While each method can be used exclusively in arriving at a sales objective, the final outcome will not be as reliable as when you apply all three approaches. By using the three different approaches, you develop sales objectives derived from three different sets of data—a safeguard against using only one set of data that might not be totally reliable or complete. If you have limited sales data available, an alternative method for setting the initial sales objective is the new product category approach, which will be explained later in the chapter.

Outside Macro Approach

In the *outside macro approach*, first look outside your immediate company environment and estimate total market or category sales for each of the next *three years*. Then, estimate your company's current and future share of the market for the next three years. Finally, multiply the total market or category projections by the market share estimate for each of the next three years to arrive at your sales objectives. You should end up with a three-year projection for both unit and dollar sales.

To arrive at these estimates, begin with a review of the past five-year trend of each marketplace in which your product, service, or retail store competes. (If five years of sales data are not available, use what data you have and supplement with available data from similar businesses to arrive at a trending of the marketplace.) If the market is trending up at a 5 percent rate, you could project the market to continue to grow at this rate for each of the next three years.

Market Trend Line Sales Projection. Rather than applying a straight percentage increase to arrive at market volume for future years, you can statistically develop a market trend line. If you were projecting sales in dollars for 2004, and you had a market change from $800,000 in 1996 to $900,000 in 2001, you would do the following:

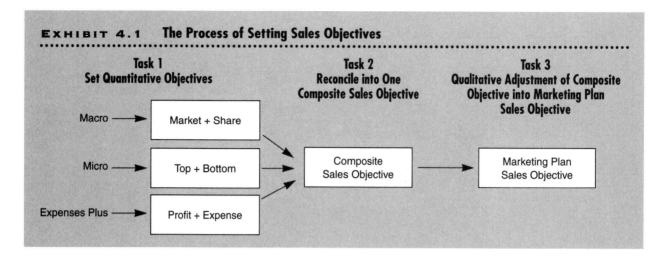

EXHIBIT 4.1   The Process of Setting Sales Objectives

Task 1
Set Quantitative Objectives

Task 2
Reconcile into One
Composite Sales Objective

Task 3
Qualitative Adjustment of Composite
Objective into Marketing Plan
Sales Objective

Macro → Market + Share

Micro → Top + Bottom → Composite Sales Objective → Marketing Plan Sales Objective

Expenses Plus → Profit + Expense

Market change 1996–2001 = $100,000 ($800,000 to $900,000)
Market change period = five years (1996–2001)
Average $ change per year = $20,000 ($100,000 ÷ 5)
$ change for eight-year period (1996–2004) = $160,000 ($20,000 × 8)
Projected $ sales for 2004 = $960,000 ($800,000 from base year 1996 + $160,000
for change over eight-year period)

This method of projecting sales, referred to as *freehand*, is the simplest method of determining trend lines. You can use this trend line approach for both dollars and unit sales. If there is a substantial fluctuation in past sales year by year, you can arrive at a mathematically generated trend line by using the least squares method. If this is necessary, we suggest you refer to a text on business statistics.

Company/Product Trend Line Share Projection. To arrive at a share of market estimate, review the change of your company's share over the past five years and project a similar share change for the future. You can estimate a percentage point change or use the same freehand approach shown in the above example. If you were estimating a share number for 2003 and your share changed from 10 percent in 1997 to 16.5 in 2002, you would do the following:

Share change 1997–2002 = 6.5 points (from 10 percent to 16.5 percent)
Share change period = five years (1997–2002)
Average change per year = 1.3 points (6.5 points ÷ 5 years)
Share change for six-year period (1997–2003) = 7.8 points (1.3 × 6)
Projected share for 2003 = 17.8 percent (10 percent share from base year 1998 +
7.8 percentage point change over six-year period)

Again, once you have arrived at a projected number for market sales and units and a projected share of the market for each, multiply the total market estimates by the estimated market shares to arrive at a sales objective for dollars and units. You would apply this macro method in each of the years for which you are developing sales objectives. Exhibit 4.2 provides an example of how this method can be used. Modify the worksheet at the end of this chapter to include transactions if you are in the retail business; modify it from units to persons/companies served if you are in the service business.

Inside Micro Approach

Having reviewed outside market sales, next review your own organization's sales history. Start at the top, and review your organization's total sales. Using the straight percentage or trend line approach discussed above, arrive at projected three-year sales for your company. From the top go further, and using the straight percentage or trend line approach, estimate sales for each product or department, adding the projected sales of each product/department

EXHIBIT 4.2   Sales Objectives: Macro Method

Market and Share Data

	Market Sales Volume				Company Share Percent of the Market			
	$ (MM)	Percent Change Previous Year	Units (MM)	Percent Change Previous Year	$	Percent Point Change from Previous Year	Units	Percent Point Change from Previous Year
Previous 5 Years								
1996	$ 952.2	13.3%	449.1	5.1%	5.0%	0.1	4.0%	0.2
1997	1,067.0	12.1	484.0	7.8	5.1	0.1	4.7	0.7
1998	1,135.1	6.4	508.2	5.0	6.1	1.0	5.2	0.5
1999	1,202.9	6.0	527.9	3.9	6.5	0.4	5.7	0.5
2000	1,275.0	6.0	544.0	3.0	6.6	0.1	6.1	0.4
Projections Next 3 Years								
2001	1,355.7	6.3	567.7	4.4	7.0	0.4	6.6	0.5
2002	1,436.4	5.9	591.4	4.1	7.4	0.4	7.1	0.5
2003	1,517.1	5.6	615.1	4.0	7.8	0.4	7.6	0.5

Three-Year Sales Projection for Company

	Dollars			Units		
Year	Market Sales Volume (MM)	× Company Share Percent of Market =	Company Sales (MM)	Market Sales Unit Volume (MM)	× Company Unit Share Percent of Market =	Company Unit Sales (MM)
2001	$1,355.7	7.0%	$ 94.9	567.7	6.6%	37.5
2002	1,436.4	7.4	106.3	591.4	7.1	42.0
2003	1,517.1	7.8	118.3	615.1	7.6	47.0

together for a three-year company total. Reconcile this total with your initial sales estimate for the entire organization to determine an ultimate top projection.

Next, review your sales by dollars and units from the bottom up to arrive at an esti-mated sales figure. *Bottom up* means estimating sales from where they are generated, such as sales by each channel, store unit, or service office/center. Based on history and changes in the marketplace, estimate sales for each bottom-up sales generator and add them together to determine each year's projection. You can use the straight percent or trend line approach for each year's projection. However, if you have either a vast amount or very little data to process, you might have to estimate, rather than calculate, each sales projection. Make sure you fac-tor in any projected price increases or decreases at this time.

Exhibit 4.3 provides an example of how to prepare a top-to-bottom sales forecast. Worksheets for the top and bottom sales forecasting needed to apply the micro method are provided at the end of this chapter.

If you are in a manufacturing business, your bottom-up generator becomes the distribu-tion channel (direct accounts, wholesaler/distributors, etc.). If you are in the retail business, build up to a total sales estimate by estimating by store, by market, and by district/region. Use this same approach if you are in the service business. It is often a good idea to have par-ticipation from the sales force or the retail/service people in the field, as they estimate sales in their area of responsibility.

EXHIBIT 4.3   Sales Objectives: Micro Method

Projection from Top: Sales Forecast for Manufacturing, Service, or Retail Category*

	Company Sales Volume			
	$ (MM)	Percent Change Previous Year	Units (MM)	Percent Change Previous Year
Previous 5 Years				
1996	$ 47.7	10.3%	20.2	6.0%
1997	54.1	13.4	22.8	12.8
1998	68.8	27.1	28.8	26.3
1999	78.0	13.3	32.7	13.5
2000	84.2	7.9	34.0	4.0
Next 3 Years' Projections				
2001	93.3	10.8	37.5	10.3
2002	102.4	9.8	41.0	9.3
2003	111.5	8.9	44.4	8.3

Projections from Bottom: Sales Forecast by Distribution Channel for Manufacturers*†

	Existing			New		
	Number	Dollars (MM)	Units (MM)	Number	Dollars (MM)	Units (MM)
Direct Accounts	25	$29.2	9.2	6	$5.6	2.4
Wholesalers/Brokers	74	62.4	26.5	6	2.1	0.9
Other	—	—	—	—	—	—
Total	99	$91.6	35.7	12	$7.7	3.3

Projections from Bottom: Sales Forecast by Store for Retailers*†

	Existing Stores	
Market	Dollars (000)	Transactions (000)
Green Bay/Store Number		
3	$ 773.7	73.6
4	276.8	25.2
5	449.8	41.8
7	285.6	23.2
8	343.5	30.5
Market Total	$2,129.4	194.3
Madison/Store Number		
1	644.1	59.5
2	396.6	35.0
6	534.7	46.0
9 (new, open 9 months)	400.0	36.0
Market Total	$1,975.4	176.5
Grand Total	$4,104.8	370.8

*Based on your type of business, include in your sales projections dollars and units/transactions/persons served, and take into consideration *new* products, distribution channels, stores or services, and price changes. Service organizations use service office/center in place of stores. Manufacturers use net dollar sales to trade/intermediate markets, and retail/service firms use dollar sales to ultimate purchasers.

†For bottom-up projections, develop projections for each year for a three-year period.

To arrive at a final micro sales objective, you must then reconcile the organization's sales estimates derived from the top with those derived from the bottom.

Expenses-Plus Approach

Once you have the outside, macro-based estimates and the inside, micro-based estimates, it makes good sense to estimate the sales level needed to cover planned expenses and make a profit. This budget-based sales objective approach is more short term in nature and is most useful in helping to arrive at your one-year sales objective. You can, however, develop sales objectives for each year of a three-year sales period by employing this approach. A sales objective derived from expense and profit expectations can differ dramatically from a sales objective generated from a market or company sales trend projection. This difference in projections may signal the need for a more conservative or aggressive marketing plan. Although very simplistic, it is also very real because it details the sales that have to be generated in order to stay in business and make a profit.

To arrive at a sales objective using this method, you will need budget data. If your company has been doing business for a number of years, it is relatively easy to estimate expenses and expected profits for the next year by reviewing your historical financial data. It is a good learning experience, particularly if you are new in the business, to review the cost of goods, operating margins, expenses, and profits within the industry and for other comparable businesses. Industry guidelines such as these are available from libraries, trade associations, and the Business Census.

A number of methods can be used to develop a budget-based sales objective. With expenses plus, a common approach that we apply in our business, you first estimate your operating expenses (marketing, administrative, etc.) in total dollars for the upcoming year. Next, subtract your expected profit (pretax) percentage from your expected gross margin percentage (Gross Sales − Cost of Goods Sold = Net Sales; Net Sales ÷ Gross Sales = Gross Margin) to determine an estimated expense percentage. The gross margin percentage is available from historical company records and/or from industry guideline data. The estimated expense percent is divided into the estimated expense dollars to determine the required sales necessary to meet expense and profit goals. Once you have developed your dollar expenses-plus sales objectives, you can arrive at a corresponding unit objective by dividing the dollar objective by the average sales unit price. Exhibit 4.4 presents an example of a review of data and calculations for the expenses-plus approach. A worksheet for your computations is provided at the end of this chapter.

Alternative: New Product/Category Approach

As mentioned earlier, you can use a target market approach to setting sales objectives when you have limited or no sales history. This approach is particularly useful for new products or product categories. Review the potential target market and work backward to a sales objective number. An example for a package goods product follows:

Potential target market consumers	2,500M
(Defined by demography, geography, usage, etc.)	
Expected trial rate	4 percent
Initial trial units	100M
Percent making repeat purchases	40 percent
Repeat purchases	40M
Number of repeat purchases	5
Repeat units	200M
Initial trial units	100M
Units sold nationally	300M
Cases (12 units per case)	25M
Gross sales (@ $10.74/case)	$268.5M

EXHIBIT 4.4   Sales Objectives: Expenses-Plus Method

Review of Historical Financial Data

Previous 5 Years	Gross Margin Percent of Sales	Profit Percent of Sales	Percent of Sales	Expenses Dollars (MM)
1996	33.4%	4.5%	29.1%	$13.9
1997	35.1	3.1	32.1	17.1
1998	37.2	3.1	34.1	23.5
1999	35.2	1.0	35.5	27.7
2000	31.3	1.0	30.1	28.0

Method Calculations

Planned Margin	33.5%
Planned Profit	−3.5%
Operating Expense	30.0%

Budgeted Expense Dollars of $28.5MM/Operating Expense of 30.0% = Sales Objective of $95.0MM

The initial estimates of the target market potential, trial, and repeat projections obviously are critical to this type of sales objectives. Unless based on historical data closely related to your product, sales objectives generated in this manner are highly speculative and thus can be highly inaccurate. It is best to use the target market approach only when data for the other forecasting methods do not exist, or in conjunction with one or all of the other quantitative methods previously discussed.

TASK 2

Reconcile Sales Objectives

Now that you have calculated your three quantitative sales objectives, you must reconcile the differences to establish the composite sales objectives for your marketing plan. After reviewing your sales objective alternatives based on the macro, micro, and expenses-plus methods, you may decide to go with a pure average of the three or a weighted average, placing more emphasis on one alternative than the other. You may use the (weighted) average of two, or just one. The important aspect of Task 2 is that you have reviewed the data from various quantitative perspectives. This will help you arrive at a sales objective with your eyes wide open and with an understanding of the dynamics that go into setting a sales objective. For the most meaningful sales projections, attempt to apply all three methods or, at the very minimum, two methods that you can use for comparison. Exhibit 4.5 shows how reconciliation of the three methods' goals into a composite sales objective(s) can be accomplished. A worksheet for your own reconciliation work is provided at the end of this chapter.

TASK 3

Make Qualitative Adjustments to Sales Objectives

Once you have arrived at quantitative sales objectives, you should review the qualitative factors that will have an impact on future sales. Put another way, you need to temper the numerically derived sales objectives with the more qualitative forecasting factors. Using the appropriate qualitative factors, you can increase or decrease the composite dollars and units/transactions/persons served sales objectives through an assignment of positive or negative percentage points, depending on the estimated degree of impact by each qualitative factor. If the economy is growing and the economic outlook is bright, you might increase the composite sales objective by two percentage points. Or, you may decrease the composite sales objective by four percentage points because an aggressive competitor moved into your trading area. If there is more than one major impacting factor, you can balance their effect through

EXHIBIT 4.5   Reconciliation of Sales Objectives

	Macro		Micro		Expense Plus		Composite Sales Objectives	
	Dollars (MM)	Units (MM)	Dollars (MM)	Units (MM)	Dollars (MM)	Units (MM)	Dollars (MM)	Units (MM)
Short Term								
2001	$ 94.9	37.5	$ 96.3	38.2	$ 95.0	37.7	$ 95.4	37.8
Long Term								
2002	106.3	42.0	103.4	40.1	104.4	40.9	104.7	41.0
2003	118.3	47.0	112.2	45.1	111.0	43.5	113.8	45.2

Qualitative Impacting Factors	Point Change	Percentage Adjustment	×	Composite Sales Objective (MM)	=	Adjusted Sales Objective (MM)
1. Economy	+2	1.02		$95.4		$ 97.3
2. Competition	–4	.96		95.4		91.6
Total						$188.9
Final Adjusted Average (Total of adjusted sales objectives divided by number of calculated factors)						$94.5

1. List qualitative factors and to what extent they will impact on the previous numerically arrived at sales objectives. Adjust composite sales objective(s) accordingly to arrive at final sales objective(s).
2. Use qualitative adjustments for units, transactions, or persons served, as well as for sales dollar objectives for each year of three-year projection. However, percentage point adjustment may differ from dollars.

averaging. Exhibit 4.6 illustrates how to calculate these factors. A worksheet for you to use in adjusting the composite sales objectives by the qualitative impacting factors is provided at the end of this chapter.

Revising Your Sales Objectives

The sales objectives will most likely be revised more than once as you write the marketing plan. You may uncover greater than expected sales potential among a target market. Or you may determine that your company does not have the necessary capital, that there is greater competition than expected, or that there is not enough consumer demand, all of which could negatively affect the estimated sales objectives.

Once your marketing plan is written (ideally, two or three months before the start of your fiscal year), it is wise to keep your sales objectives current. Review your sales objectives at two months, five months, and eight months into the marketing plan year in order to adjust the sales objectives for the second, third, and fourth quarters of your fiscal year. This will help you maximize your sales and control your expenses in a timely and profitable manner.

WORKSHEET

Sales Objectives: Macro Method
Market and Share Data

| | Market Sales Volume | | | | Company Share Percent of the Market | | | |
	$ ( )	Percent Change Previous Year	Units ( )	Percent Change Previous Year	$	Percent Points Change from Previous Year	Units	Percent Points Change from Previous Year
Previous 5 years								
1								
2								
3								
4								
5								
Projections Next 3 Years								
1								
2								
3								

Three-Year Sales Projection for Company

| | Dollars | | | Units | | |
Year	Market Sales $ Volume ( )	× Company Share Percent of Market	= Company $ Sales ( )	Market Sales Unit Volume ( )	× Company Unit Share Percent of Market	= Company Unit Sales ( )
1						
2						
3						

WORKSHEET

Sales Objectives: Micro Method

Projections from Top: Sales Forecast for Manufacturing, Service, or Retail Category*

	Company Sales Volume			
	$ ( )	% Change Previous Year	Units ( )	% Change Previous Year
Previous 5 years				
1				
2				
3				
4				
5				
Next 3 Years' Projections				
1				
2				
3				

Note: Complete a worksheet for your company's total sales and a worksheet for each individual product or department.

*Based on your type of business, include in your sales projections dollars and units/transactions/persons served, and take into consideration new products, distribution channels, stores or services, and price changes.

Use net dollar sales to trade/intermediate markets.

Projections from Bottom: Sales Forecast by Distribution Channel for Manufacturers*

	Existing			New		
Channel	Number	Dollars (MM)	Units	Number	Dollars (MM)	Units
Total						

Note: Develop projections for each year for a three-year period.

*In your sales projections, take into consideration new products, changes in distribution outlets, and price changes. Use net dollar sales to trade/intermediate markets.

Projections from Bottom: Sales Forecast by Store for Retailers*

	Stores	
	$	Transactions
Market ( ) Name/Store number	( )	( )
Market Total		

Note: Develop projections for each year for a three-year period.

*In your sales projections, take into consideration new stores, products, and services along with price changes. Service organizations use service office/center in place of stores. Use dollar sales to ultimate purchasers. Service organizations use persons served in place of transactions.

WORKSHEET

Sales Objectives: Expenses-Plus Method

Review of Historical Financial Data

Previous 5 Years	Gross Margin Percent of Sales %	Profit Percent of Sales %	Expenses Percent of Sales %	Dollars (MM) $

Method Calculations

Planned Margin		%
Planned Profit	–	%
Operating Expense		%

Budgeted Expense Dollars of $ _____ /Operating Expense of _____ % = Sales Objective of

WORKSHEET

Sales Objectives
Reconciliation of Sales Objectives

	Macro		Micro		Expense Plus		Composite Sales Objectives	
	Dollars (MM)	Units (MM)	Dollars (MM)	Units (MM)	Dollars (MM)	Units (MM)	Dollars (MM)	Units (MM)
Short-term 1-Year								
Long-term 2-year								
3-year								

WORKSHEET

Qualitative Adjustment of Quantitatively Derived Sales

Qualitative Impacting Factors	± Point Change	Percentage Adjustment	×	Composite Sales Objectives	=	Adjusted Sales Objectives

Total _____

Final Adjusted Average
(Total of adjusted sales objectives divided by number of calculated factors)

Note: 1. List the qualitative factors and to what extent they will affect the previous numerically-arrived-at sales objectives. Adjust composite sales objective(s) accordingly to arrive at final sales objective(s).
2. Use qualitative adjustments for units, transactions, or persons served, as well as for sales dollars objectives. However, percentage point adjustment may differ from dollars.

FORMAT

Sales Objectives for Manufacturers
Short-Term (One-Year)

1. Increase dollar sales _____% over previous year, from $_____ to $_____.

2. Increase unit sales _____% over previous year, from _____ to _____.

Long-Term*

1. Increase dollar sales _____% from year_____ to year_____, from $_____ to $_____.

2. Increase unit sales _____% from year_____ to year_____, from $_____ to $_____.

Rationale

Note: 1. Use this format for total company sales as well as for specific products.
2. Include profit objectives as well, using a similar format.

*List two- and three-year sales objectives separately.

F O R M A T

Sales Objectives for Retail and Service

Short-Term (One Year)

1. Increase total dollar sales _____% and transactions _____% over previous year, from $_____ to $_____ and from _____ transactions to _____ transactions.

2. Increase comparable store sales _____% and transactions _____% over previous year, from $_____ to $_____ and from _____ transactions to _____ transactions.

Long-Term†

1. Increase total sales _____% and transactions _____% for year _____ to year _____, from $_____ to $_____, and from _____ transactions to _____ transactions.

2. Increase comparable store sales _____% and transactions _____% for year _____ to year _____, from $_____ to $_____, and from _____ transactions to _____ transactions.

Rationale

Note: 1. Use this format for total company sales as well as for specific retail and service categories. Retailers might also want to use unit objectives as well. Service organizations use dollar and persons/companies served.
2. Include profit objectives as well, using a similar format.

†List two- and three-year sales objectives separately.

MARKETING BACKGROUND

1 THE BUSINESS REVIEW

Scope
Company Strengths & Weaknesses • Core Competencies • Marketing Capabilities

Product and Market Review
Company & Product Review • Category & Company Sales • Behavior Trends • Pricing • Distribution • Competitive Review

Target Market Effectors
Consumer/Business-to-Business Targets • Product Awareness & Attributes • Trial & Retrial Data

2 PROBLEMS/OPPORTUNITIES

MARKETING PLAN

3 SALES OBJECTIVES

4 TARGET MARKETS AND MARKETING OBJECTIVES

5 PLAN STRATEGIES—Positioning & Marketing

6 COMMUNICATION GOALS

7 TACTICAL MARKETING MIX TOOLS

Product	Distribution	Advertising Media
Branding	Personal Selling/Service	Merchandising
Packaging	Promotion/Events	Publicity
Pricing	Advertising Message	

8 MARKETING PLAN BUDGET AND CALENDAR

9 EXECUTION

10 EVALUATION

TARGET MARKETS AND MARKETING OBJECTIVES

IN THIS CHAPTER YOU WILL LEARN:

- HOW TO DEFINE CONSUMER AND/OR BUSINESS TARGET MARKETS.
- HOW TARGET MARKETS AND MARKETING OBJECTIVES ARE LOCKED TO SALES.
- HOW TO DEVELOP MARKETING OBJECTIVES.

TO FULFILL THE SALES OBJECTIVES you set in Chapter 4, you must now determine to whom you will be selling your product or service—the target market—and the necessary purchasing behavior needed to generate those sales. In this chapter you will learn how to identify target markets, then link those targets segments to sales through quantitative marketing objectives.

The link between target markets and marketing objectives is one of the defining differences of our marketing planning methodology. Many plans fail after sales objectives are established because there is no link back to sales in any portion of the plan. Without a direct link to sales through target markets and marketing objectives, the marketing manager should have no real expectation that the strategies and tactics will really achieve the stated sales goals. Put another way, *you can't manage what you can't measure*. You can, however, measure plans that tie marketing objectives to quantifiable target market or segment behavior that, in turn, locks back to the sales objectives.

Target Markets and Market Segmentation

A *target market* is a group of people or companies with a set of common characteristics. Target marketing allows for a concentration of effort against a portion of the universe with similar descriptors, product needs, or buying habits.

Companies don't sell products; customers *purchase* them. In effect, your company exists because of the customers or targets markets you choose to serve. Because we define marketing as the process of identifying the target market(s), determining the needs and wants of the target market(s), and fulfilling those needs and wants better than the competition, it stands to reason that determining the target market is the most critical step in the marketing planning process. Your target markets drive your marketing plan. Don't try to be all things to all people; instead, decide which target segments will form the core of the business and point your efforts and budget there.

Segmentation is a selection process that divides the broad consuming market into manageable customer or noncustomer groups with common characteristics. Segmentation allows the marketer to exploit these common characteristics through the company's marketing efforts. Instead of marketing to the "average" consumer, you are able to pinpoint specific clusters of consumers who have unique, yet similar, demographics, lifestyles, attitudes, concerns, purchasing habits, or needs and wants. The similarities inherent in a given market segment make it possible for marketers to address groups as if they were communicating with individuals, and direct communications to groups of consumers with similar characteristics via more meaningful products, pricing, and messages. Thus, segmentation allows you to realize the greatest potential sales at the lowest cost.

There are two broad segments for most businesses within which you will develop additional subsegments for targeting:

1. *Current customers*—customers and segments of the customer base with whom you are currently doing business.
2. *New customers*—segments in which you are not currently doing business or in which you feel there is potential to do more business.

Before you start developing additional target market segments within the current and new customer segments, think about what you are trying to achieve. More than simply looking for consumer or customer similarities, segment identification involves defining similarities that are tied directly to sales and profits. When you develop target market segments, you do so by grouping like segments of customers or potential customers with the objective of finding those segments that are responsible for the most dollar volume, profit, or purchases and that also demonstrate future potential. If you completed your business review, this work has been done. You now just need the parameters that will help you make the right target selections.

Primary and Secondary Target Markets

A *primary target market* is your main consuming group. These consumers are the most important purchasers and users of your product and will be the mainstay of your business. In some cases, the primary target market is the heavy user (one-third or less of the purchasers who account for two-thirds or more of the purchases). For companies that are more niche oriented, the primary target will be a smaller, though viable, section of the market that requires selective or specialized goods and services. And in some situations, a primary target market may be an intermediate channel, such as a distributor, and a primary target which is a consumer or end user. Both targets will have different ties to sales (for example, a wholesale price and a retail price, respectively), and both will require separate plans.

The following criteria should be fulfilled before you finalize a primary target market choice:

- The customer base needs to be large enough in terms of actual numbers of consumers and dollar volume of purchasers. What percent of the product category's volume does your primary target market consume? Given your projected market share, is it enough to support your business? (See Task 7, "Analyze Demand," at the end of the Target Market Segment Methodology section in this chapter.) A common reason for a plan's failure is a target market that is too small and limiting. Ideally, try to get your primary target market profile to be accountable for approximately 30–50 percent of the category volume. For example, if 18–24-year-olds accounted for only 10 percent of the consumption, the marketer would need to expand the age criteria beyond 18–24-year-olds until the age group was broad enough to account for more volume. However, if the purchase behavior or the purchasing criteria were distinctly different among 18–24-year-olds than among other age groups, the marketer would need to establish a number of smaller target markets—something that is much more difficult and expensive to execute.

  The 30–50 percent criterion can be lower if you are going to specialize against a more narrow purchaser/user base but obtain a larger market share against this segment. However, you must be certain that your company has some special tie to the narrow niche that will command loyalty.

- The target market should be profitable. Determine that the target market purchases sufficient quantity to assure profitability.

- Try to estimate the trending of your primary target market. Is it a growing or shrinking segment? If it is shrinking, will the market be large enough to support your business at its current market share in five years? If not, this should be a danger signal.

- Make sure your primary target market can be narrowly defined by one unified profile. The primary target market should be a group of individuals or companies with the same basic identifiers and purchasing behavior. This will allow your marketing effort to be focused against essentially one type of individual.

The primary target market becomes the company's reason for being. You are in business to determine the primary target market's wants and needs and to provide for those wants and needs better than your competition. This pertains to providing the product, service, shopping or sales environment, distribution channel, and price structure that is required by the customer for purchase. The better the definition and description of the consumers in your primary target market, the better you will be able to market to them.

Most plans will identify multiple target markets. The primary target markets receive priority and a majority of the marketing spending, because they will most directly influence the short-term financial success of the plan. However, the *secondary target markets* are important, too, because they provide additional sales and/or influence on the sales to the company beyond that of the primary target market as well as future sales to the company. A secondary target market can be one of the following:

- *A segment currently too small to be a primary market, but shown to have future potential.* In some cases, you may identify segments with great growth potential, but which currently are very small in absolute purchasing power. In other cases, there might be a large segment which would become a primary target as a result of fundamental marketing changes making your product or service more attractive to this market.

- *A demographic category with a low volume but a high-concentration index.* Often there is a distinct demographic category that accounts for a small percentage of the volume but contains a high concentration of purchasers. For example, 18–24-year-olds may account for only 10 percent of the total product category purchases, but 50 percent of the 18–24-year-olds may purchase the product. This may be due to popularity of the product among this age group, but fewer total purchase occasions or purchase of more inexpensive product models. In any case, a great percentage of the target uses the product, providing the opportunity for efficient use of marketing dollars and little wasted coverage in targeting the segment.

- *Subsets of purchasers or users who make up the primary target markets.* As stated in the primary target market section, your primary target market should ideally be one unified profile of customers accounting for greater than 30 percent of the category volume. This allows for a focusing of resources and message in the marketing effort. However, there are situations in which the volume of any one target market is not substantial enough to qualify it as a primary target market. In addition, each smaller target market has different demographics, needs, wants, product usage, and purchasing behavior.

  An example of this is in the target market we developed for a regional menswear retailer. The retailer was selling primarily suits and sport coats. There were many purchasing profiles, but no single profile group provided enough volume to allow for targeting against that group. The primary target market became very broad and encompassed all white-collar males who were 18–54 years of age. However, the following secondary target markets were developed, with subsequent marketing emphasis and programs against each:

  —Men, 18–24 years old, college graduates, entering the working world and looking for affordable suits

  —Men, 45 and older, higher income, at the top of their profession, interested in quality menswear and needing to update their wardrobes

—Women aged 18–34 years old; women have a great influence over men's purchases of suits and sport coats. Spouses also purchase a substantial number of sport coats as gifts and accompany men in more than 50 percent of their shopping trips, serving as advisors.

—Blue-collar males who need an all-occasion suit; price is a concern.

—Target markets were also broken out by type of profession, as this helped dictate quantity and style of suit purchases.

- *Influencers.* These are individuals who influence the purchase or usage decision of the primary target market. A good example of this is the influence children have on their parents in the purchase of many consumer goods, from toys to fast food. Influencers can be both a primary or secondary target market, though in most situations they are a secondary target market.

Influencers are of particular importance in public sector marketing, where outside forces can affect the success of an organization's marketing program. In a statewide bus transit marketing campaign, we concentrated marketing efforts against current and potential riders as our primary target, but we also targeted opinion leaders, major employers, and education leaders, all of whom affect communities' public support of the bus system, as our secondary market.

In business-to-business situations, a secondary target can often be a customer who currently does not purchase heavily from your company but who has high purchasing potential. You can delineate the potential of this customer by estimating your competitors' sales to this customer and determining what additional needs your company can fulfill for this customer.

Further, manufacturers most often include an intermediate channel as a secondary target segment. This target might be a fabricator, distributor/wholesaler, or retailer that should receive special attention in order to make sure the product is available for the end user to purchase. This is particularly true in marketing consumer goods, with minimal retail shelf space available and multiple competitors selling the same type of product. Often, so much time and money is devoted to selling to the end user that the intermediate channel is taken for granted.

Conversely, many business-to-business manufacturers, because they are selling directly to an intermediate target market (which is their primary target), push these products through the primary distribution channel (often using low prices and promotions) and put less marketing emphasis on the end user to pull the product through the channels. It might be more efficient in the short term to push the product through intermediate markets. However, the end user should not be totally ignored, as this may mean a loss of demand and loyalty for your product or brand over the long term.

Target Market Segmentation Methodology

The methodology for determining either current customer or new customer segments involves the seven tasks described below. (Note: The following methodology is designed for a target that consumes a *group of products* within the scope of an industry (i.e., shoes for the family, a range of accounting services, etc.). If you have one product, the same methodology applies except you eliminate Task 1 and Task 6, and start with Task 2 listing the segments for your one product. Worksheets designed to help you develop your target market strategies appear at the end of this chapter.

TASK 1	The target market process starts with first identifying industry and company products that demonstrate strong demand and sales growth. Go back to the business review and list the products that had the most category
Identify Strong Products

EXHIBIT 5.1 **Product Sales Volume**

Example

List the largest sales volume, profit, and fastest growth products from the category. Provide sales trends, profits trends, and percent of category sales. Provide company information (sales trends, profit trends, percent of category sales and market share) for the same leading products.

M = $000

Category 5-Year Trend

Example: Cross-Country Ski Manufacturer

Category's Highest $ Volume Products	Sales Yr. 1 Yr. 2 Yr. 3 Yr. 4 Yr. 5	% of Category Sales* Yr. 1 Yr. 2 Yr. 3 Yr. 4 Yr. 5	Profit** Yr. 1 Yr. 2 Yr. 3 Yr. 4 Yr. 5	# Transactions/Purchases Yr. 1 Yr. 2 Yr. 3 Yr. 4 Yr. 5
1) Skating skis	$100MM $120MM $110MM $150MM $160MM	10% 14% 12% 15% 16%	45% 45% 44% 44% 44%	
2) Wax touring skis				
3) No-wax touring skis				
•				
•				
•				

*In year 1, 10% of the category's sales came from product 1.
**Could be percent of profit or profit margin. In this case it is a gross margin.
Note: Dollars are not real industry figures.

Company 5-Year Trend

Company's Highest $ Volume Products	Sales Yr. 1 Yr. 2 Yr. 3 Yr. 4 Yr. 5	% of Company Sales*** Yr. 1 Yr. 2 Yr. 3 Yr. 4 Yr. 5	Profit Yr. 1 Yr. 2 Yr. 3 Yr. 4 Yr. 5	# Transactions/Purchases Yr. 1 Yr. 2 Yr. 3 Yr. 4 Yr. 5
1) Skating skis	$10MM $20MM $30MM $30MM $40MM	10% 22% 30% 30% 35%	45% 44% 44% 43% 42%	
2) No-wax touring skis				
3) Telemark skis				
•				
•				
•				

***In this example, the company's number-one selling product matches the industry's number-one selling product (skating skis). However, the company's number two and three selling products (No-wax and Telemark) differ from the category's number two and three selling skis.

Products	Company Market Share**** Yr. 1 Yr. 2 Yr. 3 Yr. 4 Yr. 5
1) Skating skis	10% 17% 27% 20% 25%
2)	
3)	
•	
•	
•	

****Company ÷ Category (Example: $10MM ÷ $100MM)

Index Company to Category

$ Volume Products	Sales % Change Company (5-year trend) Yr. 1 to Yr. 5	Sales % Change Category (5-year trend) Yr. 1 to Yr. 5	Sales Index Company/Category Yr. 1 to Yr. 5	% of Sales***** Index Company/Category Yr. 1 Yr. 2 Yr. 3 Yr. 4 Yr. 5
1) Skating skis	300%	60%	500	100 157 250 200 218
2)				
3)				
•				
•				
•				

*****Company % of sales ÷ Category % of sales (Example: 10% ÷ 10% = 100, 22% ÷ 14% = 157, etc.)

EXHIBIT 5.2 Target Market Descriptions/Target Market Behavior

Example

List the target market description for the largest industry or company product category (based upon sales volume, sales growth and/or profitability), the second largest, third largest, etc. Use a separate form for each target market description.

List the target market behavior rates for the category and company.

Target Segment Descriptions

Consumer: (demographic, geographic, use attributes); Example—College students, 18–24.
Business-to-business: (SIC, end user, channel, size, organizational structure); Example—Service Standard Industrial Code (SIC), service businesses over $1MM

Segment #1: College Students

Segment accounts for 30% of Total Category Sales* CATEGORY			Segment accounts for 25% of Total Company Sales COMPANY			Percent or Penetration COMPANY/CATEGORY	
	This Year	5-Year Growth Rate		This Year	5-Year Growth Rate		Penetration This Year
Number of users	300,000	7%	Number of users	100,000	10%	Number of users	33%
Number of purchases	850,000	5%	Number of purchases	300,000	10%	Number of purchases	35%
$ Customer	$15	15%	$ Customer	$10	5%		
Retrial rate	82%	3%	Retrial rate	70%	—		

*30% of the product category's sales is accounted for by this segment.
Note: The company has a higher purchase-per-user rate (300,000 ÷ 100,000 = 3) than the category average, but it has a lower retrial rate. Further exploration would probably demonstrate a segment of the users purchasing at very high rates and being very satisfied and another segment purchasing once and then not trying again. This information would be valuable when establishing subsequent target market and marketing objectives priorities.

and/or company sales, profits, or transactions and are demonstrating the most growth. (See Product and Market Review—Sales.) Exhibit 5.1 demonstrates this process.

TASK 2

Define Target Segments

We define target markets by first focusing on the target market segments responsible for purchasing or using the products that:
1. Account for the greatest industry and company product sales volume, and/or profits, and/or transactions, and/or number of customers (see Product and Market Review—Sales and Target Market Effectors—Target Market in the business review).
2. Are industry or company growth products that are trending up in sales, and/or profits, and/or transactions, and/or customers, and that are estimated to be major volume producers in the future.

Review the business review to determine the number of current customers and noncustomers who consumed the products identified in Task 1. List the number of customers and potential customers in the target market, the average dollar-per-purchase occasion, the dollar purchased per customer, the number of purchase occasions/number of purchases per year, the penetration (customers as a percent of the potential total category consumers), the retrial rate, and the growth trends in terms of customers/consumers using or purchasing the product.

Now break the large segments (customers and noncustomers) into smaller segments looking for characteristics that predict volume. Note the volume of each segment along with the specifics just identified (number in target market, number of purchase occasions, the dollar purchased per customer, etc.) for each of the segments. Finally, list the segment description that accounts for the most purchases, sales, profits, transactions, and/or customers; the second most for each of the top-performing products. Exhibit 5.2 demonstrates this process.

If your current customer segments (based upon expected retention rates) and their respective dollar volume do not add up beyond your sales goal based upon historical purchasing averages, develop new customer segments to include in your marketing effort.

New customer segments may be identical to current customer segments if you find you still have plenty of customer market share or penetration potential. For example, a customer target market may be 18–24-year-old college students, yet your business review shows that you have only 20 percent of a particular state's college students as customers. Obviously, the target market can still be mined for new customers in that state. New trial segments may also be strong industry category segments in which you don't do well but where the segment's purchasing needs or criteria match your product's attributes. Therefore, it makes sense to target poorer performing customer segments that are relatively strong performing industry segments, especially if the competitive environment is not fiercely intense.

Based upon your findings, you may want to alter your initial target market profile description to more closely mirror the product category's target market in order to expand your current customer base. For example, through an analysis for a retail client experiencing low sales per store, we found that its customer target market was primarily blue collar with an annual income of under $30,000, while the majority of purchases in the total category were white collar with annual incomes over $40,000, skewing to $60,000 plus. The analysis involved in this exercise may also point out the major differences between the customer profiles of your company's product and those of the category and provide insight as to why your company is successfully capturing a specific segment of the product category and how to attract even more of the same consumers.

On the other hand, based upon your analysis, you may want to target a smaller, but growing, segment not targeted by the competition. Factors such as the size and growth of the market, above-average expenditures per customer, and the strong awareness and positive attribute ratings of your company might lead you to focus on a segment that does not mirror the category's heavy-user target segment.

A final word of caution: Before you go on to develop a new market or modify an existing target, make sure you have fully exploited the profit potential of your current customer base. This is particularly true in retail, service, and business-to-business marketing, where you have personal contact with your customers. In most cases, your own customers are your most important and potentially most profitable target market, because they are responsible for your firm's current existence and are a prime target for future sales. Target your current customers not only to retain their purchase loyalty but also to motivate them to make more and bigger purchases and to refer new customers. (See Target Market Effectors—Target Market and Behavior sections in business review, and Exhibit 5.2.)

The following segmentation categories were reviewed in the business review under the Target Market section of Target Market Effectors. Use these as you develop your target market segments against the high-performing products in Task 1.

Consumer Tenure
Existing customers often display different purchasing habits (number of purchases, amount of purchases, different product mix) based upon the number of years they have been a customer, known as customer tenure. In addition, the retrial or renewal rate is often different by tenure. For example, AAA's renewal rate was significantly higher for members with five or more years of membership than for those with four or less. The new members used the organization significantly less (fewer services and usage amounts per service), which was a major factor in the smaller renewal rate. These findings resulted in establishing specific target market segments, objectives, and strategies against customers with zero to four years of tenure.

Demographics

Demographics include descriptors such as age, income, education level, marital status, employment/job classification, race, and home ownership. Most of the purchasers of consumer products are predicted by demographics. The purchase of household products and childrens' games are two examples.

Buying Habits/Product Use

Segmentation can be based upon how the product is purchased or used, the number of times purchased per year, the time of year the product is purchased, loyalty, or tenure of product use. For example, we defined a target for the AAA Chicago Auto Club around the product users of Triptiks (routing maps) and maps. We discovered these customers were using a travel service (the Triptik or map provided by AAA for members) but were then booking the majority of their trips through alternative travel agencies. Therefore, we targeted users of Triptiks and maps (provided through the AAA Chicago club membership), with the objective of cross-selling this target into a package travel purchase. This idea was translated into the Triptik Plus program.

Many consumer goods firms target consumers based upon buying habits, specifically the consumer's propensity for multiple purchases. We worked with a game company in the puzzle business whose heavy users purchased eight to 12 puzzles per year. Much of our target market segmentation work and many of the subsequent marketing objectives were developed around this purchasing behavior. We developed objectives to increase the number of company puzzles purchased per year, and strategies that called for series of puzzles and incentives to generate loyalty to this particular company's puzzles.

In addition, there are many product categories where the product is used/consumed differently by different target market groups. This is common in the business-to-business area, where spray-dried cheese is used very differently by Frito Lay in the processing of snacks than by Swanson in its TV dinners. Segmentation by different levels of consumption use is also common in consumer package goods marketing. For example, the snack industry segments users by individual, family, and party size, among others, when developing its package sizes.

Lifestyle Characteristics

Psychographics (values, lifestyles, interests, attitudes) often are used in conjunction with demographics to identify target market descriptors. One example would be a new five-blade propeller that we helped Mercury Marine introduce to the marketplace. We targeted against two lifestyle or interest psychographics—waterskiing and bass fishing. The five-blade prop provided significantly better "hole shot," or acceleration. Both of these segments had a need for this type of product, and they were predicted to account for a significant percentage of the sales volume for the five-blade propeller. They were targeted in terms of media, advertising (testimonials from expert waterskiers and bass fishermen), distribution of the product, and point-of-sale merchandising.

Geography

Purchasing rates often differ according to geography. Segmentation can be based upon climate, the consumption habits of certain regions, and other factors that cause differences in volume and usage by geography.

In your business review you should have determined regions, markets, and/or areas of markets that have the greatest consumption potential for your product by comparing the overall category sales to the sales of your product in comparable geographic areas. (See discussion of BDI and CDI in the Target Market Effectors—Trial Behavior section of chapter 2.) Based on this analysis, you may want to expand, reduce, or merely refine the geographic focus of your target market.

EXHIBIT 5.3 Awareness and Attribute Rankings

Example

List the awareness of the target markets for the company and the leading competitors. List the top purchase attributes for the target markets and the relative ranking of the company versus the leading competitors.

TARGET SEGMENT AWARENESS RATINGS

Target Segment: Women 18–34, Single, Income of $40M+

	Yr. 1	2	3	4	5
Company	10%	12%	15%	17%	18%
Leading Competitor	28%	35%	36%	32%	30%
Leading Competitor	16%	15%	16%	15%	16%
Leading Competitor	15%	14%	13%	12%	10%

TARGET SEGMENT ATTRIBUTE RATINGS

Target Segment: Women 18–34, Single, Income of $40M+
Note: 1 = best; 5 = worst

Top 5 Attributes	Company Ranking					Leading Competitor A Ranking					Leading Competitor B Ranking					Leading Competitor C Ranking				
Yr.	1	2	3	4	5	1	2	3	4	5	1	2	3	4	5	1	2	3	4	5
1) Quality*	3	3	2	2	2	2	2	3	3	3	1	1	1	1	1	4	4	4	4	4
2) Selection	2	2	2	2	1	1	1	1	1	2	3	3	4	3	4	4	4	3	4	3
3) After-Sale Service	2	2	2	2	2	4	3	3	3	4	3	4	4	4	3	1	1	1	1	1
4) Price	3	3	2	3	2	2	2	3	2	3	4	4	4	4	4	1	1	1	1	1
4) Location	4	4	4	4	4	3	3	3	3	3	1	1	1	1	1	2	2	2	2	2

*The data demonstrates that competitor B ranks best on quality over all five years and with the company dominating second place over the last three years, having moved past competitor A. Competitor C ranks worst on quality, the most important attribute to the segment.

Attribute Preference

Different consumer groups purchase different product categories due to product attributes and benefits. With a retailer marketing fabric to sewers, product attributes or benefits became the primary means of defining the target market. Because not all sewers consider both large selection and low prices of fabrics to be equally important when choosing one fabric store over the other, the retailer made "selection shoppers" its primary target, as it could not profitably deliver the price benefit as well as selection.

Heavy User or Purchaser

Analyze the target market data in your business review to determine if there is a heavy user for your product. As a guideline, you have a heavy user in your product category if approximately two-thirds or more of total product is consumed by approximately one-third or less of the total users. A few percentage points below 67 percent of total usage and a few points above 33 percent of users is acceptable.

With a one-third user to two-thirds consumption determination, this heavy user usually becomes your primary target. Define the heavy-user segment based on descriptive data available to you. For the consumer market, the heavy-user descriptor could include demography, geography, and/or possibly lifestyle and product benefit/usage information, if available. For business-to-business markets, the heavy user might be a specific industry type (SIC code), a relatively small number of distributors, or the customer group that has been ordering for more than 10 years.

| **TASK 3**
| *Determine Awareness Level* | Review the business review to determine if there is average to above-average awareness for your company and/or products among the segments you are considering for your target market(s). If not, you will need to spend considerable dollars increasing awareness. Remember: *Share of mind leads to share of market* (see Target Market Effectors—Awareness). Exhibit 5.3 demonstrates this process.

| **TASK 4**
| *Analyze Attitudes* | Go back to the business review and determine whether the segments developed in Task 2 have positive attitudes across the most important purchase criteria for each segment. If not, you will need to make a significant effort to change attitudes across the most important purchase attributes in order to convince the segment to purchase in meaningful numbers. Remember: It's always easier to build on strengths than to change a weakness (Target Market Effectors—Attitudes).

| **TASK 5**
| *Narrow the List* | Make a decision to target all or some of the segments that provide you with as many as possible of the following:

- Strong industry and company sales or growing company or industry sales.
- Strong awareness.
- Positive attitudes toward your company or brand.
- Large size or large potential size (smaller numbers of company customers but large industry category consumers or potential customers).
- Strong dollar-per-customer average, more profit per customer, or high number of transactions per customer.
- Loyal segments with strong retrial rates.

If the market segments defined in Task 2 do not meet all of the criteria listed above, look for those that have the greatest combination of them.

| **TASK 6**
| *Analyze Product Mix of Targeted Segments* | Look at the mix of products consumed by the market segments you listed in Task 5. Not all of the products in the mix will be the highest volume, fastest growing, or most profitable products, but since that's where you started (originally defining the segment around the largest volume products in Tasks 1 and 2), you will be assured that the final product mix will be of significant volume.

This task forces you to develop *target market plans*, not simply product marketing plans. By looking at the natural mix of products the target market consumes within the scope of your business, you are forced to analyze your company's mix of product offerings to the target market later in the plan. Target market plans lead you to market a mix of product/service offerings to the consumer, while product plans are much more focused on selling only what you have—one product or service at a time. Ideally, you will pick final segments that perform positively on a majority of the above steps. This allows you to minimize the number of weaknesses that must be addressed and to market to segments that have the greatest potential to be profitable and are predisposed to purchase your product.

Task 6 is critical because it moves you back to developing target market plans rather than product plans. If you looked only at the largest volume products (Task 1) and defined the target markets from those products (Task 2), you essentially would be developing plans on a product-by-product basis. But in Task 6, you review what group or mix of products these customers of the high volume purchase. Once we detail the mix of products, you are now in a position to write a target market plan that attempts to affect target market behavior towards the entire mix of products this segment consumes.

TASK 7	The last task in determining target markets is to calculate the demand for
Analyze Demand	

The last task in determining target markets is to calculate the demand for your product in your chosen target market segments. The *demand analysis* is a check to make sure that the target segment is large enough to warrant your effort. The conclusions will be directional and are intended to provide you with a rough estimate of the size of your market and the potential business you might generate. This is a first check to make sure the sales goals you set in the plan are realistic and obtainable. The final check will be when you quantify your marketing objectives at the end of this chapter.

The following outlines the procedures to take in estimating demand for your product.

1. *Target Market:* How many consumers are there in your target market? Define the target market in terms of numbers of potential customers. For example, if your target market is women 25–49, provide the total number of women 25–49. This is the top-level figure of potential customers. It can be used for calculating future or potential demand.

2. *Geographic Territory:* How many consumers are in your defined trading area or geographic market territory? Define your geographic territory and determine the number of your target market customers in this area.

3. *Consumption Constraints:* What consumption habits exist that limit the potential customer base of your target market? Determine if there are consumption constraints that will reduce the target market for your product. For example, apartment dwellers have no real need for garden tools or lawn mowers. From this review, develop a final estimate of customers in your geographic territory.

4. *Average Purchase per Year per Customer:* Determine the average number of purchases of your product per year. From the business review and the purchase rates/buying habits section, you should have access to the average number of purchases per year for your product category.

5. *Total Purchases per Year in Category:* What is the total number of purchases made by the target market in your geographic territory per year? Multiply the number of customers in your territory by the average number of purchases per year to get total purchases.

6. *Average Price:* Determine the average price of your product. Utilize the pricing section of the business review to obtain this information.

7. *Total Dollar Purchases:* What are the total dollar purchases of your product category in your geographic target market? Multiply the total purchases (number 5) by the average price (number 6) to determine total dollar purchase.

8. *Your Company's Share of Purchase:* What is your company's market share? Is it trending up or down? Review market share data and trends from the sales analysis and competitive market shares, strengths, and weaknesses from the Competitive Analysis section of your business review. Also, consider loyalty measures from the Target Market Effector/Trial and Retrial section of the business review. Multiply your market share by the total dollar purchases (number 7). Adjust this number up or down depending upon the increases or decreases of your company's market share versus the competition over the past five years (e.g., if your company has been losing 5 percent market share per year over five years, project this average loss into your market share projection).

9. *Additional Factors:* What additional factors strongly affect demand for your product? What competitive factors will affect demand? How and why will recent or expected changes in these factors change demand for your product? Additional factors that correlate to the demand for your product, such as a new competitive set, the state of the economy, demographic fluctuations, and changing consumer tastes and lifestyles, should be analyzed for their effect on

EXHIBIT 5.4   Demand Potential

1.	**Target Market**	
	DMA population	2,000,000
	Target market male 18–65	720,000
2.	**Geographic Territory**	
	Target market male 18–65 in trading area of stores 1 and 3	400,000
3.	**Consumption Constraints**	
	None	
4.	**Average Purchases per Year per Customer**	
	Average customer purchases .40 suits/sport coats per year	.40 suits/year
5.	**Total Purchases per Year in Category**	
	.40 × 400,000	160,000 suits/year
6.	**Average Price**	
	Average price is $150	$150/suit
7.	**Total Dollar Purchases**	
	$150 × 160,000 suits per year	$24,000,000
8.	**Your Company's Share of Purchases**	
	Estimated market share is 15 percent	$3,600,000
9.	**Additional Factors**	
	None	
Final Demand Expectations for Your Company		$3,600,000

the demand for your company's product. For example, the influence of rising or falling interest rates on demand should be analyzed if your product is extremely interest-rate sensitive and there is good probability that interest rates are going to rise or fall within the next year. Likewise, if your product's sales are teen oriented, determine whether the number of teens is growing or shrinking and project the effect this will have on sales. Based upon this information, adjust the final share of purchase figure you derived (number 8). At this point you should have a fairly reasonable estimate of your company's potential share of total dollars and customers.

Exhibit 5.4 presents an example of how a demand analysis can be calculated for a men's clothing retailer. The chart provides the retailer with a rough projection of demand for suits in stores 1 and 3. Using figures derived in the above calculations, the chart could easily be expanded to include demand information for the total market. Use a similar procedure for other types of businesses.

Further analysis should be done using information developed in the business review, such as competitive factors, store location and analysis, competitive advertising expenditures, store loyalty, and the future economic factors affecting the purchase of suits, to provide input for the final adjustment up or down of the demand expectation generated in the above calculations.

Business-to-Business Target Market Segmentation

The target market segmentation methodology described above can be used for all types of businesses—consumer, service, retail, and/or business-to-business. The following is another methodology specifically designed for business-to-business firms. See the formats designed for your own applications at the end of this chapter.

<table>
<tr><td>

TASK 1

Define Existing Core Customers

</td><td>

Through your target market analysis in the business review, you should have a clear understanding of your current customer companies in terms of Standard Industrial Classification (SIC) size, geography, application of your product, organizational structure, and new versus repeat usage. You must decide whether to focus your marketing efforts on selling more to your pri-

</td></tr>
</table>

mary customers or to lesser-purchasing customers who have high purchase potential. Toward this end, list your customer segments in order of total sales, average dollar per customer, and number of customers. What segment is most efficient? What holds more short- and long-term potential?

Make sure you segment your current customer base into heavy and light users of your product to determine where you should concentrate your marketing energies and dollars.

<table>
<tr><td>

TASK 2

Target High-Potential New Customers

</td><td>

After redefining your current customer target market to fully exploit its buying potential, compare your target customer to the marketplace (national and state SIC charts in the business review), selecting those customer SIC categories (or other applicable segments) with the greatest potential in terms of new customers, average dollar per customer, and total segment sales.

</td></tr>
</table>

New Potential Customers in SIC Categories with Which Your Company Does Business

In each SIC category with which your company does business, target companies that best match your high-volume customers in terms of size (sales dollars, employees, number of outlets if retail) and geography, not neglecting application of product and organization structure (one location versus branches). You can select these potential companies from the individual state industrial directories (available from state government), which provide a complete listing of in-state commercial and industrial firms.

As a case in point, Famous Fixtures, a company that manufactures and installs new store fixtures for retailers, segmented its current, high-potential retail SIC category by size and geography using their current customer profile as a guide. The company targeted retail companies with five or more outlets in a contiguous three-state area, so it could market to larger, regionally concentrated store chains that would be most profitable and easy to service.

Potential Customers in SIC Categories with Which Your Company Does Not Do Business

Do not neglect the SIC categories in which your company has no or minimal market share if it sells a product or service that would fulfill the needs of companies in those categories. In working with a statewide CPA firm that was strong in serving the accounting needs of companies in the financial field, we found it was also very effective to market the firm's services to retailers, even though this firm originally had only a small share of this category.

<table>
<tr><td>

TASK 3

Define the Decision Maker(s) and the Decision-Making Process

</td><td>

Once you have segmented the customer and noncustomer companies, target the specific decision makers and determine their function and influence in the decision process. Next, determine the decision sequence and the purchase criteria. Which decision maker does the initial screening of your product? Who makes the final decision? Is the decision maker looking for the very best quality product and then the best price, or vice versa? Is service most important?

</td></tr>
</table>

EXHIBIT 5.5   Target Market for a Packer of Canned Vegetables

Primary Market

Consumer: heavy users (35 percent of the users and 65 percent of the total consumption) who store large quantities of inexpensive food for their families

Female homemakers

Age 25–49

Blue-collar occupation

Household income $15M to $30M

Reside in size B and C counties

High school education

Family size 3+, skewing to 5+

Eastern and Midwest regions

Trade: buyers for chain supermarkets and independent grocers that cumulatively represent a minimum of 65 percent of total canned vegetable sales; current brokers/wholesalers

Note: In the above example, there would be two potential primary target markets—one leading to a consumer marketing plan and the other to a trade marketing plan. Emphasis would be dependent upon the importance of each target and the overall budget.

EXHIBIT 5.6   Target Market for a Retail Casual Apparel Chain

Primary Target Market: value-conscious purchasers of casual apparel for the family

Married women

Age 18–49

Household size 3+

Household income $25M+

Employed

Reside in size B and C counties

High school education

Secondary Target Market: purchasers of durable, value-oriented casual/work apparel for self

Men 18–49

Income $25M+

Reside in B and C counties

Better education than women's apparel purchasers

Many times you cannot answer these questions unless you first define who the real decision maker is and determine if there is more than one. In working with a firm that manufactured computer paper, we found through quantitative research that it was not the manager of the computer department alone who made the purchasing decision; the purchasing agent manager was also part of this decision process, providing an important final approval role. The purchasing agent's decision was based primarily on price, while the computer department manager's decision was based primarily on the quality of paper and the service. As a result of this information, each decision maker was then targeted with a tailored direct mail and personal selling program.

Target Market Descriptors

Once you have arrived at your final target market selection(s), you can use the worksheets provided at the end of this chapter to list your target market(s). Include a brief rationale under the final target market selection and reference additional supporting data in the business review. Exhbit 5.5, 5.6, 5.7 illustrate the format for writing target market descriptors for a package good, retail, and business-to-business firm.

Locking Sales Objectives, Target Markets, and Marketing Objectives Together

Our marketing planning methodology quantitatively locks marketing objectives to target markets and then back to the sales objectives. This is where most marketing plans begin to lose focus and become soft and subjective. Think of each of the three components (sales objectives, target markets, and marketing objectives) in the following manner:

    Sales are the reason you are in business.

    Target markets provide sales. Satisfying the target markets is the way a company stays in business.

    Marketing objectives define the target market behavior required to produce sales — behavior such as retention of current customers, increased purchases from existing customers, trial from new customers, or repeat purchase from new customers.

EXHIBIT 5.8 **Disciplined Marketing Planning Interlocking Overview**

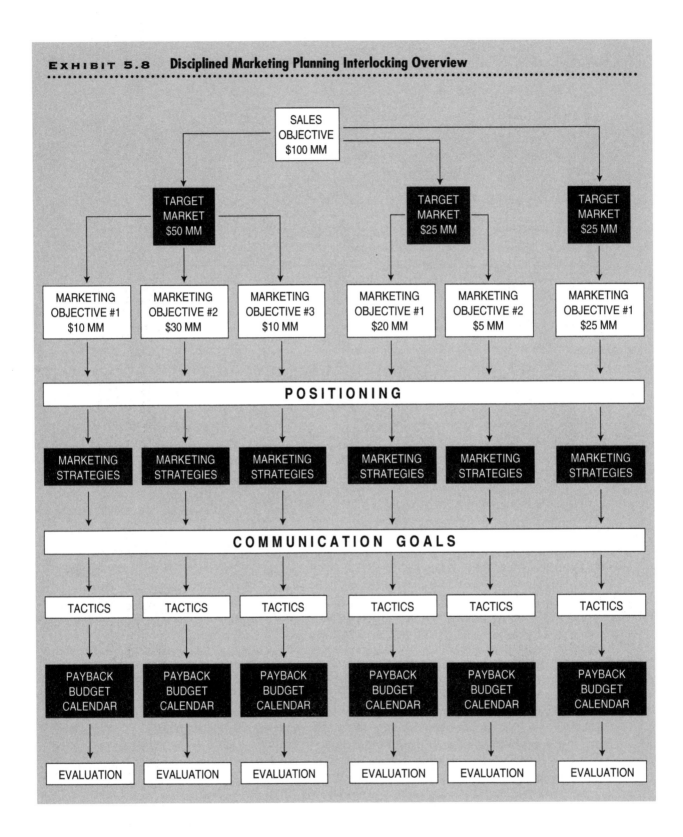

Understanding the target market is the key to marketing planning. All too often, however, the target market is not closely linked to each step of the marketing planning process. As illustrated in Exhibit 5.8 in our methodology, target markets are locked to sales through marketing objectives that define the behavior needed to achieve the sales. Thus, the marketing objectives quantify the target market behavior needed to deliver the required sales results. The end result is that the marketing objectives under each target market sum to a sales result, and combining the target market sales sum to the aggregate sales objective. Target markets and their corresponding marketing objectives are also locked directly to the remaining portions of the plan through the strategies developed to accomplish the marketing objectives. Finally, the marketing plan communication awareness and attitude goals are locked to delivering the behavior of the marketing objectives and are fulfilled by the cumulative communication generated by each marketing tactical tool. (This method will be explained in Chapter 8, "Communication Goals.")

Marketing Objectives. A marketing objective defines what needs to be accomplished. Differentiating between marketing objectives and marketing strategies is not always easy and is a source of confusion even for marketing professionals who have been in the business many years. We believe a marketing objective must:

- *Be specific.* The objective should focus on a single goal.
- *Be measurable.* The results must be quantifiable in terms of a target market's behavior and the resulting sales.
- *Relate to a specific time period.* This can be one or more years, the next six months, or even specific months of the year.
- *Focus on affecting target market behavior* (retaining customers, trial of a product, repeat purchase of a product, larger purchases, more frequent purchases, etc.).

One key to disciplined marketing planning is to make sure each marketing objective can be quantified back to a sales number. If this can be done, the marketing objectives under each target market can be summed to provide a target market sales number. Ultimately, the total sales objective can be derived by either adding all the marketing objectives together or adding the worth of each target market. Thus the disciplined marketing planning system is interlocking, linking marketing objectives to target markets to sales.

Marketing objectives relate to target markets and focus on influencing their behavior. Objectives will therefore fall into one of two target market categories: current users/customers or new users/customers. There are several possible objectives to be achieved within each category.

Current Users/Customers

For your current client or customer base, marketing objectives will relate to either retaining that client base and/or increasing their purchases.

Retaining Current Users. An important marketing objective is to retain the customer base at its current size from both a number and a dollar standpoint. This objective is defensive in nature. If your company has been losing customers over the past year or two, it becomes necessary to reverse this trend and maintain your customer base. You need to first direct total focus towards determining why business has been lost and then towards stabilizing the customer base.

Increasing Purchases from Current Users. If your customer base is loyal, the objective can take a more offensive direction, with strategies designed to obtain additional business from existing customers. This can be accomplished in three different ways by getting your customers to purchase:

- More often or more times in a given month or year.
- A more expensive product or service.
- Greater volume or amounts of product during each purchase.

New Users/Customers

If your objectives are aimed at new users, then they will most likely relate to increasing trial of your product or obtaining repeat usage after the initial trial.

Increasing Trial of Your Product or Service. For retailers, this equates to first getting traffic of a specific target segment into the store. Most retailers have a fairly consistent purchase ratio (percentage of times a consumer purchases versus leaves without purchasing), which means that the retailer can usually rely on a certain percentage of the increased traffic actually making a purchase. Increased trial for package goods, service, and business-to-business firms equates to actual use of the product from new target segment consumers. However, in both the retail situation and in package goods, service, and business-to-business, trial relates to obtaining new customers.

Obtaining Repeat Usage After Initial Trial. If your company has obtained high degrees of initial trial, it is important to make sure that you establish continuity of purchase and loyalty. Often, large amounts of trial exist, but the repeat purchase ratio is very low. If this is the case, establish an objective to increase repeat purchase and product loyalty and develop a fact-finding program to determine why repeat purchase rates are low and what can be done to increase them. Even if repeat purchase rates are fairly strong, there is usually some need to make sure they are maintained. Remember: It is far less expensive and more profitable to keep your new customers than it is to prospect, yet again, for new ones.

Developing Marketing Objectives

Developing realistic marketing objectives involves four tasks: reviewing the sales objectives and target markets sections of your marketing plan, as well as the problems and opportunities summaries of your business review, then quantifying the actual objectives in terms of sales and target market behavior.

TASK 1

Review Sales Objectives

Sales objectives provide a guideline for determining marketing objectives, as marketing objectives are established specifically to achieve the sales goals. All marketing objectives are quantifiable and measurable. The numerical quantifier used in the marketing objectives must be large enough to assure success of the sales goals.

Assume the sales objective for a large package-good firm is to increase sales 8.7 percent, or $26MM, from $300MM to $326MM. If the marketing objectives are to retain 70 percent of the current customer base and to increase current customer purchases from 3 to 3.2 times a year over the next 12 months, we would have to assure that this action will guarantee a sales increase of $26MM. In order to calculate this, we need to know the customer base size and the average purchase price of the target market. This leads us to the next step.

TASK 2

Review Target Market

The target market is the generator needed to achieve the sales goals. By reviewing the target market sections of the business review (Chapter 3) and of the work you did earlier in this chapter (Exhibit 5.2), you will be able to define:

- *The potential size of your target markets.* This will allow you to determine the number of people in your primary and secondary target markets, or the actual potential universe of category customers.
- *The size of your current customer base.* This will allow you to determine the number of customers you have versus the number of potential customers across each target market segment.
- *The purchasing rates of your company target market, including average purchase price and number of purchases per year.* This will provide you with the behavior or transactional data needed to quantify the target market behavior back to sales numbers.

Recall the current customer objectives mentioned in Task 1, to retain 70 percent of the customer base and increase purchase rates from 3 to 3.2 times per year. Unless we know how many customers there are and the average purchase price, we can't translate these objectives to actual sales dollars. If, on the other hand, we know there are 5MM (M = 000) customers who purchase three times per year at $20 per purchase, both of these objectives can now be quantified.

By reviewing your sales goals and your target market size, you have the potential to calculate the total effect of your marketing objectives and determine whether they are realistic in terms of helping your company reach its sales goals.

TASK 3	The problem and opportunity summaries of the business review (Chapter 3) provide insight into the content of the marketing objectives. Review
Review Problems and Opportunities	each problem and opportunity that relates to the target market's behavior. Solving these problems or exploiting these opportunities will be the basis for your marketing objectives.

One of the opportunities we discovered while working for a national package goods firm was stated in the following manner: Though trial of the product is very low, repeat purchase is above average when compared to the industry standard.

The implication from this opportunity was that, although trial was low, consumers liked the product's benefits and there was a high degree of product acceptance and loyalty. Thus, the new customer marketing objectives from this opportunity become:

1. Increase new trial of the product by 3MM customers (86 percent increase over the estimated 3.5MM existing customers) among the target audience over the next 12 months or obtain another 3MM new customers, 6 percent of the total 50MM potential target market.
2. Achieve repeat purchase of 70 percent from new users over the next 12 months.

TASK 4	The last step is to quantify the objective in terms of sales and target market behavior. Assume the product is in the early stage or second year of its prod-
Quantify Marketing Objective	uct life cycle; the sales objective is to increase sales 8.7 percent, or $26MM. Here, the work you did in reviewing your sales objectives and target market becomes important.

A major problem has been low trial of the product (10 percent of the target market). However, while trial was very low, repeat purchase among users was high (over 70 percent). Thus, consumer acceptance of the product was very positive, and the major problem to overcome was low overall trial of the product by consumers.

The sales objectives will be fulfilled by the following marketing objectives:

- *Existing customer marketing objective:* Retain 70 percent of existing customers and increase purchases among current customers from 3 to 3.2.
- *New customer marketing objective:* An incremental 86 percent increase (3MM new customers over the 3.5MM base after retention is calculated) in new customers, with a repeat of one purchase at 70 percent.

Exhibit 5.9 illustrates an example for quantifying your marketing objectives, while the format provided at the end of this chapter will help you create short- and long-term objectives.

EXHIBIT 5.9   Quantifying Your Marketing Objectives

Sales Objectives   Increase dollar sales 8.7% over the previous year from $300MM to $326MM

Target Market   Women 25–49
— total potential target market size   50MM
— existing customers   5MM

Marketing Objective Current Customers

Retention of 70%
Increase purchase rate from 3 times per year to 3.2 times per year at current average price per purchase of $20.

Projected Sales Dollars
$5MM \times 70\% = 3.5MM$
$3.5MM \times \$20 \times 3.2 = \$224MM$

Marketing Objective New Customers

Obtain 3MM new customers at the current average purchase rate of $20.
Obtain a 70% repeat purchase of one time at the current purchase rate of $20.

Projected Sales Dollars

3MM customers $\times$ $20	$60MM
3MM $\times$ 70% $\times$ $20	$42MM
Total	$102MM

Current and New Customers

Total Sales Last Year	$300MM
Total Projected Sales	$326MM
Customer Retention	$224MM
New Customers	$102MM
	$326MM

Product Sales Volume for Development of Target Market

List the largest sales volume and fastest growth products from the category. Provide sales trends, profits trends, and percent of category sales. Provide company information (sales trends, profit trends, percent of category sales and market share) for the same leading products.

M = $000

Category 5-Year Trend

Category's Highest $ Volume Products	Sales Yr. 1 Yr. 2 Yr. 3 Yr. 4 Yr. 5	% of Category Sales Yr. 1 Yr. 2 Yr. 3 Yr. 4 Yr. 5	Profit Yr. 1 Yr. 2 Yr. 3 Yr. 4 Yr. 5	# Transactions/Purchases Yr. 1 Yr. 2 Yr. 3 Yr. 4 Yr. 5
1)				
2)				
3)				
•				
•				
•				

Company 5-Year Trend

Company's Highest $ Volume Products	Sales Yr. 1 Yr. 2 Yr. 3 Yr. 4 Yr. 5	% of Company Sales Yr. 1 Yr. 2 Yr. 3 Yr. 4 Yr. 5	Profit Yr. 1 Yr. 2 Yr. 3 Yr. 4 Yr. 5	# Transactions/Purchases Yr. 1 Yr. 2 Yr. 3 Yr. 4 Yr. 5
1)				
2)				
3)				
•				
•				
•				

Products	Market Share Yr. 1 Yr. 2 Yr. 3 Yr. 4 Yr. 5
1)	
2)	
3)	
•	
•	
•	

Index Company to Category

$ Volume Products	Sales % Change Company (5-year trend) Yr. 1 to Yr. 5	Sales % Change Category (5-year trend) Yr. 1 to Yr. 5	Sales Index Company/Category Yr. 1 to Yr. 5	% of Sales Index Company/Category Yr. 1 Yr. 2 Yr. 3 Yr. 4 Yr. 5
1)				
2)				
3)				
•				
•				
•				

Target Market Descriptions/Target Market Behavior

List the target market description for the largest industry or company product category (based upon sales volume, sales growth, and/or profitability), the second largest, third largest, etc. Use a separate form for each target market description.

List the target market behavior rates for the category and company.

Target Segment Description #1

_____

_____

_____

Segment accounts for ____ of Total Category Sales	Segment accounts for ____ of Total Company Sales	Market Share
CATEGORY	**COMPANY**	**COMPANY/CATEGORY**
Growth Rate This Year Past 5 Years	**Growth Rate** This Year Past 5 Years	**Penetration** This Year
Number of users	Number of users	Number of users
Number of purchases	Number of purchases	Number of purchases
$ Customer	$ Customer	
Retrial rate	Retrial rate	

Target Segment Description #2

_____

_____

_____

Segment accounts for ____ of Total Category Sales	Segment accounts for ____ of Total Company Sales	Market Share
CATEGORY	**COMPANY**	**COMPANY/CATEGORY**
Growth Rate This Year Past 5 Years	**Growth Rate** This Year Past 5 Years	**Penetration** This Year
Number of users	Number of users	Number of users
Number of purchases	Number of purchases	Number of purchases
$ Customer	$ Customer	
Retrial rate	Retrial rate	

WORKSHEET

Awareness and Attribute Rankings

List the awareness of the target markets for the company and the leading competitors. List the top purchase attributes for the target markets and the relative ranking of the company versus the leading competitors.

TARGET SEGMENT AWARENESS RATINGS

Target Segment:

	Yr. 1	Yr. 2	Yr. 3	Yr. 4	Yr. 5
Company					
Leading Competitor					
Leading Competitor					
Leading Competitor					

TARGET SEGMENT ATTRIBUTE RATINGS

Target Segment:

Top 5 Attributes	Company Ranking Yr. 1 Yr. 2 Yr. 3 Yr. 4 Yr. 5	Leading Competitor Ranking Yr. 1 Yr. 2 Yr. 3 Yr. 4 Yr. 5	Leading Competitor Ranking Yr. 1 Yr. 2 Yr. 3 Yr. 4 Yr. 5	Leading Competitor Ranking Yr. 1 Yr. 2 Yr. 3 Yr. 4 Yr. 5
1)				
2)				
3)				
4)				
5)				

FORMAT

Target Market for Consumer — Short-Term (Package Goods, Retail, Service)

Primary Market

Secondary Market (Where Applicable)

Rationale

FORMAT

Target Market for Consumer — Long-Term (Package Goods, Retail, Service)

Primary Market

Secondary Market (Where Applicable)

Rationale

FORMAT

Target Market for Business-to-Business—Short-Term

Primary

Secondary (Where Applicable)
Intermediate

End User

Other

Rationale

FORMAT

Target Market for Business-to-Business—Long-Term

Primary

Secondary (Where Applicable)
Intermediate

End User

Other

Rationale

Marketing Objectives

Short-Term Objectives

Rationale

Long-Term Objectives

Rationale

Step 5: Plan Strategies

MARKETING BACKGROUND

1 THE BUSINESS REVIEW

Scope
Company Strengths & Weaknesses • Core Competencies • Marketing Capabilities

Product and Market Review
Company & Product Review • Category & Company Sales • Behavior Trends • Pricing • Distribution • Competitive Review

Target Market Effectors
Consumer/Business-to-Business Targets • Product Awareness & Attributes • Trial & Retrial Data

2 PROBLEMS/OPPORTUNITIES

MARKETING PLAN

3 SALES OBJECTIVES

4 TARGET MARKETS AND MARKETING OBJECTIVES

5 PLAN STRATEGIES—Positioning & Marketing

6 COMMUNICATION GOALS

7 TACTICAL MARKETING MIX TOOLS

Product	Distribution	Advertising Media
Branding	Personal Selling/Service	Merchandising
Packaging	Promotion/Events	Publicity
Pricing	Advertising Message	

8 MARKETING PLAN BUDGET AND CALENDAR

9 EXECUTION

10 EVALUATION

POSITIONING 6

- WHAT POSITIONING IS, AND WHY IT IS IMPORTANT.
- WHAT TO CONSIDER WHEN YOU ARE DEVELOPING POSITIONING STRATEGIES.
- HOW TO DEVELOP POSITIONING STRATEGIES.

THE MARKETING OBJECTIVES ESTABLISHED in Chapter 5 state what you want to accomplish in terms of marketing behavior. The next step in the marketing planning process is to develop the strategies that will state *how* you will accomplish your objectives. Two types of strategies will be developed: positioning and marketing. In this chapter, you will develop a positioning strategy, an umbrella strategy that guides the marketing strategies (Chapter 7) and is the glue that provides for a unified image execution of the marketing plan.

Positioning

By *positioning*, we mean creating an image for your product in the minds of the people to whom you are attempting to sell your product. Positioning establishes the desired perception of your product with the target market relative to the competition.

No matter what you are marketing, salient positioning is necessary. It is the basis for all of your communications—branding, advertising, promotions, packaging, sales force, merchandising, and publicity. By having one meaningful, targeted positioning as a guide for all communications, you convey a consistent image. By conveying a common positioning, each vehicle of communication will reinforce the others for a cumulative effect, maximizing the return of your marketing investment. Accordingly, everything you do from a marketing perspective must reinforce one positioning; otherwise, you will undermine your marketing efforts and confuse the target group as well.

To arrive at a successful long-term positioning, you must take into consideration these factors:
- The inherent drama of the product you are selling.
- The needs and wants of the target markets.
- The competition.

All the work you have done thus far will help you arrive at the right positioning strategy. You must understand the strengths and weaknesses of your product versus that of the competition. Where is your product comparable to the competition and where is it different? Where is it unique? Most important, what do these competitive differences, if any, mean to the target market? If the positioning reflects a difference that your product cannot deliver or that is not important to the target group, your positioning will not be successful. Even if your product possesses a meaningful difference, your positioning will not be effective if the target group does not perceive it as meaningfully different. The key point is that as you develop your product positioning, you must deal with the target group's *perception* of the competing products, even if it is not altogether accurate, because they are the buyers, and consequently, *their perception is truth.*

To arrive at a specific positioning, closely evaluate how your product ties to the target market relative to the competition. Three step-by-step positioning methods are outlined here: matching, mapping, and emotional relationship.

Positioning by Matching

Simply stated, the positioning-by-matching method matches your product's inherent and unique benefits or competitive advantage to the characteristics and needs/wants of the target market.

TASK 1

Analyze Your Product versus Competitors'

A good place to start the matching method is with an analysis of your product and your competition. Based on your business review, list your competition on the top left side of the worksheet provided at the end of this chapter (Exhibit 6.1 provides an example). The competition could be one major competitor, a number of key competitors, a specific business category, or a number of key business categories. In the positioning of an off-price menswear retailer, it was determined that specific competition varied by geographic market, but the competitive business categories remained the same in all markets—department stores, specialty men's clothing stores, and off-price/discount stores.

TASK 2

Identify Product Differences versus Competitors'

Next, write down the key positive and negative differences of your product versus those of the competition relative to your primary target market. These differences should be listed as they relate to key elements of the marketing mix that are appropriate to what you are selling.

A meaningful difference can be just about anything that makes your product unlike your competitors'. Coors beer is different because it is unpasteurized and fresh, with the beer shipped from the brewery refrigerated. Cheer laundry detergent was made different because it washed all types of clothes in hot, warm, and cold water. For a retail ski client of ours, being new to a market and offering innovated customer service was a difference, leading to its positioning as "the new age of ski shops." Sometimes a seemingly negative difference can actually be a positive. For instance, a small retailer with limited square footage and, thereby, limited variety of product offering can position itself as offering specialty selection and personal attention.

As you consider your product differences, ask yourself, How is my product different and how is it better? Is it different through product superiority? Innovation? Size (number of customers, volume of goods sold, number of outlets)? Whenever possible, use quantitative research for objectivity.

TASK 3

List Key Target Market / Characteristics

Insert your key target market on the top right side of the same worksheet (see Exhibit 6.1). Now, list the characteristics of your target market in terms of wants and needs on the right side of the worksheet. With or without research, ask yourself the following questions, listing brief answers below each question:

- What is the target market really purchasing? Is the product to be used by itself or in conjunction with a number of products (i.e., Are women purchasing dress shoes separately or as part of a fashion ensemble?)? For what purpose is the target using the product (i.e., Is the baking soda for baking a cake, deodorizing the refrigerator, or brushing teeth?)?
- Where is the target market purchasing/using it—by geography (i.e., in sunny, warm climates) and/or by place (i.e., in the home or car)?
- When is the target market using it—time of the year, month, week, day, during or after work?

Retail Fabrics Chain Example

Competition

1. Specialty chains
2. Mass merchants

Differences from Competitor
Product/Store/Service Attributes

Larger selection of fabrics and notions

Slightly better quality

Favorite store of sewers

Always new merchandise

Carries variety of goods for sewing, home decorating, and crafting

New Products/Improvements

Greater expansion into craft and home-decorating merchandise

Packaging/Store Appearance

Best store layout

Larger stores

Does not have promotional appearance

Branding/Name/Reputation

Established reputation

Distribution/Penetration

Greater number of outlets in most markets

Price

Perception of higher prices and less value

Advertising

Have more advertising

Key Target Market

Practical and creation sewers

Women 25–54

Average household income

3+ household size

Characteristics—Needs/Wants
What

Wide selection of merchandise from which to choose

Be able to purchase everything at one store

Lowest prices/good values

Quality fabrics

Where

Sews at home

When

After work and on weekends (seen as recreation)

Throughout the day (considered part of family responsibilities by practical sewers)

Why (Benefit)

For fun and as a hobby

To express creativity

For herself and children

To save money

For better fit of garments

For feeling of accomplishment

How Purchased/Used

Usually sew alone

Visit a fabric store on average every two weeks

Like to shop for deals

Shop for enjoyment

How the Target and Its Needs/Wants Are Changing

Less sewing to save money

More sewing for fun and recreation

Not enough time to sew

More sewers working out of the home

Using fabrics not just for sewing garments but for crafting and decorating the home

Buying more fabric-related merchandise for special occasions/holidays

- Why is the target market purchasing and/or using the product, or why is the target purchasing from one store over another? Is it because of a particular feature? Is it a convenient location or greater selection? Does the product save time or money?

- How is the product purchased/used? Is it purchased/used alone or with other people? Is it a frequent or infrequent purchase? How is it used (i.e., Is the tissue used to wipe one's nose or clean the windows? Is the beer used to relax after work or celebrate and party?)?
- How is the target changing? Is the market changing by demographics, lifestyle, size, or SIC classification? How are purchasing/usage habits of the product changing (i.e., Is fashion becoming more important than durability, value more than price, service more than just product quality?)?

TASK 4

Match Product's Characteristics to Target Market's Needs/Wants

Having listed the differences of your product and the key needs/wants of the target market, now try to match what is unique about your product to the meaningful needs and wants of the target market.

In Exhibit 6.1, using a retail fabric chain as an example, we have listed the specific competition and retailer's competitive differences on the left and the target market and its characteristics on the right. Based on the listing of the competitive differences, it would appear that this fabric retailer has a competitive advantage by offering an abundance of fabric-related merchandise in larger, better-designed stores. The merchandise selection appears superior not only in the amount but also in the variety of merchandise offered to complete a sewing project, as well as related crafting and home-decorating projects. This retailer could be viewed as a leader with an established reputation offering a variety of quality merchandise, though not at the lowest prices or greatest values.

The target market, on the other hand, is a mix of both practically and recreationally motivated sewers who want a large selection of all types of fabric-related merchandise that is very competitively priced and is a real value. This retailer definitely has the desired selection and quality but not necessarily the lower prices and value. The target also wants all of the required merchandise under one roof in order to enjoy a fun and rewarding shopping experience, as well as to fulfill the needs for both practically and recreationally motivated projects. Further, the listing indicates changes occurring within the target market. It appears that sewers have less time or need to sew regularly, are creating fewer garments, and are becoming more recreationally oriented, with interest growing in craft and home-decorating projects.

In this example, there appear to be a number of competitive advantages coming together under "superior selection offering" (wide variety, quality, fashionable, growing selection, and larger stores). These advantages would seem to match the target's growing desire for a fabric store with a large and complete offering of sewing, craft, and home-decorating merchandise. By matching the key differences to the key target market needs/wants of the positioning listings, the following positioning statement could be written for this fabric retail chain: "Each store provides *everything* a woman needs to fulfill fabric-related sewing, crafting, and home-decorating expectations."

After you have prepared your own positioning worksheet, draw lines from the major competitive positive differences to the paralleling want/need characteristics of the target market. Ask yourself again what really is important to the target market in terms of how your product is different and better. Based on this, eliminate lines until you have the two or three most meaningful potential positioning connections between product and target market.

In some cases you might combine two product differences or advantages to fill an important want. If you are a retailer, you might combine the attributes of brand name products and very competitive prices to arrive at a value positioning, which ties to an important consumer desire.

In some situations you will draw lines between product and target market characteristics and find that a most important consumer need/want is not being fulfilled by your product or the competition. For example, Virginia Slims, cigarettes for women, were created to fill a consumer gap. Going to the other extreme, you might find that all of the competing products fulfill the target's need/want, but no one product including yours, has claimed that need/want as its reason for being. Or, it might be that there are changing needs that are not being met and evolving needs that will provide positioning opportunities.

Positioning by Mapping

The positioning-by-mapping approach is a practical application of mapping methodology based on multidimensional models. Using this approach, you visually map out what is important to your target market in terms of key product attributes. The competition's products, including your own, are then ranked on these attributes.

Positioning by mapping is extremely useful in positioning a product and is most effective when based on quantitative research that is representative of the marketplace. Your preconceived notions about what the target market thinks can differ dramatically from what quantifiable research reports. However, if you do not have market research, it is still helpful to use this method to help sort out what you believe is important to the target market. Further, this positioning approach will help you to more clearly evaluate how your product and your key competition are perceived on each attribute. Because this mapping method is somewhat involved and you will most likely not have research to assist you, read through the three tasks outlined below before beginning the actual mapping process.

TASK 1 *List Product Attributes by Importance*	Acknowledging your built-in bias while being as objective as possible, the first step is to list, in order of importance, the product category attributes on the right side of the mapping worksheet provided at the end of this chapter. Move from top to bottom, from most important (10 value) to least important (0 value).

As shown in Exhibit 6.2, in the retail category the most important attribute to the consumer might be quality, followed by selection, price, service, and fashion, with location listed at the bottom. In the business-to-business category, reliable delivery might be ranked most important, followed by product consistency, quality, price, and favorable reputation, with knowledgeable sales force being least important.

TASK 2 *Rate Your Product and Competitors' Products for Each Attribute*	Once you have listed the key target market attributes, rate each competitor from best to worst for each attribute. For each rating, place the initial of each key competitor, including your product, on the line of each attribute ranking. Make a master listing of these keys under company/product/store code.

In Exhibit 6.2, our client, shoe retailer Famous Footwear, is coded as H, while its competitors are coded as D, E, L, and U. At the time this mapping was done, Famous Footwear rated second-to-last competitively on the two most important attributes for the retail category: quality and value.

In your plotting of the competitive market, you might have great disparity between competitors on one attribute and no differences on another. Ideally, you want your product ranked the best versus the competition on all attributes, but particularly on those that are most important to the consumer. The more you see your product's initial on the right, especially on those attributes at the top of the chart, the stronger the position of your product in the marketplace.

If quantitative research is not available before you begin mapping, it's a good idea to gather a number of people knowledgeable about your product category and have each one of them list the most important attributes. Next, as objectively as possible, have them independently assign a number from 0 to 10 (10 being most important and 0 least important) for each attribute. Take an average of these estimates for each ranking. Based on each composite estimate, rank-order the attributes.

After ranking attribute importance, ask the participants to agree on the top three to five market competitors, including your product. Then have each of them independently assign

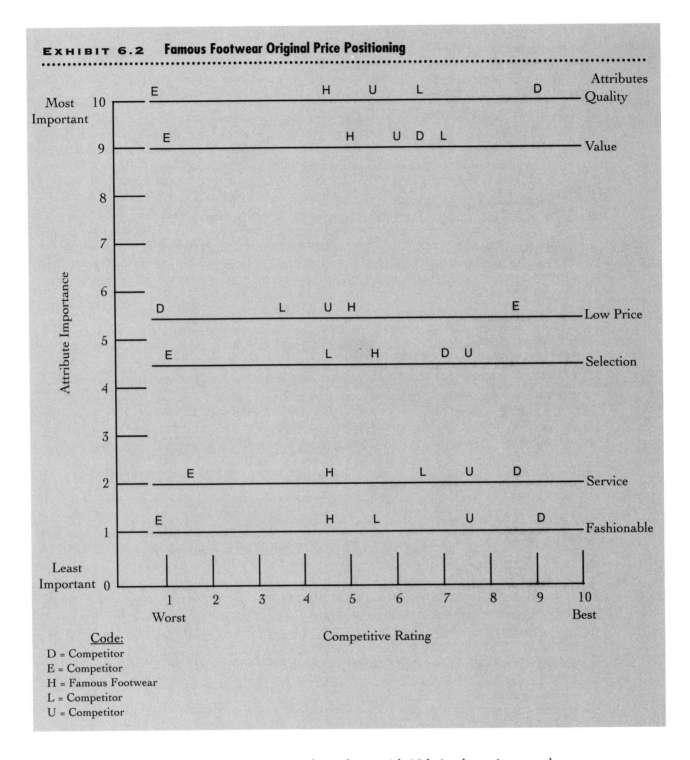

EXHIBIT 6.2   Famous Footwear Original Price Positioning

Code:
D = Competitor
E = Competitor
H = Famous Footwear
L = Competitor
U = Competitor

a rating of 1–10 for each competitor on each attribute, with 10 being best. Average the ratings for each competitor and insert a rating for each competitor, by initial, in line with each attribute ranking.

A note of caution: Using a knowledgeable group of people to assist in arriving at key attributes and competitive ratings is not as accurate as using survey research that will quantify the perceptions of the users and/or purchasers. However, with no research available, this approach will at least give you more perspective than if you positioned by matching only.

EXHIBIT 6.3   **Famous Footwear Original Price versus New Value Positioning**

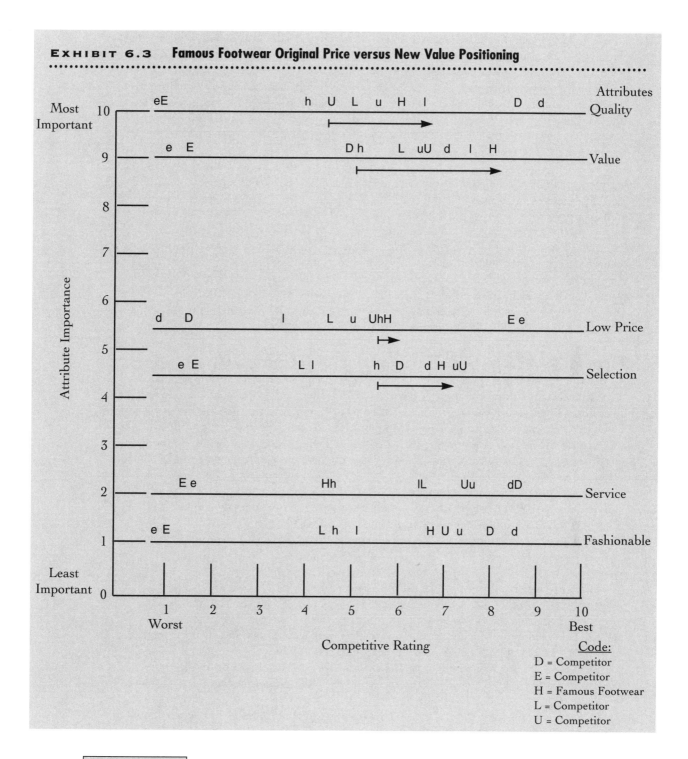

TASK 3

Visualize Desired Position on Map for Your Product

Once your positioning map is complete, review how your product ranks on the more important attributes relative to the competition. Next, visualize where you want your product positioned on the map based on what the consumer wants and what your product can provide relative to strengths and weaknesses of the competition. Finally, from the various types of positionings previously discussed, select the positioning approach that will positively affect the target market's perceptions and attain your visualized positioning.

Returning to the Famous Footwear example, declining sales had prompted this 20-store chain to conduct market research among consumers. The research indicated that, although price was important, quality and value were most important to consumers. Based on this data, the company changed its position from a "store with low prices" to "the value shoe store"—a store with quality merchandise at competitive prices. Translating this goal to the map visually would mean it would be the first store from the right for the value attribute. Accordingly, this retailer upgraded its merchandise mix and the appearance of its stores. The advertising was also changed to convey a value image.

The results of this value positioning versus the former low price/discount price positioning were dramatic. Comparable store sales for the year increased more than 30 percent. Market research conducted 18 months after the benchmark research study revealed dramatic positive shifts in how the consumer perceived this retailer versus the competition on the key attributes. As you can see in Exhibit 6.3, the retailer's competitive rating (H) on *quality* moved from second-to-last to second. Further, its competitive *value* rating moved from second-to-last to first, while the *price* rating remained virtually the same. Even the retailer's competitive rating on *selection* showed considerable positive movement from third to second place. This change in positioning resulted in a 30+ percent store-for-store sales increase in each of the two years following the value positioning. Today this once-floundering chain of 20 stores is now nationwide and growing, approaching 1,000 stores.

Positioning by Emotional Relationship

All positioning efforts seek to establish a connection between product and target market. But the emphasis can differ dramatically. Positioning by mapping focuses on the target's attribute positioning—the rating of the product relative to the competition; it focuses more on attributes like value, quality, or convenience. Emotional relationship positioning on the other hand, emphasizes the *feelings* of the target market—their feelings about the product, about themselves or about others, towards the company's personality, and about the meaning of the product in their lives.

The emotional approach offers a number of advantages:

- It is harder for competitors to attack emotional relationships than specific product attributes once a relationship is established.
- You can maintain the relationship despite radical changes in technology or product features.

There are also some disadvantages to this approach:

- If your product has a unique advantage (for example, a patented process), this approach may not focus enough on the product.
- If you cannot afford the media dollars to establish and defend this position, a larger, better-funded competitor can steal it from you.
- You must be able to deliver on the emotional promise. If you promise "friendly" and deliver "indifferent," you will make matters worse.

In many business categories, the marketing battleground already has seen some movement from rational benefits to emotional relationships. The reason? The consumer now faces a bewildering array of product choices. Unique product features or technical breakthroughs are quickly duplicated. The result is that the consumer does not have the time or energy to know everything necessary to make the right choice. He or she needs a simple relationship with a company that can be counted on, over time, to be a good choice.

The value of an emotional relationship with the company is even greater when:

- There is high emotional involvement in product selection, as in the perfume category.
- The competitive frame is saturated and complex, for example, soft drinks.

- The degree of personal, financial, or emotional risk is great, for example, cars.
- The business category is perceived as a commodity, for example, sugar.

Many of these emotional relationships are subconscious and irrational. They may even sound silly when stated out loud. You will probably never hear someone say, "I feel like a rich man when people see me in my Cadillac." But that is how they feel. Such feelings can be powerful motivators to buy your product.

Building an emotional relationship starts with the consumer rather than with your company or product. The goal is to build on his or her feelings, perceptions, and emotional needs. You will have to live in the consumer's hidden emotional world. Get ready to be surprised!

Emotional relationship marketing requires the use of fairly sophisticated qualitative research techniques, the ability to listen "behind" or "below" what consumers are saying, and the ability to create a wide range of positioning hypotheses to test. Before you undertake emotional relationship positioning, you may want to seek the assistance of a marketing communications firm, an advertising agency, or a marketing research firm with proven experience in this area.

TASK 1

Develop Individual Profile of Your Highest-Opportunity Consumer

The individual profile contains things like demographics, lifestyle, values, emotional needs, life experiences, philosophies, hobbies, and interests of the heavy purchaser. This profile is then contrasted with that of the person who is the lowest-opportunity consumer or the light purchaser. This contrast will often point to the key underlying motivator. DeanCare, a medical enterprise, used many different sources of information to develop its individual profile: national studies, trade magazines, local demographic information, focus groups, quantitative studies, and even direct experience.

TASK 2

Brainstorm for Motivators

Brainstorm with your staff or people knowledgeable about the product to develop a wide range of underlying, feeling-generated motivators to test with consumers. It is even valuable to include motivators that you know are wrong in order to get clearer feedback that points you in the right direction. For example, when DeanCare extended the positioning to cardiac care, they tested several emotional motivators (fear of dying, joy of living) against several attribute motivators (experience, physician expertise, mortality rates).

TASK 3

Rank the Motivator Choices with Target Consumers

Conduct focus groups (at least two) to determine which of the above-established motivator choices work with consumers. For example, DeanCare focus-group members were shown positioning statements both in writing and as tape-recorded patient statements. Participants then ranked their most favorite and least favorite statements.

TASK 4

Identify the Consumer's Primary Emotional Motivator(s) Based on the Above Rankings

Motivations can differ significantly depending on the purchasing occasion, the stage of your life, or the role the product plays in your life. For DeanCare's pediatric customers, contrasting their good and bad doctor experiences helped reveal the key motivator—the need to be treated like a human being with feelings.

TASK 5

Validate Qualitative Analysis with Quantitative Survey Results

If at all possible, use survey research to test several different positionings (both emotional and attribute) to verify the results of the focus groups regarding the appeal of the key motivator relative to the size of the market. This will prevent you from selecting a key motivator that is very strong but that is significant only for a small group of people.

This will establish a relationship with your target person and also establish a core brand personality for your company or product. DeanCare used "human feelings." Finally, based on the qualitative and quantitative research you have conducted, write a positioning statement using the strongest emotional motivator.

Preparing a Positioning Strategy

Having gone through the matching, mapping, and emotional relationship methods with your product, you should now have some direction or thoughts on how you want your product to be perceived as meaningfully different from the competition by the target market. With this, you are ready to write alternative positioning strategies. It is wise to write more than one positioning strategy in order to make a comparison of strategies and evaluate which positioning best reflects your product relative to the competition and fulfills the needs/wants of the target market. Your alternative positioning statements should vary by the degree of emphasis placed on the product advantage, the competition's weaknesses, and the target market benefit.

The key word is *focus* when writing a positioning statement. The tendency is to write a positioning statement that reads like a litany, rather than keeping it simple and straightforward. The shorter and more to the point, the better the positioning strategy. A succinct positioning will provide clear and specific direction for the employment of the tactical marketing mix tools. For this reason, choose each word thoughtfully. Once you have prepared the alternative positionings, select the one that will best suit the target market and fulfill the marketing strategies using the format provided at the end of this chapter. Below are some examples of positioning:

Consumer Package Goods
Funny Face: the *kids'* powdered soft drink for summertime fun.
Miller Lite: the only beer with superior taste and low caloric content.

Business-to-Business
W. T. Rogers: the *established office supply leader,* improving the look and efficiency of the office environment.

Service
Stark Realtors: the *most professional realtor* for home buyers and sellers *throughout Dane County.*

WORKSHEET

Positioning—Matching Product Differences to the Target Market's Needs/Wants

Key Competition

Key Target Market

1

2

3

4

5

Differences from Competitor
Product/Store/Service Attributes/Benefits

Characteristics—Needs/Wants
What

New Products/Improvements

Where

Packaging/Store Appearance

Branding/Name/Reputation

When

Distribution/Penetration

Price

Why (Benefit)

Advertising (Message/Media)

How Purchased/Used

Promotion

Merchandising

How the Target and Its Needs/Wants Are Changing

Personal Selling and Service

Publicity

Positioning—Mapping Product Importance by Competitive Ranking

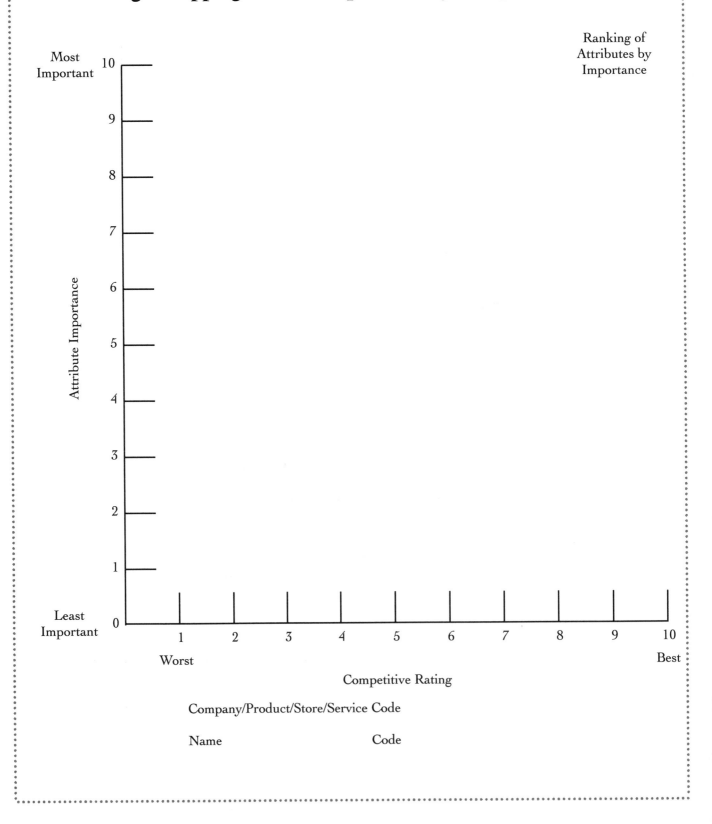

Ranking of
Attributes by
Importance

Most
Important

Attribute Importance

Least
Important

Worst

Best

Competitive Rating

Company/Product/Store/Service Code

Name   Code

FORMAT

Positioning Strategy

Strategy Statement

Qualifier/Descriptors (Only if necessary)

Rationale

Step 5: Plan Strategies

MARKETING BACKGROUND

1 THE BUSINESS REVIEW

Scope
Company Strengths & Weaknesses • Core Competencies • Marketing Capabilities

Product and Market Review
Company & Product Review • Category & Company Sales • Behavior Trends • Pricing • Distribution • Competitive Review

Target Market Effectors
Consumer/Business-to-Business Targets • Product Awareness & Attributes • Trial & Retrial Data

2 PROBLEMS/OPPORTUNITIES

MARKETING PLAN

3 SALES OBJECTIVES

4 TARGET MARKETS AND MARKETING OBJECTIVES

5 PLAN STRATEGIES—Positioning & Marketing

6 COMMUNICATION GOALS

7 TACTICAL MARKETING MIX TOOLS

Product	Distribution	Advertising Media
Branding	Personal Selling/Service	Merchandising
Packaging	Promotion/Events	Publicity
Pricing	Advertising Message	

8 MARKETING PLAN BUDGET AND CALENDAR

9 EXECUTION

10 EVALUATION

MARKETING STRATEGIES

- WHAT MARKETING STRATEGIES ARE, AND WHAT ROLE THEY PLAY IN THE MARKETING PLANNING PROCESS.
- THE 18 MARKETING STRATEGY ALTERNATIVES, AND WHEN TO EMPLOY THEM.
- HOW TO DEVELOP AND WRITE MARKETING STRATEGIES.

ONCE YOU HAVE ESTABLISHED MARKETING OBJECTIVES (Chapter 5) and a positioning strategy (Chapter 6), the next step is to develop marketing strategies. We will describe the process of developing marketing strategies in this chapter.

A *marketing strategy* is a broad directional statement that describes how marketing objectives will be accomplished. Within your marketing plan, the marketing strategies represent a first overview of various marketing tools and how they will be used to achieve the marketing objectives. While marketing objectives are specific, quantifiable, and measurable, marketing strategies are descriptive.

The most commonly addressed strategy issues are listed here and described in more detail later in the chapter:

Build market or steal share	Pricing
National, regional, or local markets	Distribution/penetration or coverage
Seasonality	Personal selling/service/operations
Spending	Promotion/events
Competition	Advertising message
Target market	Advertising media
Product	Merchandising
Branding	Publicity
Packaging	Marketing research and testing (R&T)

In some cases, the marketing strategies section of your plan may be the only place where some of these issues, such as building a market or spending, are discussed directly. In such cases, the strategies you develop here will provide guideposts for a variety of tactical decisions later in the plan. For example, you may establish a market-building strategy with the introduction of a new product. Such a strategy provides the context for advertising and promotion plans, among others, as you will need to build a high level of awareness and generate trial through a high level of activity for your new product.

Many of the marketing elements addressed in this chapter are reconsidered from a specific tactical perspective later in the plan. The marketing strategies developed here serve as a reference for the tactical tools that follow. They provide the general strategic direction to accomplish the marketing objectives, but they do not include such specifics as "use television," for example, which belongs in the tactical media segment of the marketing plan.

The following provides a review of alternative strategy approaches around which to develop marketing strategies, as well as marketing strategy examples to get you started. You should consider all the strategy alternatives and then prepare marketing strategies that fulfill the marketing objectives of your plan. A format for developing your marketing strategies is provided at the end of this chapter.

Alternative Marketing Strategies

Build the Market or Steal-Market-Share Strategies

A critical strategic decision facing all marketers writing a plan is whether to build the market or steal share from competitors in order to achieve sales goals. The information regarding product awareness and attributes in your business review, and the product life cycle specifically, will help provide answers to this fundamental question.

If you have a relatively new product, a small current user base but a large potential user base, and little competition, you may want to build the market. Many times, the company that creates the market maintains the largest market share long into the future. An example of this would be Miller Lite, which created demand for low-calorie beer. Miller established the light beer category and was the market share leader for two decades. However, as Miller Lite can attest, it is usually easier to steal market share than to build the market. Accordingly, Bud Light and Coors have passed Miller Lite in sales by stealing share of the light beer market Miller built. Because it is a two-step process, building a market takes additional time and money. You have to develop a need for the product and then convince a target market to purchase your particular brand.

In a situation where the product is a mature one with minimal growth (i.e., few new customers entering the marketplace), stealing market share from competitors is often called for. In this situation, you have to convince product category users that your product is superior to that of your competition. In some cases, the market may be growing, which allows your firm to grow along with it. In this case, the question becomes, "Is the market growing at the same rate I want to grow?" If the answer is no, then you will still need to steal share from your competition. All of these scenarios would be described in the market share strategy.

The decision to build the market or steal share must be made upfront in your marketing strategy section, as this is a fundamental strategic decision that will affect all other areas of the marketing plan. A stealing-share strategy, such as "steal market share from the leading competitor," requires that your company's target market definitions closely approximate those of the current market leader's customer profile. Also, the advertising will most likely communicate benefits or an image of your product that the market leader doesn't possess. To the contrary, a "build the market" strategy often requires educating new customers about the benefits of product usage, then convincing them to use your company's products.

Build-the-Market Example: Build the market for the new Quicksilver variable-pitch propeller as a replacement for a damaged propeller, as an upgrade to a current propeller, and as a propeller bought with new engines. *Rationale:* The new variable-pitch technology is unknown to the consumer market, and Quicksilver must develop a market for this new type of prop. Their marketing objectives called for gaining trial of new customers in years one and two of the launch.

Steal-Share Example: Steal share from the premium segment of the green and ripe olive category. *Rationale:* Introduce a new ripe olive product at a premium price and, at the same time, increase the price of the existing green olive product to the same premium price in order to steal share from the premium-priced olive competition.

National, Regional, and Local Markets Strategies

This strategy helps the marketer determine whether there will be a core national marketing plan or a combination of national, regional, and local marketing plans. It recognizes regional DMA (designated market area or television viewing area) and even local trading area differences by allowing for the application of specific territorial marketing programs. Such an approach allows the marketer to tailor the media, message, and spending levels to specific markets.

National, Regional, and Local Markets Example: Concentrate marketing efforts for a printing company located in Wisconsin to customers who purchase directly versus those who purchase through advertising/design agencies in Wisconsin first, then in the immediate Midwest (Michigan, Minnesota, and Illinois), followed by the remainder of the United States. *Rationale:* All objectives have a local (Wisconsin), regional (Michigan, Minnesota, Illinois), and national component, and marketing efforts will mirror that. This "pyramid" essentially allows the marketer to focus on areas of high potential nearby, where its sales force can most effectively reach, and follow up with farther-reaching efforts by targeting key industries and corporations in locations beyond the Midwest.

Seasonality Strategies

Strategic decisions must be made about when to advertise or promote your product or store and whether you are going to advertise and promote all year, during stronger selling periods, or during weaker selling periods. You also need to decide if you are going to advertise and promote prior to, during, or between peak selling periods.

Seasonality Example: Promote heavily during major back-to-school periods of late summer, as well as Christmas vacation and spring vacation periods. *Rationale:* A national paper-products marketer targeted mothers of school-aged children with its travel-sized tissue product. Positioned as the tissue to keep in your desk at school, the school season influenced the purchase timing.

Spending Strategies

Spending strategies outline how the marketing dollars will be spent. To achieve your marketing objectives, you need to decide on spending strategies regarding issues such as investment spending for a new product; whether to increase sales of weaker-selling brands, stores, or regions of the country; and whether to attract more customers to your stronger brands or stores. In order to make these decisions, you need to determine spending levels by brand, store, or regions of the country.

Overall spending should also be addressed. Does your company plan to spend at a percent of sales for marketing and advertising consistent with past years? Or, because of new aggressive sales projections and marketing objectives, do you need to increase marketing spending from, for example, 5 percent of gross sales to 8 percent? The actual spending detail will be highlighted in the budget section of the marketing plan (Chapter 18).

Spending Example: Allocate marketing expenditures between two different tiers geographically. In tier 1, increase spending by 25 percent; in tier 2, maintain spending levels comparable to the previous year. *Rationale:* This national retailer recognized that certain markets were particularly competitive and that additional spending would be necessary to maintain share growth.

Competition Strategies

The business review may reveal that a single competitor is almost totally responsible for your company's decline in market share, a new competitor is entering the market, or a single company or group of competitors may have preempted your unique positioning in the marketplace. If this is the case, you will need to develop a competitive marketing strategy in your marketing plan.

Competition Example: Target the second- through tenth-ranked competitors by aligning with Pioneer, the market leader, as the second hybrid choice. *Rationale:* This hybrid seed producer recognized Pioneer's dominance (40 percent market share) by aiming at the next level of competitors. To do this, the company capitalized on the fact that most farmers use two or more brands on their farms and positioned itself as the second seed with Pioneer.

Target Market Strategies

The target market section of your business review detailed primary and secondary target markets. You must now discuss the emphasis you will place against the various target markets and how you will market to them based on your marketing objectives, which defined the purchase behavior you intend to gain from the target.

Target Market Example: Target women 25–54 with children through emphasis on pediatrics expertise and leadership. *Rationale:* Women make 75–80 percent of all health care decisions in a family. Mothers tend to align their health care decisions around a pediatrician's choice. This medical center, associated with a regional HMO, was rated highly on its pediatric care and aimed to take advantage of this target.

Product Strategies

You must make strategic decisions regarding new products, product line extensions, product improvement, product elimination, and/or whether to build or improve weaker product lines or continue to maximize stronger selling product lines.

Product Example: Combine product offerings as packages based on bundles of benefits consistent with consumer purchasing needs. *Rationale:* High turnover plagued this national auto club due to low awareness of its full product line, including a travel agency, auto insurance, financial services, and more. Known merely for its road service, the best method to gain renewal of a club member was to use cross-selling of products.

Branding Strategies

If you are introducing a new product or line extension, you will want to provide direction for the branding or naming of these products. Should the new product stand by itself or be under the umbrella of the family name? Should the brand name exclusively target current customers or current and new customers? If you are going to enter a new channel, you might want to change the name of your product line to appeal to different targets, or you might need a new name for stores carrying your products in discount outlet malls versus regional malls.

Branding Example: Develop a new product name appealing to existing customers first and potential customers second. *Rationale:* The largest segment of potential purchasers are existing customers.

Packaging Strategies

If you are developing a packaging plan later in the marketing plan, establish a general direction for your packaging strategy. Here you will need to consider and address the following issues regarding your product's packaging, referring to your problems and opportunities for direction:

1. Function—Is your product's packaging serving its primary function of holding or protecting the product?
2. Value-added—Does your packaging add value to the product purchase and enhance its use experience for the consumer?
3. Communication—Does your packaging stand out in the retail environment compared to competitors'? Does it communicate the inherent drama of the product?

Packaging Example: Develop packaging to reflect value positioning, distinct from the current product line offerings, while drawing attention on the dealer's shelves. *Rationale:* A new line of accessories from this manufacturer was positioned differently from its traditional quality-oriented product line. In order to avoid confusion or the possibility of eroding the equity of the original brand, packaging for the new line needs to provide differentiation both from the competition and from the company's original line.

Pricing Strategies

Address whether you will use high or low prices relative to your competition or whether you will simply match the competition's price and depend upon service or superior product attributes for a competitive edge. Will you maintain margins with high-price strategies, or will you allow for lower margins and lower prices to develop trial?

Pricing Example: Maintain a parity pricing approach (based on appropriately fitting printing jobs to capabilities) to existing customers, where service and quality are more important than price. Use competitive pricing to gain trial and entry with noncustomers. *Rationale:* Research indicated that price was an important element of a customer's decision as to whether or not to try a printer. Further, the research also revealed that the decision to continue a relationship with a printer was based primarily on print quality and service and less on price. However, a high-price strategy may allow a competitor to "buy" a customer's business. Therefore, a strategy of parity pricing seems most appropriate for this commercial printer.

Distribution of Product/Penetration or Coverage Strategies

The strategic decisions that must be made in this area are different for consumer goods and business-to-business firms than for retailers and service firms. Consumer goods and business-to-business firms must decide in what areas of the country to target their distribution efforts. They also must decide on the type of channels/outlets that will carry their product and on the desired market coverage among the targeted outlet category.

Retailers and service firms must strategically decide if marketing objectives can be achieved through existing outlets, whether new stores need to be added in existing markets without cannibalizing existing stores, or whether new stores need to be added through entering new markets.

Distribution of Product/Penetration or Coverage Example: Focus distribution through large retailers nationally. *Rationale:* This distributor and publisher of alternative comic books recognizes that the vast majority of comics are sold through the larger comic retailers, who tend to carry alternative comics more than smaller retailers. National distribution is necessary to achieve sales goals.

Personal Selling/Service/Operation Strategies

Determine whether you want to address a structured personal selling program through this marketing plan. You may want to address basic elements of that sales program, including whether you will use sales incentives; establish sales goals relative to pure dollar objectives, a particular product, or target market emphasis in terms of calls made, etc.; and define a sales methodology (e.g., soft sell versus hard sell). If you are a retailer, note whether your subsequent selling plan should include specific sales ratios (e.g., develop sales ratio of purchasers versus walkers based upon past history and future expectations).

Personal Selling/Service/Operation Example: Develop detailed target volume objectives with the field sales organization to establish a forecast and performance criteria. *Rationale:* This strategy for a national manufacturer of recycled paper products, which holds the market share lead in certain market segments, addresses the lack of quantifiable sales goals among the sales force in spite of aggressive overall sales objectives.

Promotion/Events Strategies

Promotions, along with events, should be channeled to meet specific needs and must be incorporated into the overall marketing plan in a disciplined fashion. These promotion strategies will set the areas of emphasis for the specific promotion plan later in the marketing plan, providing direction for the promotional and event efforts aimed at addressing specific marketing objectives.

Promotion/Events Example: Develop a promotional program to encourage existing advertiser customers to purchase more ad space. A tactic later in the plan, directed by this strategy, could be: Introduce a 13th edition in the year with special page rates. *Rationale:* The problems and opportunities section for this monthly magazine indicated that the publication was a secondary buy among advertisers, that the advertisers typically purchase more in a special issue, and that the current customer advertiser had a relatively low purchase level. This strategy addresses all of these issues.

Advertising Message Strategies

Provide an overall focus for the advertising communication. It is important to state upfront in your marketing strategy section how you are going to use image, promotional, regional, or national advertising to fulfill your marketing objectives.

Advertising Message Example: Develop an aggressive and comprehensive consumer advertising program to build awareness for the new product and educate the consumer about its unique features. *Rationale:* The strategy for a new variable-pitch propeller responds to the need to build a market through consumer education and to generate maximum support from the trade to carry and merchandise the product.

Advertising Media Strategies

The strategies developed in this section should be consistent with the direction established in the product, competitive, and spending marketing strategies. The primary goal in establishing an overall media strategy is to provide direction for the upcoming media plan and to establish geographic and product spending emphasis.

Advertising Media Example: Advertise throughout the year to maintain awareness among all key targets. *Rationale:* Multiple decision makers represent the target for this producer of anesthesia machines: anesthesiologists, biomedical engineers, materials management directors, hospital administrators, and financial managers, among others. Because the purchase of such equipment is not seasonal, awareness must be maintained among these segments on an ongoing basis.

Merchandising Strategies

A strategy is needed to set the tone for what will be done from a merchandising standpoint. This applies to all nonmedia communication; for example, in-store signage for retailers, point-of-purchase displays for package goods firms, and personal presentation sales aids such as brochures and sell sheets for business-to-business firms.

Merchandising Example: All in-store communication materials should be developed to reinforce the positioning themeline. This may include collateral materials, signage, and continuing service reference materials for buyers. *Rationale:* A themeline based on the positioning had been developed for this large auto dealership. Considering the propensity for car purchase decisions to be made at the dealership, point-of-sale materials communicating this theme are extremely important.

Publicity Strategies

Determine if you are going to make publicity or nonpaid mass media communication part of your marketing plan, as you will need to consider publicity opportunities when you develop the other specific tactical tool segments of your plan. Then there will be an overall direction established when it comes time to develop a specific public relations tactical segment later in the plan.

Publicity Example: Utilize editorial programs to help build awareness and provide legitimacy to building a leadership peer position in the high-end commercial printing category. *Rationale:* Primary competitors for the high-end commercial printing segment have established reputations among the target. This firm must build awareness and a reputation as a major player in the high-end segment through targeted publications and other "newslike" formats.

Marketing Research and Testing (R&T) Strategies

Research can help define your product's problem(s) and help determine the potential and needs of the target market, optimum pricing, effective advertising messages, and much more. If you plan to conduct primary research, now is the time to establish a research strategy. You may develop a research strategy to solve a specific problem that will help you to build sales and accomplish a marketing objective. Or you may decide to conduct an ongoing awareness, attitude, and behavior tracking study to assist with next year's plan and to provide a benchmark to evaluate the results of current and future marketing plans.

Testing keeps you ahead of the competition and helps you avoid costly mistakes. It can help you develop a new product or marketing activity, make it better, provide evidence of your program's effectiveness, and eliminate those ideas that aren't going to work before a costly investment has been made. You can test any part of a marketing program, from a product change and price increase to a new promotion, television commercial, or store format.

Once you have committed to some form of marketing R&T, this section should be used to define what you will be researching and testing—new products, services, merchandising programs, store layouts, packaging, media strategies, advertising messages, pricing, promotions, etc. Incorporate what you will research and test in the appropriate plan segments later in the marketing plan. To help you develop these strategies, refer to Chapter 21, Marketing R&T.

Marketing Research and Testing Example: Test among dealers the pricing elasticity and promotion programs for the variable-pitch propeller. *Rationale:* As the variable-pitch propeller is a new product with a premium price, there is little knowledge of how consumers will respond to this price and how dealers would respond to the promotional efforts by the manufacturer. Testing would help provide answers prior to rolling the product introduction out nationally.

Developing Your Marketing Strategies

To develop marketing strategies, review the problems and opportunities, target market, and marketing objectives as well as your positioning strategy. Then use your problems and opportunities as a guide in writing strategies that solve each problem and exploit each opportunity.

1. Review your problems and opportunities.

    Read through your problems and opportunities and make notes regarding ideas you have on how to solve the problems and take advantage of the opportunities. Be creative in this exercise and identify multiple solutions for each problem or opportunity.

2. Review your target market and marketing objectives.

    Review your target market and marketing objectives, then reread the problems and opportunities, along with your notes on how to solve the problems and take advantage of the opportunities. Determine which of the ideas will form strategies capable of achieving the marketing objectives.

3. Review your positioning strategy.

    What is the product image you want to instill in the minds of the target market relative to the competition? It is this meaningful image that must be reinforced individually and cumulatively by your marketing strategies.

4. Develop your strategies.

    Review the 18 alternative strategy considerations and determine which issues you need to address. As stated before, use the strategy approaches that fit your product's or company's particular situation—not all strategy alternatives will apply in every situation. Then, based on what you know from the problems and opportunities, develop clear and concise directional statements about how you intend to address each issue.

Remember that the strategies developed here should provide the direction for use of the marketing mix tools throughout the marketing plan. For example, your spending and seasonality strategies established here will be reflected in the detailed media plan later in your marketing plan.

In summary, after reviewing the marketing strategies, upper management should have a good understanding as to how you are going to achieve your marketing objectives from a strategic standpoint. However, the details of these strategies will be fully developed in the subsequent tactical marketing mix tool segments of the marketing plan.

Writing Your Marketing Strategies

Make sure to focus on one single idea at a time when writing your strategies. The strategies should be very descriptive and focus on how you are going to utilize a particular tool, such as promotions or packaging, to achieve the marketing objectives. Following each strategy should be a brief rationale drawing information from the business review, problems and opportunities, target market and marketing objectives, and market positioning sections to support the strategy.

FORMAT

Marketing Strategies
Build-the-Market or Steal-Market-Share Strategies

National, Regional, and Local Marketing Strategies

Seasonality Strategies

Spending Strategies

Competitive Strategies

Target Market Strategies

Product Strategies

Packaging

Branding Strategies

Note: Provide rationale for each strategy.

Pricing Strategies

Distribution of Product/Store Penetration or Coverage Strategies

Personal Selling/Service/Operations Strategies

Promotion Strategies

Advertising Message Strategies

Advertising Media Strategies

Merchandising Strategies

Publicity Strategies

Marketing R&T (Research and Testing) Strategies

Step 6: Communication Goals—Positioning & Marketing

MARKETING BACKGROUND

1 THE BUSINESS REVIEW

Scope
Company Strengths & Weaknesses • Core Competencies • Marketing Capabilities

Product and Market Review
Company & Product Review • Category & Company Sales • Behavior Trends • Pricing • Distribution • Competitive Review

Target Market Effectors
Consumer/Business-to-Business Targets • Product Awareness & Attributes • Trial & Retrial Data

2 PROBLEMS/OPPORTUNITIES

MARKETING PLAN

3 SALES OBJECTIVES

4 TARGET MARKETS AND MARKETING OBJECTIVES

5 PLAN STRATEGIES—Positioning & Marketing

6 COMMUNICATION GOALS

7 TACTICAL MARKETING MIX TOOLS

Product
Branding
Packaging
Pricing

Distribution
Personal Selling/Service
Promotion/Events
Advertising Message

Advertising Media
Merchandising
Publicity

8 MARKETING PLAN BUDGET AND CALENDAR

9 EXECUTION

10 EVALUATION

COMMUNICATION GOALS

IN THIS CHAPTER YOU WILL LEARN:

- THE FOUR A'S OF COMMUNICATION AND BEHAVIOR.
- HOW TO LOCK SALES OBJECTIVES TO COMMUNICATION GOALS.
- HOW TO DEVELOP COMMUNICATION GOALS THAT WILL DELIVER THE POSITIONING.
- HOW TO ALLOCATE THE NECESSARY AWARENESS AND ATTITUDE VALUES FOR EACH TACTICAL TOOL THAT FULFILLS THE OVERALL COMMUNICATION GOALS.

ONCE YOU HAVE DETERMINED THE OVERALL ELEMENTS (marketing objectives and positioning and marketing strategies), it is time to build a bridge that will link these elements to the tactical tools that will be used in the execution of your marketing plan. As shown graphically below, the bridge between marketing objectives and tactics is the *communication goals*. While the plan strategies fulfill the marketing objectives and guide the direction of the tactical tools, the communication goals of awareness and attitude quantitatively lock the required communication to delivery of the marketing objectives. These communication goals also lock to the tactical tools that follow by providing the allocation of the required communication among each of the tactical tools.

In this chapter, we will explain how the communication process works and how communication goals can positively affect target market behavior. We will also describe how to allocate the necessary communication values for each tactical tool that fulfills the overall communication goals.

The Four A's of Communication and Behavior

Everything about a successful marketing plan begins with *fulfilling the target market needs and wants*, not just selling the product. Therefore, we must begin with an explanation of the communication process and how it can positively affect the target market behavior that you have previously quantified in your marketing objectives. The question to keep in mind is, How do we use communication to affect target market behavior?

The answer to this question is the Four A's of Communication and Behavior: Awareness, Attitude, Action, and Action[2]. In order to have continual target market purchase, it is necessary to have communication down, then up the Four A's axis (as shown in Exhibit 8.1), with attitude affecting action (behavior) and action (behavior) affecting attitude. Let's start at the top of the axis and work our way down.

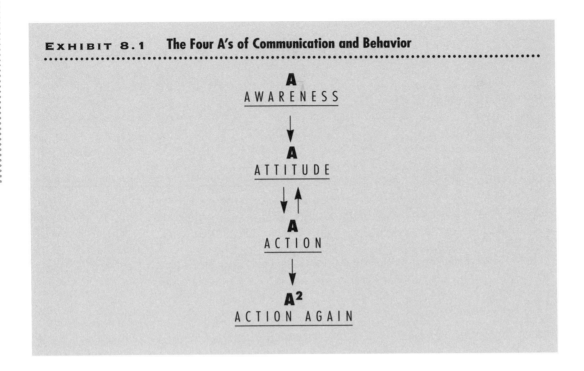

EXHIBIT 8.1   The Four A's of Communication and Behavior

A
AWARENESS

↓

A
ATTITUDE

↓ ↑

A
ACTION

↓

A²
ACTION AGAIN

While it may seem basic, in nearly all cases you must have *Awareness* of a product in order to form an attitude about it or take action to purchase it. Recall from Chapter 2 that the three different types of awareness, from most- to least effective, are top-of-mind, unaided, and aided. *Top-of-mind awareness* is the first product name given by an individual when asked what product comes to mind in a particular category. *Unaided awareness* includes all the brands in a category a person can think of without assistance. *Aided awareness* is an individual's recognition of branded products when their names are given or products are shown.

In the next step, awareness creates *Attitude.* This could involve a long-term attitude development process, such as the process most people go through when buying a new car, or low attitude involvement, such as that leading to the impulse purchase of a pack of gum at the check-out register in the grocery store. Your attitude toward a product could be formed by brand name, packaging, price, or some previous action or experience, such as sampling, but not buying, a product or calling for a brochure. You also might have had a previous experience with a product, causing you to form an attitude—positive or negative—toward it. Accordingly, *attitude affects action and action affects attitude;* hence, the two-way arrow in the Four A's model in Exhibit 8.1.

Action represents the initial purchase or trial of the product. If this initial action is not a purchase, it must be an action that could lead to a potential purchase, such as sampling the product. If the targeted person has not acted on your product in the past year, there still may be attitude that has to be dealt with because of a relationship with your product, such as having been a previous purchaser of your product or a user of a competing brand.[1]

The bottom of the axis, *Action Again*, represents one repeat purchase in the past year to a loyal customer who has made multiple purchases of your product. This, of course, is the ultimate goal of the communication process.

[1]Don E. Schultz, Stanley I. Tannenbaum, and Robert F. Lauterborn, *Integrated Marketing Communications: Putting It All Together and Making It Work* (Lincolnwood, Ill.: NTC Publishing Group, 1993.)

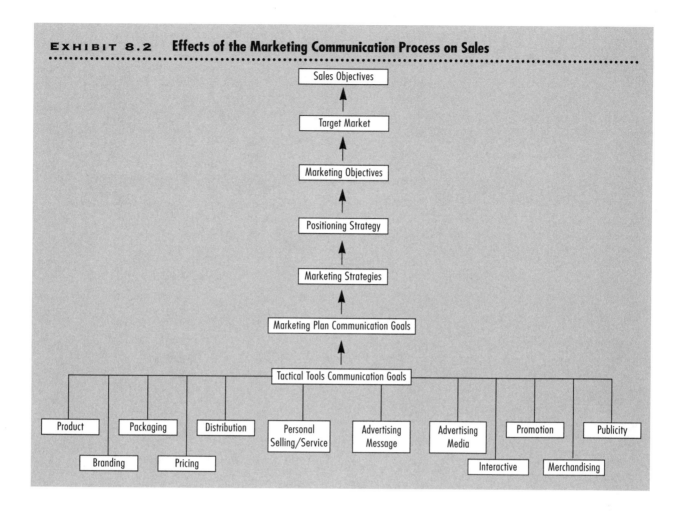

EXHIBIT 8.2   Effects of the Marketing Communication Process on Sales

Locking Sales to Communication

Now that you have an understanding of the Four A's communication and target market behavior process, we will explain how this process interfaces with other plan elements and the ultimate goal of generating sales. This approach is graphically depicted in Exhibit 8.2. Looking from the bottom, the cumulative effect of the specific awareness and attitude generated from each tactical tool fulfills the overall marketing plan communication goals. The overall marketing plan communication delivers the positioning via the marketing strategies, which fulfill the marketing objectives of target market behavior. This behavior will, in turn, fulfill the sales objectives.

While Exhibit 8.2 shows graphically the effects of the marketing communication process on sales, Exhibit 8.3 provides an example of how you can *numerically lock* the projected sales from the target market to the marketing objectives and to the required plan and tactical tool communication goals.

Looking at Exhibit 8.3, notice that the total sales objective of $5.5MM will be generated from the defined total target market, quantified at 664.1M. This total market is then segmented into 206.0M previous purchasers and 458.1M nonpurchasers, with each segment receiving its own sales objective. The marketing objectives, which have been previously delineated in the marketing plan, call for retention of 41.3 percent of previous purchasers and trial by 3.1 percent of nonpurchasers. The estimated average number of annual purchases and average purchase dollar amount (1.8 × $32.15 for previous purchasers and 1.3 × $33.00 for nonpurchasers) multiplied by the total number of retention purchasers and trial purchasers equals the $4.9MM and $0.6MM segmented target sales, respectively. In order to fulfill these

EXHIBIT 8.3 Locking Sales from Target Market to Marketing Objectives and Communication

Footwear Store Target Market Example

Total Sales
$5.5MM

Total Target Market
664.1M

	Previous Purchasers (206.0M)		Nonpurchasers (458.1M)	
Segmented Target Sales Objectives	$4.9MM		$0.6MM	
Marketing Objectives	**%**	**#**	**%**	**#**
Purchasers (via retention and trial)	41.3	85.1	3.1	14.2
# of Annual Purchases	(Retention)	1.8	(Trial)	1.3
Average $ Purchase		$32.15		$33.00
Purchase Intent	**%**	**#**	**%**	**#**
Believe They Will Definitely Purchase	55.0	113.3	7.0	32.1

	Unaided Awareness		Positive Attitude		Unaided Awareness		Positive Attitude	
	%	**#**	**%**	**#**	**%**	**#**	**%**	**#**
Marketing Plan Communication Goals	95.0	195.7	69.0	142.1	29.0	132.8	12.0	55.0
Tactical Tool Communication Goals								
Product	10.0		16.0		2.0		3.5	
Branding	5.0		3.0		0.5		0.5	
Packaging	5.0		3.0		0.5		1.0	
Pricing	1.0		5.5		1.0		1.0	
Distribution/Penetration	7.0		3.0		2.0		0.5	
Personal Selling/Service	9.0		5.0		2.1		1.0	
Promotion/Events	14.0		8.0		2.5		0.8	
Advertising Message	12.0		8.0		3.1		1.6	
Advertising Media	17.0		6.0		3.8		0.5	
Merchandising	15.0		11.5		10.0		1.6	
Publicity	—		—		1.5		—	
Interactive Communication	—		—		—		—	

specific sales objectives, 55 percent and 7 percent of each respective target market must have a definite intent to purchase. As you can see, there is a falloff from the percent that definitely intends to purchase versus those who are projected to purchase. Using previous purchasers as an example, in order to have 55 percent purchase intent, a positive attitude is projected at 69 percent of the target, which falls off from the total unaided awareness projection of 95 percent. In order to deliver the projected 95 percent unaided awareness and 69 percent positive attitude goals, these totals are then allocated among each tactical tool. Each tool is then planned and executed to generate its share of the required marketing plan awareness and attitude communication goals.

We are exposing you to this overview of the complete method in order for you to understand how the completed plan elements will lock together; both the process and locking mechanics will be explained in detail later in this chapter. After you apply this methodology, you should be able to construct a top-down, sales-to-tactical tool communication grid, as shown in Exhibit 8.3, which quantitatively delineates how the ultimate sales objective will be delivered from the specific target market segments. A worksheet similar to this exhibit is included at the end of this chapter.

Developing and Applying Communication Goals

Now that you have a basic understanding of the relationship between communication and behavior, we will describe the process of developing and applying communication goals. The four tasks involved in this process are:

1. Reviewing awareness, attitude, and action/behavior experiences for your product, the competition, the category, and related categories.
2. Reviewing the previously established target market behavior for both purchasers and nonpurchasers, as well as the marketing position and strategies.
3. Determining the overall marketing plan communication goals.
4. Setting specific awareness and attitude value goals for each tactical tool that will fulfill the overall marketing communication goals.

TASK 1
Review Awareness, Attributes, and Action/Behavior Experiences for Your Product, the Competition, the Category, and Related Categories

Literally all small, medium, and even large businesses lack much of the described information needed to apply the ideal communication goals strategy method. We expect, however, that much of the data you have gathered in your business review can be used as a basis in the application of this method. Most of these data will be found in your product history, as well as through primary and secondary research.

Specifically, look for information that provides insight into the effectiveness of each tactical tool's ability to deliver awareness and positive attitude to generate behavior and/or make the sale. Try to get some indication of what percentage of the target market is aware of your product and holds key attitudes toward your product, such as a "best quality" or leadership and how these communication factors relate to the percentage of your target market that purchases the product.

If possible, you would like to know the awareness, attitude, and behavior of both customers and noncustomers in your target market, because you will find that the relationship between communication and behavior will vary dramatically between purchasers and nonpurchasers.

Your Own Product History

Begin your review of awareness, attitude, and behavior data with your own product, store, or service. You should have uncovered some of this communication and behavioral data in the preparation of your business review. Next, review your business data for cause-and-effect relationships. For example, when a manufacturer secures display placements in 25 percent or more of the retail outlets in his service area, he sees an increase in sales from 30–50 percent. Or, when a business-to-business manufacturer receives a feature article placed in a major industry trade publication, he generally sees an increase of 60–70 percent in inquiries. With this same manufacturer, over half of the inquiries each year can be tracked back to those trade shows at which he had a booth or when a retailer runs a test in which only the execution of one tool was changed (promotion tool changed from couponing to sampling), the retailer might record a 15 percent sales increase in test markets as compared to the control markets where no change was made.

If you have not been measuring and recording the effectiveness of the various tools or testing their effectiveness, it is something you will want to include in next year's plan. While the above observations measure cause and effect and do not answer the awareness and attitude questions, you can use this basic information to help estimate what percentage of the target market's unaided awareness and attitude caused the behavior. For example, if running twice the number of ads in a given period increased calls by 50 percent, the inference would be that there was a minimum of 50 percent increase in awareness created by doubling the number of ads. These types of inferences are far from empirical research, but they do provide some direction.

Primary Research

While being able to relate cause and effect is a start to learning, it is necessary to conduct primary research to determine more accurately the awareness, attitude, and behavior levels of purchasers and nonpurchasers for your product and that of the competition. In most cases, the awareness, attitude, and behavior data derived from survey research will be cumulative in nature and will not provide specific information for each tool. However, by applying the cause-and-effect information you have collected, you might be able to learn directionally about each tool's effect on awareness and attitude. For example, let's say your primary research indicated a 40 percent unaided awareness for your product among the target market and that, by applying only three tactical marketing mix tools (personal selling, merchandising, and publicity), it was shown that 70 percent of your noncustomer inquiries came from editorial messages in trade publications—the direct result of your publicity programs. If this were the case, you could surmise that 70 percent of the total awareness came from the publicity tool and, therefore, that one could allocate 28 points ($0.70 \times 0.40 = 28$ points) of current awareness to this tool. This is a very rough approach to allocation, but again, it demonstrates how you can use the interpolation of cause-and-effect data with research-derived awareness, attitude, and behavior data to arrive at an individual communication value for a tactical tool.

Secondary Sources

In addition to conducting primary research, review industry and trade association publications for research studies that might have been implemented. Also review studies done within specific disciplines, such as *Advertising Age* for the advertising message, *Inside Media* for the advertising media, and *Promo* for the promotion tool. You can review some of the publications oriented to the academic world, such as the *Journal of Consumer Research* and *Journal of Advertising Research*, for insight into the impact of tactical tools, both individually and cumulatively, on various types and levels of awareness, attitude, and behavior.

From this type of review you will arrive at specific quantitative information that you can apply when determining your marketing plan communications goals and values for each tool. Be aware, however, that in most situations your review of this type of information will lead only to broad, directional inferences that you can apply in the "value method."

To help organize, catalog, and summarize this diverse information from many sources as it pertains particularly to the tactical tools, use a structured format like the one shown in Exhibit 8.4 and refer to the appropriate worksheet at the end of this chapter.

TASK 2

Review Marketing Objectives, Positioning, and Strategies

To set the tactical tool values and then lock them into the marketing plan communication goals, you must understand the requirements of the marketing behavior objectives, and the direction provided by the position and marketing strategies.

Marketing Objectives

First review the specific behavior required in terms of retention of current purchasers, trial by new purchasers, and the amount of annual product purchase by both current and new purchasers. Ask yourself the following questions:

- Where is the greatest emphasis in terms of required behavior versus the previous years? Is the greatest emphasis on retention or trial? If the emphasis is

EXHIBIT 8.4 **Communication Values Review Examples**

Tactical Tool	Activity	Results	Directional Implications
Product			
Branding			
Packaging			
Pricing			
Distribution/Penetration			
Personal Selling/Service			
Promotion/Events	Trade show sampling of product	Received 180 responses from this trade show handout requesting sales presentations. This is double the rate from same show last year with no sampling.	Sample products at all trade shows.
Advertising Message			
Advertising/Interactive Media			
Merchandising			
Publicity	Feature product stories Product news releases	—Generated 50 to 150 phone calls per story. —Generated minimal, if any, phone inquiries	—Place greater emphasis on product feature stories even if it means fewer news releases —Don't expand product news release program

on trial and new customers, you will need greater awareness among nonpurchasers for your marketing plan communication goal, and accordingly, you will potentially require more support from specific tactical tools designed to generate greater exposure for your product, such as advertising media and publicity. If the emphasis in on retention, your efforts should be concentrated on your current customers.

- What is the total amount of product to be purchased by the current and new customers as called for in the marketing objectives? If the objectives call for substantial increases in the amount of purchases by small numbers of target companies or persons, you might consider greater support from tactical tools that are close to the point-of-purchase, such as personal selling or merchandising through store displays that encourage impulse purchase, and "loading" types of promotions (i.e., buy two, get one free). If, on the other hand, the objectives call for small increases by large numbers of the target market, you will use tactics that reach mass numbers of the target market.

- What are the expectation levels for repeat buying and building loyalty among new customers who have tried the product? In this case, product performance and personal service could be tools used for more support.

Market Positioning

What are the specific drivers of the positioning of your product? What are key attributes around which your product is built? What is the attitude you want within your target market regarding these attributes relative to the competition? In the positioning chapter, we gave the example of Famous Footwear concentrating on the "value" attribute, with emphasis on creating the attitude among the target person that Famous Footwear has the best value on branded shoes for the whole family. Accordingly, these are the types of positive attitudes that Famous Footwear instills through all of its communication to generate a high purchase interest in the relatively broad target market of women 25–49 with families of household incomes of $40,000+.

Marketing Strategies

Each of your marketing strategies will provide direction indicating which tactical tools will be used and how they should be used to help communicate the position in terms of building awareness, presenting a positive attitude, and, in turn, fulfilling the marketing objectives.

TASK 3	The third step in developing and applying communication goals is to determine the overall goals. This is accomplished by estimating purchase intent, reviewing attitude and awareness, and considering the relationship between them.
Determine Overall Marketing Plan Communication Goals	

Purchase Intent

To estimate purchase intent, you must estimate what percent of the target market believes it will *definitely* continue as purchasing customers and what percent of the target noncustomers believes it will *definitely* become new purchasers. If your research database does not indicate this information, make this estimate based on the information reviewed in Task 1, above. To help you make this estimate, break down each target segment into the following categories: definitely will not purchase, possibly will not purchase, possibly will purchase, and definitely will purchase. We will discuss goal estimation in more detail shortly.

Attitude and Awareness

Next, based on your review of the data in Task 1, determine what percent of the target purchasers and nonpurchasers will have to hold a specific attitude toward the product in order to arrive at the specific percentage of each base that definitely will purchase.

Then, determine what percent of the target customers and target noncustomers must have unaided awareness of the product in order to affect the intended attitude and the predetermined purchase intent. "First mention" or "top-of-mind" awareness can also be used as a goal in place of total unaided awareness; aided awareness should not be used as a goal because it is not a reliable awareness measurement to use in the projection of attitude and purchase intent goals.

In setting attitude and awareness goals and projecting purchase intent, review the level of change in the target market behavior from the previous years and compare it to the marketing objectives of the plan you are preparing. Let's say in previous years you have been averaging 3 percent trial of new purchasers, and your plan now requires that you generate 10 percent trial. The more aggressive the marketing objectives in terms of a change in behavior, the greater the increase in awareness and attitude goals and purchase intent. The more dramatic the increase in awareness and positive attitude for the competition's product as compared to the previous year, the greater the need for an increase in awareness and attitude goals for your product.

It is difficult to recommend what the awareness, attitude, and purchase goals should be for a new product or a product for which you have no quantitative awareness and attitude data. However, some basic awareness principles to keep in mind are:

- Target market unaided awareness exceeds target market purchase.
- The higher the percent of the target market required to purchase, the higher the awareness required.
- The greater the number of major competitors in a category, the greater the difference between the percent of a target market that has unaided awareness and the percent that purchase.
- Purchaser unaided awareness is dramatically higher than nonpurchaser unaided awareness—it can vary from up to two to five times or more in amount.
- The greater the one-product dominance of a target market and the fewer major competitors, the closer the percentage of purchasers to the percentage with unaided awareness of the product.

Relationship of Actual Purchase to Intent, Attitude, and Awareness

While general principles are difficult to provide, a starting point—and only a starting point—for defining the total target market goals (purchaser and nonpurchaser) for percent to purchase, purchase intent, attitude, and unaided awareness is the *50 Percent Happening* premise. As shown in the example below, this subjective premise suggests you take the percent of the total target market that you project to purchase (including purchaser and previous nonpurchaser) and add 50 percent of each level to the next level of the sequence.

Total Target Market = 200,000

	Target Market Effected	
	#	%
To purchase	10,000	5.0
"Definite" purchase intent	15,000	7.5
Specific positive attitude	22,500	11.3
Unaided awareness	33,800	16.9

There are more exceptions than rules to this 50 Percent Happening premise, but it is a beginning sequence to follow if you have no data. Keep in mind that if there is a large number purchasing, if the product is established, and if there is a great deal of positive trending in the marketplace, you will need to add less than 50 percent for each increment. Likewise, you will need to add more than 50 percent if you discover findings opposite the above in the marketplace.

Remember, the 50 Percent Happening approach is for the total target market. When you break out the target market purchaser and nonpurchaser separately, you will find the actual percentages in terms of intent to purchase, attitude, and awareness for *purchasers* to be substantially higher, with a "less than 50 Percent Happening" for each level, as shown in the next exhibit. On the other hand, there can be closer to 100 percent difference between the percent purchasing and those who say they "definitely will purchase" for *noncustomers* and the total target market, as shown in Exhibit 8.5. You will modify the percentage levels at each increment based on your review of Task 1. Also, keep in mind that applying a percent to a percent is not mathematically correct and is directional only. To be totally accurate, apply

EXHIBIT 8.5 **Method to Set Marketing Communication Goals to Fulfill the Marketing Objectives**

Footwear Store Target Market Example

	Target Market		
	% Current Purchasers	% Nonpurchasers	% Total
Marketing Objectives Purchasers (via retention and trial)	41.3	3.1	4.5
Purchase Intent Believe they will definitely purchase	55.0	7.0	10.0
Marketing Communication Goals *Attitude* Rate store as having high-value shoes	69.0	12.0	14.5
Awareness Unaided awareness of footwear store	95.0	29.0	31.0

your 50 percent factor to actual target market whole numbers, as shown in the previous example.

An example of determining quantitative goals by beginning with the required target market behavior in the marketing objectives and then working back to purchase intent, attitude, and awareness is shown in Exhibit 8.5. To simplify the demonstration of setting marketing communication goals to meet marketing objectives, this example shows total target market purchasers by purchaser retention and trial by nonpurchasers. A worksheet to help you estimate the purchase intent, attitude, and awareness levels needed to fulfill the marketing objectives is included at the end of this chapter.

Although Exhibit 8.5 has precise numbers for calculation, marketing communication goals are directional. Remember that marketing is not a science, so you should use these calculations as estimates and temper them with common sense. The point to keep in mind in your evaluation is that once the plan has been implemented and you review the target market purchaser and nonpurchaser intent to purchase, attitude, and awareness levels (via survey research), it is not important whether each goal was perfectly met. However, it is important to recognize the significance of reaching only half of the levels of your goals. If you missed your communication goals by 50 percent, it is safe to say that you most likely did not fulfill your marketing objectives and, consequently, did not deliver the required sales.

TASK 4

Set Awareness and Attitude Value Goals for Each Tactical Tool

The final task is to set specific awareness and attitude goals for target customers and noncustomers for each tactical tool. The value goals you assign each tool are important because each tactical segment of the marketing plan will be developed to fulfill its respective value goals. The values assigned to each tool will be dependent upon what you are marketing and where your product is in the product life cycle. Most important, you will set value goals for each tool based on your specific product situation and its competitive set in the marketplace. Accordingly, review Task 1 again before you begin setting tactical tool value goals.

Tactical Tool	Awareness		Attitude	
	Purchaser	Nonpurchaser	Purchaser	Nonpurchaser
Product	VI	MI	I	MI
Branding	I	VI	I	VI
Packaging	I	VI	I	VI
Price	I		I	
Distribution/Penetration	I	VI	I	VI
Personal Selling/Service	MI	MI	I	MI
Promotion/Events	MI	MI	VI	VI
Advertising Message	VI	MI	VI	VI
Advertising Media	MI	MI	VI	MI
Merchandising	MI	VI	VI	MI
Publicity	—	I	—	I
Interactive Communication	—	—	—	—

EXHIBIT 8.6   Tactical Tool Importance Ranking Example

VI = Very Important   MI = Moderately Important   I = Important

Tactical Tools by Importance

Having reviewed Task 1 and knowing that the value goals you set are subjective and only a starting point, attempt to rank the tactical tools based on their importance in fulfilling the marketing communication goals. To do this: 1) review your tactical experience via the worksheet shown in Exhibit 8.4, and 2) review each tactical tool against the overall marketing strategies and against the respective strategy for each tool, such as personal selling/service, promotion, and advertising. This will help you determine the degree of emphasis to place on each tool.

For example, if the personal selling strategy states "maintain sales force effectiveness comparable to that of the previous year," and the promotion strategy states "increase promotion activity to stimulate trial from new purchasers," the promotion tool would be given greater importance than in the past relative to the personal selling strategy. The key point to remember is that if your strategic direction does not call for a change in marketing approach for a particular tool, that tool should not be given more or less importance in this year's plan versus the previous marketing plan.

Having compared one tool to the other, list "important" (I), "moderately important" (MI), or "very important" (VI) next to each tool to indicate its awareness and attitude value. As shown in the example in Exhibit 8.6, rank these values by importance as they relate to target purchasers and nonpurchasers. Usually, every tool has some importance, but if you believe a particular tool has no importance relative to awareness and attitude, do not give it an importance ranking. For example, you might decide that while the "price" tool is "very important" in affecting attitude, it really has no importance in building the overall awareness for the product. A worksheet designed to help you rank importance is provided.

Values by Importance

Based on the importance rankings determined above, assign awareness and attitude percentage point values to each tool for purchaser and nonpurchaser so that they total to the awareness and attitude marketing communication goals. An example of this assignment of value point goals is shown in Exhibit 8.7, and a comparable worksheet is included at the end of this chapter. In this example, the totals of the awareness and attitude generated by the tactical tools equate to the total unaided awareness and positive attitude estimated to fulfill the ultimate sales objective as outlined in Exhibit 8.3.

EXHIBIT 8.7 **Individual Tactical Tool Value Goals for Your Product by Awareness and Attitude**

	Awareness		Attitude	
	Purchaser % Point	Nonpurchaser % Point	Purchaser % Point	Nonpurchaser % Point
Product Design	10.0	2.0	16.0	3.5
Branding	5.0	0.5	3.0	0.5
Packaging	5.0	0.5	3.0	1.0
Pricing	1.0	1.0	5.5	1.0
Distribution/Penetration	7.0	2.0	3.0	0.5
Personal Selling/Service	9.0	2.1	5.0	1.0
Promotion/Events	14.0	2.5	8.0	0.8
Advertising Message	12.0	3.1	8.0	1.6
Advertising Media	17.0	3.8	6.0	0.5
Merchandising	15.0	10.0	11.5	1.6
Publicity	—	1.5	—	—
Interactive Communication	—	—	—	—
Total	95.0	29.0	69.0	12.0

The value point goals total to the marketing communication awareness and attitude goals shown in Exhibit 8.5.

If you have gone through Tasks 1, 2, and 3 thoroughly, as well as the importance ranking process in your assignment of values, you will find some of your tactical tool goals virtually the same, while others will have major disparity between them. These results are dependent upon what contributions you expect each tool to make in fulfilling the marketing communication goals.

Expect to revise these value goals as you prepare and interface the tactical tool segments of the plan. For example, you might assign more weight to the advertising media tool after determining that effectively communicating a specific promotion will require not only the merchandising tool via store displays, but also more media via newspaper ads. Further, as you finalize the marketing budget and reconcile it with the sales objectives and bottom-line goals, there most likely will be an adjustment in tactical tool values.

A major question still to be answered is, Among all the tools, what is the multiple progression effect of integrated communication that truly reinforces the market positioning and drives behavior? We acknowledge that, because this multiplier effect is virtually impossible to measure, it serves as your communication bonus for the plan, providing the safety margins to compensate for any shortfalls in those tactical tools that do not deliver the expected awareness and attitude communication. Think of it as your "goals insurance policy" in your overall plan delivery of the marketing communications.

Finally, even if you have no data (which is unlikely) or minimal data from which to develop your overall marketing communication goals and tactical value communication goals, it will still be worthwhile in the marketing plan preparation to arrive at estimates of awareness, attitude, and intent to purchase to fulfill your marketing objectives.

Locking Sales from Target Market to Marketing Objectives and Communication

Total Sales

Total Target Market

	Previous Purchasers				Nonpurchasers			
Segmented Target Sales Objectives								
Marketing Objectives	%	#			%	#		
Purchasers (via retention and trial)								
# of annual purchases								
Average $ purchase								
Purchase Intent	%	#			%	#		
Believe they will definitely purchase								

	Unaided Awareness		Positive* Attitude		Unaided Awareness		Positive* Attitude	
	%	#	%	#	%	#	%	#
Marketing Plan Communication Goals								
Tactical Tool Communication Goals								
Product								
Branding								
Packaging								
Price								
Distribution/Penetration								
Personal Selling/Service								
Promotion/Events								
Advertising Message								
Advertising Media								
Merchandising								
Publicity								
Interactive Communication								

*List specific primary attitude to be affected for previous purchasers and nonpurchasers:
Previous purchasers   _____
Nonpurchasers   _____

Communication Goals Application

Target Market _____ Total Target Market #

Purchasers _____ %

Definitely Purchase Intent _____ %

Specific Positive Attitude _____%

Unaided Awareness _____ %

WORKSHEET

Communications Values Review

Tactical Tool	Activity	Results	Directional Implications
Product			
Branding			
Packaging			
Price			
Distribution/Penetration			
Personal Selling/Service			
Promotion/Events			
Advertising Message			
Advertising Media			
Merchandising			
Publicity			
Interactive			

Method to Set Marketing Communication Goals to Fulfill the Marketing Objectives

	Target Market		
	Current Purchasers	**Nonpurchasers**	**Total**
	%	%	%

Marketing Objectives

Purchase Intent

Marketing Communication Goals

Specific Positive Attitude

Unaided Awareness

WORKSHEET

Tactical Tool Importance Ranking

Tactical Tool	Awareness		Attitude	
	Purchaser	Nonpurchaser	Purchaser	Nonpurchaser
Product				
Branding				
Packaging				
Price				
Distribution/ Penetration				
Personal Selling/ Service				
Promotion/ Events				
Advertising Message				
Advertising Media				
Merchandising				
Publicity				
Interactive Communication				

VI = Very Important
MI = Moderately Important
I = Important

Individual Tactical Tool Value Goals for Your Product by Awareness and Attitude

	AWARENESS		ATTITUDE	
	Purchaser	**Nonpurchaser**	**Purchaser**	**Nonpurchaser**
	% Point	% Point	% Point	% Point
Product				
Branding				
Packaging				
Price				
Distribution/ Penetration				
Personal Selling/ Service				
Promotion/ Events				
Advertising Message				
Advertising Media				
Merchandising				
Publicity				
Interactive Communication				
TOTAL*				

*Total % for purchaser and nonpurchaser for awareness and attitude should sum to awareness and attitude communication goals previously set.

Step 7: Tactical Marketing Mix Tools

MARKETING BACKGROUND

1 THE BUSINESS REVIEW

Scope
> Company Strengths & Weaknesses • Core Competencies •
> Marketing Capabilities

Product and Market Review
> Company & Product Review • Category & Company Sales •
> Behavior Trends • Pricing • Distribution • Competitive Review

Target Market Effectors
> Consumer/Business-to-Business Targets • Product Awareness &
> Attributes • Trial & Retrial Data

2 PROBLEMS/OPPORTUNITIES

MARKETING PLAN

3 SALES OBJECTIVES

4 TARGET MARKETS AND MARKETING OBJECTIVES

5 PLAN STRATEGIES—Positioning & Marketing

6 COMMUNICATION GOALS

7 TACTICAL MARKETING MIX TOOLS

Product	Distribution	Advertising Media
Branding	Personal Selling/Service	Merchandising
Packaging	Promotion/Events	Publicity
Pricing	Advertising Message	

8 MARKETING PLAN BUDGET AND CALENDAR

9 EXECUTION

10 EVALUATION

PRODUCT, BRANDING, AND PACKAGING

9

IN THIS CHAPTER YOU WILL LEARN:

- HOW TO DEVELOP PRODUCT OBJECTIVES AND STRATEGIES.
- HOW TO DEVELOP A BRANDING PLAN.
- HOW TO DEVELOP A PACKAGING PLAN.

WITH ALL OF YOUR STRATEGIC INFORMATION IN PLACE—sales objectives, target markets and marketing objectives, positioning and marketing strategies, and communication goals—you can now begin to consider what role each tactical marketing tool will play in your marketing plan. In the next nine chapters we will discuss the following tools: product, branding, and packaging; pricing; distribution; personal selling and service; promotion and events; advertising message; advertising media; merchandising; and publicity.

We begin in this chapter with a discussion of the product, its brand identity, and its packaging—the most fundamental elements of the entire marketing mix. These interrelated elements make up the reality of the positioning: The attributes and attitudes consumers have about your product are what define your brand relative to the competition; the product's name and packaging are components of its attribute composition and help communicate the brand identity.

Before you write the product/branding/packaging segment of your marketing plan, review the direction provided by the problems and opportunities, positioning, and marketing strategies affecting each of the three areas. If you are not modifying or developing a new product, brand name, or package, there is no need to address these marketing mix tools in your plan. It is recommended, however, that you read this chapter to help determine your needs for the product, branding, or packaging modifications; their tactical tool value contributions to the plan's awareness and attitude goals; and for additional background in writing the remainder of the marketing plan.

Developing a Product Plan

While your product, its brand identity, and its packaging all have a major impact on the contribution of awareness and attitude in fulfilling the positioning to deliver on marketing objectives, the product is the key. Effective communication of a positioning may induce trial of a product, but nothing will ruin a company faster than advertising and selling a poor product or a product that is not consistent with its positioning. Customers may be convinced to purchase once, but they won't be fooled again.

As a point of clarification, a *product* is something that is marketed to customers in exchange for money or another unit of value. In the case of consumer package goods, retail, and business-to-business companies, the product is a tangible object. For service businesses, however, the product takes the form of some intangible offering, such as a future benefit or future promise. Thus, while all products are offerings to the customer, there is an inherent difference between what is sold by a retailer or manufacturer and what is sold by a service firm.

TASK 1 *Establish Product Objectives*	Product objectives center around one or more of the following five areas: 1. *New products.* A new product is one that has not been marketed previously by your firm. We use this definition because, even if a product is not new to the market, if it is new to your firm, it presents unique marketing challenges for your company.

A new product may be a product with an entirely new function. Generally, such new products grow out of a technical innovation against an existing consumer need. For example, the first television was a product with an entirely new function (broadcast of picture and sound), but it served an existing consumer need for information and entertainment.

New products may also offer improved performance against an existing function/need. These products perform an existing function in a better way. For example, our client Mondial Industries markets the Diaper Genie, an odor-free system for disposing of disposable diapers—a vast improvement over the old diaper pail.

2. *Line extensions for existing brands.* This adds to the breadth of your product line with the addition of new flavors, scents, colors, sizes, or the like. Line extensions can provide an effective way to reach new customers by leveraging the existing equity in your product's brand name, both at the consumer level and at the trade level, to assist in selling the product at retail.

3. *New uses for existing products.* This entails changing customer perceptions of the personality and/or usage of your product. The classic example is Arm & Hammer's positioning of its baking soda product as a refrigerator deodorizer as well as a baking ingredient.

4. *Product improvement.* This is essentially an upgrade of an existing product that improves or expands its performance against consumer needs. An example is Mercury Marine's introduction of the High Five Propeller, a five-blade stainless steel prop that gets skiers out of the water faster than conventional three- or four-blade props.

5. *More efficient ways to produce the product, in the case of manufacturers, or purchase the product, in the case of retailers.* Many times the development of more efficient manufacturing or purchasing mechanisms leads to the company's ability to market higher value products or better quality at a lower price.

In addition to addressing one or more of the above, product objectives should incorporate specifics on when the product will be available for distribution or inventory.

An example of a product objective for a manufacturer would be:

In the upcoming fiscal year, modify the product to reflect the current purchasing habits of consumers interested in low-salt foods.

TASK 2 *Establish Product Strategies*	Your new product strategies should help your firm focus its product development activities against one of the following five approaches: 1. *Developing a new positioning for an existing product.* This entails changing consumer perceptions of the personality and/or usage of your product. Some of the strategies associated with a new positioning include developing a new application for an existing product, aiming an existing product at a new target market, or reintroducing an existing product with a new price/value mix.

2. *Developing line extensions.* As discussed above, line extensions can provide an effective way to reach new customers by leveraging the existing equity in your product's brand name,

3. *Developing flanker products.* Flankers are complementary products marketed under an existing brand umbrella. As with line extensions, flankers can be an

effective way to increase sales by leveraging existing strengths. An example would be Gillette's capitalizing on the strength of its brand in the shaving products market to offer other health and beauty aids products, such as deodorant, under the Gillette name.

4. *Developing entirely new products.*
5. *Acquiring another firm or the rights to another firm's products that address your company's product strategies.*

An example of a product strategy would be:

Expand product line offerings to include three new flavors based on product attribute research indicating flavor preferences.

Developing a Branding Plan

Some product categories, such as automobiles, are defined by a relatively high level of differentiation between competing product offerings, while other categories, such as paperclips, are relative commodities. It is the points of differentiation between your product and the competition, whether real or perceived, extensive or relatively few, and how you communicate those differences that comprise your brand.

It is your task to develop your brand in terms of the name, graphic identity, and maintenance of marketing mix elements consistent with that identity and your positioning. If successful, the brand will be considerably more valuable to you than the sum of physical attributes that comprise your product.

In simplest terms, a *brand* is merely the identification of a product's or service's source, whether it is the manufacturer, a wholesaler, or some other entity. In slightly broader terms, the brand is composed of the title or name by which the product is commonly known and graphic forms of identification, including symbols, logotypes or signatures, tag lines, or characters. For example, we know through our work with the American Automobile Association (AAA) that the AAA brand is one of the most known and respected brands in America today. The AAA brand covers a vast number of products and services—from towing to maps to insurance to travel. All these services fall under the well-recognized AAA logo.

In another example, Betty Crocker is a brand name applied to a number of products. Betty Crocker products can also be identified by the white type treatment in the red spoon symbol or by the Betty Crocker female character. Betty Crocker, which is owned by General Mills, is an example of a *manufacturer's brand*—a name other than the producer's provided specifically for a product or collection of products. Use of a manufacturer's brand is typical in consumer packaged goods. By contrast, many products bear the name of the manufacturer, such as Xerox copiers, Black and Decker tools, or American Family Insurance. These *trade names* are common among consumers durables, service industries, and business-to-business products.

In some cases, the manufacturer of the product is not identified either with its own name or with a brand name it owns. Rather, a manufacturer might sell the product to wholesalers or retailers who provide their own brand names, known as *private labels*. Sears was built around the private labels of Kenmore appliances and Craftsman tools. *Generic products* bear no brand at all. Generic products were popular among consumers in the late 1970s as a means of saving during an inflationary period.

Branding is a process of establishing and managing the images, perceptions, and associations that the consumer applies to your product, based on the values and beliefs associated with your product. These are managed through application of the brand elements (name and graphic components) and consistency with the product's positioning in all consumer communications relating to the product. The more effective you are in your branding efforts, the greater value your brand holds for you. The value of the brand, above and beyond the cumulative physical attributes of the product itself, represents *brand equity*.

Developing a brand and building equity in that brand are the broad components of the branding process. In this process, you have one goal for the brand: to generate consistent purchase behavior among a consumer base (thus providing you with a consistent return on the investment of capital in that asset). In other words, you seek to build and maintain *brand loyalty*. In our work with McDonald's and Coors beer we know that both the fast-food retailer and beer manufacturer have strong, loyal consumer bases, but this loyalty is tested constantly by competitive efforts. It is only through careful management—to avoid erosion of the brand equity by their competitors or by their own actions—that McDonald's and Coors are able to reap the rewards of the successful brands they market.

The process of branding is complex and ongoing, involving all elements of the marketing mix. In this section of your marketing plan, focus on your branding needs in terms of a brand name and graphic identity. Keep the other aspects of branding in mind, however, as you approach each of the subsequent tactical plan elements.

TASK 1

Establish Branding Objectives

The first task in developing a branding plan is to arrive at objectives for your brand name, graphics, and legal protection of the brand. It is important to state the objectives of the brand in terms of the product strategies defined in the previous section. What are your objectives for how the new name and graphic will be used? Is this a new product, a repositioned product, an existing product, etc.? State your objectives and include a final decision date for selection of the name, completion of a legal search, and adoption of graphics.

Examples of branding objectives are:

> Develop a name by March 1 and logo graphic by June 1, for the new value-oriented line of accessories.

- Develop a final list of name options by November 1.
- Complete legal name search based on this list by December 1.
- Complete consumer research of names by February 1.
- Make final name selection by March 1.
- Develop a logo graphic for the new name by June 1.

> Develop a new name to replace Big Jake's for the new family apparel store by the end of the fiscal year.

TASK 2

Establish Branding Strategies

Before proceeding to develop a new name and/or graphic, it is important to develop strategies for the brand. Development of a branding strategy increases the likelihood that you will arrive at a name that is consistent with the product and its positioning, and takes into consideration all of the users of the name over the long and short term. The branding strategy should highlight those components that will communicate the key perceptions to the key targets.

Your strategy should flow directly from the positioning statement and the product strategies. For example, if you are developing a new product and see long-term potential for line extensions, your branding strategy should address this so that the new name you develop accommodates it. For instance, it is reasonable to imagine the Alpo brand of dog food products extended into cat food products, but Milk-Bone brand cat food products probably wouldn't work. (There really is an Alpo cat food.) Further, the name and graphic treatment should be developed on the basis of the breadth of products to which they will apply. In an earlier example, we saw that the Betty Crocker brand applies to a wide variety of cooking and baking packaged goods. The name is not specific to one product, and the red-spoon graphic acts as a unifying element across the product line.

Example branding strategies include:

> Name the new line of marine accessories to reflect the value-oriented positioning: quality products at lower prices relative to the competition.

Develop a logo for the marine accessories line that can be used across the wide variety of marine products in the line (with the potential of additional products to be added in the future).

TASK 3

Establish Branding Property Parameters

The branding strategies should be followed by a list of parameters for the new name and graphic application. These parameters are an extension of the branding strategy and provide specific guideposts for name and graphic development.

Name parameters for consideration:

Reflects positioning of the product, and product attributes or benefits.

Provides generic identification and clearly identifies with its functional category.

Is preemptive.

Contributes to awareness and knowledge of its purpose.

Is simple.

Is memorable.

Elicits a mental image and emotion.

Provides potential for growth under its umbrella (new entities, products, etc.).

Possesses a positive connotation in meaning, pronunciation, and visualization.

Reflects the personality of the product.

Has intrinsic meaning of its own (i.e., is not an acronym or a set of letters that signifies nothing).

Is not limited geographically or topically as the organization grows.

Lends itself to and allows for creative development both visually and in copy.

Works with current signage and packaging sizes.

Is legally acceptable and protectable.

Graphic parameters for consideration:

Reproduces in large or small form.

Reproduces in black and white and in color.

Incorporates attention-getting colors that reflect the positioning.

Has visual impact in print and broadcast media.

Allows for umbrella look applied to a variety of products and packages.

TASK 4

Name Generation and Selection

Using the branding strategy and name property parameters as a guide, begin the name development process by generating a multitude of name alternatives. One first step would be to outline all of the qualities, characteristics, or descriptors that you would like to have associated with your product. Such an outline for a toothpaste might include words like "protective" or "refreshing." It might also include characters, animals, or objects that maintain similar qualities, such as "honey bee." This outline acts to translate the product positioning into simple, everyday words and associations and will help to stimulate ideas for names and graphics.

If you are not in a position to develop the names on your own, seek help. You can share the task with others in your organization, an agency, or with a professional brand identity development organization.

From here, it is conceivable that your name alternatives could number into the hundreds. Next, using the branding strategy and name parameters as the decision criteria in the screening process, pare back the names in a disciplined manner to approximately five to ten names. Follow this process with a legal name search for trademark availability among your choices. Finally, you would be wise to research the remaining screened name alternatives, as well as graphic representations you ultimately develop, with the target market(s) before making final brand decisions.

Developing a Packaging Plan

Earlier we defined the product as the object or service the consumer purchases and uses, and we defined the brand as the collection of associations the consumer holds about your particular product. An important element of every product, which serves as a vehicle for the brand, is the *packaging*. The package bears the responsibility of holding or maintaining your product and communicating the essence of your brand.

As you prepare to develop a plan for your product's packaging, review your positioning, appropriate marketing strategies, and product and branding plans. Your packaging plan should reflect your positioning and flow from the objectives and strategies for the product and brand.

TASK 1

Develop Packaging Objectives

Establish objectives for your packaging that focus on the following issues:
1. Communication of brand positioning and image to contribute to building equity in your brand.
2. Generating awareness and drawing attention to the product at the point of purchase.
3. Encouraging trial.
4. Providing protection for and enhancement of the product by making usage easier or adding value to the purchase.
5. Communicating promotional offerings.

Provide a time frame for the development and production of your new packaging. An example packaging objective might be:

Have new packaging ready for introduction by March 1 of next year that demonstrates the following:

- Communicates the family-oriented positioning and extra servings per container.
- Protects the product while displaying the product fully prepared.
- Emphasizes the new brand name and graphic scheme.
- Addresses the three flavors clearly, yet maintains a consistent look for the brand.

TASK 2

Develop Packaging Strategies

Your packaging strategies suggest direction for achieving your objectives. They should address specifics about the packaging, such as:
- Physical attributes of the package — What size is the container going to be, or how many sizes will be provided? What is the type and strength of the package material? What color and design scheme will be utilized? What shape should it be? What copy elements should it contain?
- Whether an outside packaging firm, design firm, or agency will be called upon to assist in your new packaging efforts, and if so, when and to what extent it will be involved.

Example packaging strategies include:

Develop a uniquely shaped plastic package in a 12- and 16-ounce size that will accommodate extensive home and office use.

Use bright, bold graphics and provide product attribute statements to communicate a value orientation.

Assign an agency to the packaging project by October 1 to assist in design and research.

FORMAT

Product

Product Objectives

Product Strategies

Rationale

FORMAT

Branding/New Name

Branding Objectives

Branding Strategies

Branding Parameters

Rationale

FORMAT

Packaging

Packaging Objectives

Packaging Strategies

Rationale

Step 7: Tactical Marketing Mix Tools

MARKETING BACKGROUND

1 THE BUSINESS REVIEW

Scope
Company Strengths & Weaknesses • Core Competencies •
Marketing Capabilities

Product and Market Review
Company & Product Review • Category & Company Sales •
Behavior Trends • Pricing • Distribution • Competitive Review

Target Market Effectors
Consumer/Business-to-Business Targets • Product Awareness &
Attributes • Trial & Retrial Data

2 PROBLEMS/OPPORTUNITIES

MARKETING PLAN

3 SALES OBJECTIVES

4 TARGET MARKETS AND MARKETING OBJECTIVES

5 PLAN STRATEGIES—Positioning & Marketing

6 COMMUNICATION GOALS

7 TACTICAL MARKETING MIX TOOLS

Product	Distribution	Advertising Media
Branding	Personal Selling/Service	Merchandising
Packaging	Promotion/Events	Publicity
Pricing	Advertising Message	

8 MARKETING PLAN BUDGET AND CALENDAR

9 EXECUTION

10 EVALUATION

PRICING *10*

- WHAT IMPORTANT PRICING CONSIDERATIONS TO BEAR IN MIND.
- HOW TO DEVELOP PRICING OBJECTIVES AND STRATEGIES.

P*RICE* IS THE MONETARY VALUE OF YOUR PRODUCT (or service) to your target market — the primary cost to the consumer for obtaining your product. While it represents one of the most basic elements of the marketing mix, pricing is also one of the most difficult elements for which to develop a plan because it has implications for your firm, your product, the competition, the target market, and the individual consumer. As a result of this complexity, setting prices is as much an art (perhaps more so) as it is a science.

In this chapter we will discuss how the price you select will directly affect sales and profits, how it will affect the target consumer's attitude toward the product, and thus its impact in fulfilling the plan communication goal.

Pricing Considerations

A myriad of factors need to be taken into consideration as you begin to develop your pricing plan. In addition to reviewing all of you strategic information (problems and opportunities, marketing objectives, positioning, marketing strategies, and communication goals related to price), the following factors also must be considered. A worksheet designed to help you work through these elements is included at the end of the chapter. Exhibit 10.1 shows an example worksheet partially completed.

Breakeven

Barring the use of loss-leader pricing to drive sales, there is a point below which it would be unreasonable to price your product. This point is know as the *breakeven*. The following formula allows you to determine breakeven points to help ensure expenditures do not exceed sales.

$$PX = FC + VC(X)$$

Where: P = Price
VC = Variable costs
FC = Fixed costs
X = Volume of units produced at breakeven point (the number of units that must be sold)

Price Sensitivity

The effect of a price on sales volume is the result of change in consumer demand determined by the market's willingness or capacity to pay that price for the product. This concept is known as *price sensitivity*, and it is influenced by two major factors: consumer attitudes and attribute preferences, and the status of alternatives (competition or other substitute).

EXHIBIT 10.1 Pricing Considerations

Consideration	Specific Situation	Pricing Implication	Potential Price Approach
Problems/Opportunities	The company's "standard" line is continually underpriced by the competition.	This line is losing share and losing distribution.	Match price of top three competitors.
Marketing Objectives	Increase new customer trial by 15% over previous year.	Price is an important attribute sought by first-time customers.	Provide price incentives around new customer promotions.
Positioning	Position as the most affordable competitive option.	Looking to position based on a price relative to competition.	Maintain price just below top three competitors.
Marketing Strategies	Build sales volume in off-season months of May and September.	Price incentives could be used to pump sales during off-season.	Use price promotions to tie off-season sales to seasonal purchases.
Price Communication Goals			
Breakeven			
Price Elasticity			
Product Life Cycle Stage			
Product Differentiation			
Business Goals			
Competition Pricing			
Other			

The degree to which consumer demand is sensitive to price changes is referred to as *price elasticity*. After reviewing your pricing problems and opportunities you may find that demand for your product is *elastic*—sales go down when the price is raised and up when the price is lowered—or *inelastic*—sales are not significantly effected by price changes.

Product Life Cycle Stage

The stage of your product in the product life cycle has an important influence on the pricing structure in the industry and presents various implications for your pricing decisions. In each stage, a high- or low-price strategy may be appropriate for different objectives, as shown below.

Life Cycle Stage	Low-Price Strategy	High-Price Strategy
Introductory	Penetration pricing—encourage trial and mass consumption.	Premium pricing—generate profits to cover investment costs.
Growth	Build market share and deter competitive entries.	Build profits
Maturity	Compete and maintain market share.	Reap profits to finance new products.
Decline	Recover variable costs and provide some contribution to overhead.	

Product Differentiation

In industries where products are not highly differentiated in terms of attributes, pricing and service become the only real points of differentiation. In some cases, particularly in growth markets, pricing can contribute to maintaining differentiation of a brand. This effort usually requires a higher-price strategy to generate revenues to finance product improvements and R&D. The higher price also connotes a quality image consistent with a differentiated product.

Business Goals

Your final pricing decision should take into consideration what you need to accomplish in other areas of your business. Such goals, including sales and profitability objectives, can be aided by the appropriate pricing approach or derailed by an inappropriate one.

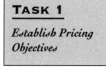

TASK 1

Establish Pricing Objectives

The first major step in the development of a pricing plan is to establish your pricing objective—whether you intend to implement a lower, higher, or parity pricing approach relative to the competition. All other objectives, such as increased sales, higher margins, and the like are overall goals of your business or marketing plan to which pricing contributes.

Parity versus Higher or Lower Pricing

How you price your product or service has a significant impact on many aspects of your overall marketing efforts. Used in conjunction with the other elements of your plan, a given price approach supports your product's positioning, while contributing directly to consumer demand (thus sales volume) for your product and providing income to cover costs and contribute to the profitability of your firm. Following is an overview of each of the three approaches to pricing.

Parity Pricing. Often referred to as a "going rate" strategy, the parity pricing approach maintains pricing levels at or near those of the competition. This is appropriate where other means of differentiation are common or are considered more important by the target. These other forms of differentiation often include specific product features and attributes, non-product advantages such as service, guarantees, location (for retailers), or additional distribution channels. Interestingly, it is also used when product differentiation is low and price is the basis of competition.

Lower Pricing. Lower pricing involves maintaining a price lower than the competition. One specific execution of this approach includes discount pricing, a direct result of a low-price positioning. This approach aims for a high volume of sales to offset typically low margins to achieve desired profit levels (low margin dollars but high volume). It also requires appropriate capacity and distribution channels to support the volume requirements. The reasons for a low-price objective are usually:

- To expand the market, allowing new consumers who couldn't purchase at higher prices to become purchasers.
- To increase trial and/or sales due to price incentives.
- To take advantage of a strong price-elastic product where a low price results in increased demand. The result is lower margins but increased profits because of the increased volume.
- To preempt competitive strategies, helping to steal market share. This is often necessary in a mature market.
- To remain competitive with your competition. If a majority of the competitors have reduced their prices, oftentimes you will need to do so, especially if you are in a price-sensitive product category. If a strong competitor also is offering an attribute such as service with which you cannot compete, you may need to lower your price to counter the service offering.
- To keep competitors from entering the marketplace by having a price that is difficult for a new company with high initial investment costs to match. This policy of expanded market pricing allows a company to develop a large, loyal consumer base while keeping competition to a minimum.

Higher Pricing. A premium price—a higher price relative to the competition—supports a quality positioning and provides high margins to support higher product and promotional expenditures. The reasons for a high price objective are usually:

- A need for a fast recovery of the firm's investment.
- A need for faster accumulation of profits to cover research and development costs. The profits can then be used to improve the product and to sustain competitive marketing tactics once competitors enter the market.
- The company wants to substantiate a quality image positioning.
- The product is price inelastic, where the demand or sales decrease only marginally with higher pricing.
- The product or service is in the introductory phase of its product life cycle and represents a substantial innovation within the product category. Also, the company may wish to cream profits while there are no substitute products to force competitive pricing.
- The company is stressing profits rather than sales, thus, margins must remain high.
- The product has a short life span. An example would be fad products, which last for a relatively short time. This necessitates a high-price policy, which will help recover the firm's research and development costs in a short time period.
- The product is difficult to copy and reproduce or has patent protection.

Determine Your Price Approach

Based on your list of pricing considerations (see Exhibit 10.1), you should be able to establish a price objective that is either one of parity, lower, or higher pricing for your product or company. Your product, its positioning and other marketing communications goals, the target market's perceptions and behavior, the competition, and the industry, will all suggest the most appropriate course of action. Once you have determined which approach you wish to take, it becomes the basis of your pricing objectives. A format to help you set your pricing objectives is provided at the end of the chapter.

Address Geography and Timing

Many times a company's or industry's pricing structure is not consistent across the entire country. One market may have greater competition, greater price sensitivity, or higher distribution costs, for example, than others. Thus, your objectives should state any differences that exist from market to market. Finally, timing should be addressed in your price objectives. Are the sales increases to be addressed by a particular price approach needed constantly or just up to a certain point in time? Will price changes for promotional purposes take place during certain seasonal periods or for another, specific, period? While timing relates to the changing of your price on a seasonal basis, it also relates to the changing of prices in a timely fashion to address competitive price changes, cost changes, market changes, and the like.

Writing the Price Objectives

The following examples present the appropriate style of pricing objective statements, including geography and timing considerations:

> Utilize higher pricing relative to the direct competition (minimum +10 percent) within the first year of the plan in all markets, consistent with a quality positioning.

> Increase prices during the strong tourist months of May to September, then lower prices during the off-season, while maintaining a relative parity-price approach.

TASK 2

Establish Price Strategies

Pricing strategies state how you will achieve your pricing objectives. They provide the specifics you need to finalize your pricing plan. In developing your pricing strategies, the following steps should be taken:

1. *Review your pricing objectives.* As the strategies are intended to provide direction for achieving price objectives, it is important to truly understand what price approach you need to achieve, when, and where.
2. *Review your marketing strategies.* Again, relate your pricing decisions not only to the direction provided in the pricing portion of your marketing strategies, but also to the effect your pricing will have on the implementation of other strategies.
3. *Review the product category and competition.* What is the competitive price structure of the industry? At what stage is the category in terms of the product life cycle, and what is the competitive structure? What are the costs and pricing strategies of your competition?
4. *Review your product.* Determine whether your firm has the capacity and/or capability to maintain a low-price strategy. Determine if your product has unique and defensible product attributes that could support a high-price objective. What are your costs associated with the product, and what is the breakeven at various price points? Calculate at what price you are most likely to break even.
5. *Review the marketplace.* Consider the target market makeup and segmentation, and determine the price sensitivity among the segments. What attitudes does the target hold with regard to the product category and the importance of price?

6. Finally, develop strategies that address how price levels, geography, and timing objectives will be accomplished. Using the information acquired in the tasks above, detail specifics as to your pricing strategy. Consider the following two marketing strategies:

Marketing Seasonality Strategy: Increase sales among current customers during the off-season.
Marketing Pricing Strategy: Maintain a 45 percent margin for the year.

The pricing objective might be to utilize a parity pricing structure relative to the competition during the strong selling season nationally and a low price relative to the competition during the off-season nationally. Price then would be one of the tools used to execute the seasonality marketing strategy along with promotion and advertising. And pricing certainly would be used to execute the pricing marketing strategy.

The subsequent pricing strategies might be:

Utilize a price consistent with the top three market leaders in the northern markets and the top market leader in the southern markets during the months of August through December.

Utilize a price at 5 percent below the top three market leaders in the northern markets and 7 percent below the market leader in the southern markets during the off-season of January through July.

WORKSHEET

Pricing Considerations

Consideration	Specific Situation	Pricing Implications	Potential Price Approach
Problems/Opportunities			
Marketing Objectives			
Positioning			
Marketing Strategies			
Price Communication Goals			
Breakeven			
Price Elasticity			
Product Life Cycle Stage			
Product Differentiation			
Business Goals			
Competition Pricing			

FORMAT

Price

Price Objectives

Price Strategies

Rationale

Step 7: Tactical Marketing Mix Tools

MARKETING BACKGROUND

1 THE BUSINESS REVIEW

<u>Scope</u>
Company Strengths & Weaknesses • Core Competencies •
Marketing Capabilities

<u>Product and Market Review</u>
Company & Product Review • Category & Company Sales •
Behavior Trends • Pricing • Distribution • Competitive Review

<u>Target Market Effectors</u>
Consumer/Business-to-Business Targets • Product Awareness &
Attributes • Trial & Retrial Data

2 PROBLEMS/OPPORTUNITIES

MARKETING PLAN

3 SALES OBJECTIVES

4 TARGET MARKETS AND MARKETING OBJECTIVES

5 PLAN STRATEGIES—Positioning & Marketing

6 COMMUNICATION GOALS

7 TACTICAL MARKETING MIX TOOLS

Product	Distribution	Advertising Media
Branding	Personal Selling/Service	Merchandising
Packaging	Promotion/Events	Publicity
Pricing	Advertising Message	

8 MARKETING PLAN BUDGET AND CALENDAR

9 EXECUTION

10 EVALUATION

DISTRIBUTION

11

IN THIS CHAPTER YOU WILL LEARN:

● WHAT ISSUES CAN AFFECT A DISTRIBUTION PLAN.
● HOW TO DEVELOP DISTRIBUTION PLAN OBJECTIVES AND STRATEGIES.

U P TO THIS POINT, your efforts have been focused on developing plans to persuade the target market to purchase your product. *Distribution*—the transmission of goods and services from the producer or seller to the user—focuses on making sure there is accessible product for the target market to purchase once you have initiated demand.

Distribution Considerations

In developing your distribution plan, five main areas should be addressed: penetration or market coverage, type of outlets or channels, competition, geography, and timing.

Penetration or Market Coverage

Retailers and service firms need to review the Distribution section of the business review to determine whether the market is *underpenetrated*—not enough stores or offices in the trading area—or *overpenetrated*—too many stores or offices in the trading area. Manufacturers need to consider the number of potential outlets or distribution centers that carry your product, the All Commodity Volume (ACV) of the stores that carry your product, and the amount of shelf space allocated your product. Business-to-business firms should undertake the same process as manufacturers, except the focus should be intermediate channel targets and percent of product purchased by each distributor, wholesaler, and other outlet type.

Type of Outlets or Channels

Going back to the Distribution section of the business review, consult the data that traces sales by distribution outlet for your product category. Note which channels have the most volume and which are a growing influence in your industry. Are there any trends your firm should take advantage of during the next year? Then, list the different attributes of each distribution choice in terms of customer segmentation, customer service provided, and price orientation (discount, full price, etc.) to help you make the correct choice for your product.

Competition

Review competitors' distribution patterns when making decisions regarding penetration/market coverage, type of outlet, geography, and timing. Consult your business review to determine competitive distribution patterns. This knowledge is helpful when deciding what markets to further penetrate. What channels does the competition dominate? Are these channels/outlets so important to the way the target market purchases in the category that you cannot afford to not be in these channels? Or can you seek distribution in alternate channels in which your product could have a dominant position?

Geography

Consider the Brand Development Index (BDI) and Category Development Index (CDI) data developed in the business review. A low BDI in any given market coupled with a penetration or coverage analysis that shows a firm is underpenetrated points toward potential geographic expansion in those markets. Geographic expansion should be considered for those markets that are underpenetrated and have high CDIs. Consult the simplified BDI/CDI matrix shown below before you set your distribution objectives.

	High CDI	**Low CDI**
High BDI	—Strong market with good market potential and product sales worthy of continual development. —May require strong support to limit competitive entry.	—Cash cow (don't spend marketing dollars to level of sales; use these dollars to fund development of other markets). —Will need to look to other markets for growth.
Low BDI	—May be a market right for development or a competitor's stronghold to be avoided.1	—Not promising; generally markets to be avoided unless your firm can develop a dominant (and profitable) share of this limited market.

Timing

Finally, state whether the objectives are to be completed in a matter of months or years. Because distribution involves a commitment to actual construction, long-term leases, or the development of working relationships with outlets and distributors, the distribution timing is often longer term than some of the other tactical tool considerations.

Developing a Distribution Plan

A format for developing your distribution plan is provided at the end of this chapter.

TASK 1

Establish Distribution Objectives

Establish quantifiable distribution objectives for the following four categories:
1. Penetration or market coverage/shelf space.
2. Type of outlet(s) or channel(s).
3. Geography.
4. Timing.

Distribution objective examples for a retail firm would be as follows:

Fully penetrate the firm's two largest BDI markets (Chicago and Detroit, which account for 25 percent of the firm's business) to attain the ratio of one store for every 100,000 households within the next two years (eight stores in this plan year and 10 stores the following year).

Continue to utilize strip centers in existing markets, testing outlet centers in new markets.

TASK 2

Establish Distribution Strategies

Your distribution strategies should describe how you will accomplish your distribution objectives. The following points should be considered by each business category:

Retail and Service Firms

- Describe the criteria or methodology for penetrating markets or adding new locations. Where will you locate new stores? What demographic, location,

cost per square foot, competition, or other criteria will you use to make these decisions?
- If you are expanding geographic penetration, detail if this will be done on a systematic, market-by-market basis or will occur wherever the opportunity develops within the total system.
- If a change is warranted, describe how you will make the change from one type of outlet to another.
- Describe your purchase or lease strategies.

Manufacturers

- Describe how you will attain market coverage goals and/or shelf space goals. Some of your strategies to achieve these goals will be incorporated into your promotional plan. If your business review details that your product does not differ from your competition's, your product is not established with the trade, and your product does not make a large impact on the trade in terms of profits, then you will have to rely more heavily on promotions and trade deals to meet aggressive market coverage and shelf space goals.
- If your objective is to increase market coverage, describe how you will choose the type(s) of channel to target for increased coverage and detail specifically what stores you plan to target.
- Outline whether you are going to use a push or pull strategy. A *push strategy* focuses on marketing to the intermediate targets, such as distributors and the outlets, to obtain distribution and shelf space. A *pull strategy* involves marketing to the ultimate purchaser or directly to consumers to build demand, forcing the outlets to stock the product.
- Describe how you will enter new distribution channels if this is an objective. Will you try to place your entire line or one top-selling product in the stores? What kind of merchandising and advertising support will you provide? Will you offer return privileges or lower your minimum order requirements? If storage, display, dispensing, price marking, or accounting specifics are important to the new channel, describe how you will make allowances to gain distribution trial. Will you provide special introductory pricing?

Assume a distribution objective for a package goods firm is to increase ACV market coverage 20 points among grocery stores in all top 100 markets over the next year. The strategies to achieve this objective might be:

Place additional sales emphasis against large independents with multiple store outlets.

Concentrate on first establishing the top-selling line of frozen foods before attempting to gain distribution of the entire line of frozen and canned foods.

Utilize special promotions developed in the promotion plan to help sell-in product, such as special display allowances designed to encourage initial trial and special introductory pricing incentives.

FORMAT

Distribution

Distribution Objectives

Distribution Strategies

Rationale

Step 7: Tactical Marketing Mix Tools

MARKETING BACKGROUND

1 THE BUSINESS REVIEW

Scope
Company Strengths & Weaknesses • Core Competencies •
Marketing Capabilities

Product and Market Review
Company & Product Review • Category & Company Sales •
Behavior Trends • Pricing • Distribution • Competitive Review

Target Market Effectors
Consumer/Business-to-Business Targets • Product Awareness &
Attributes • Trial & Retrial Data

2 PROBLEMS/OPPORTUNITIES

MARKETING PLAN

3 SALES OBJECTIVES

4 TARGET MARKETS AND MARKETING OBJECTIVES

5 PLAN STRATEGIES—Positioning & Marketing

6 COMMUNICATION GOALS

7 TACTICAL MARKETING MIX TOOLS

Product	Distribution	Advertising Media
Branding	Personal Selling/Service	Merchandising
Packaging	Promotion/Events	Publicity
Pricing	Advertising Message	

8 MARKETING PLAN BUDGET AND CALENDAR

9 EXECUTION

10 EVALUATION

PERSONAL SELLING AND SERVICE

12

IN THIS CHAPTER YOU WILL LEARN

- THE ISSUES AFFECTING A PERSONAL SELLING AND SERVICE PLAN.
- HOW TO DEVELOP A PERSONAL SELLING AND SERVICE PLAN.

P ERSONAL SELLING AND SERVICE involve the personal, one-on-one contact your company has with the specific target person. Whether it's business-to-business or consumer marketing, personal selling is an important tool that incorporates the critical human factor into the marketing mix. *It is the one personal and direct link between the target market and the organization selling the product.* Further, the degree of personal contact with the target person affects the level of impact the personal selling and service functions have on the awareness and attitude toward your product.

For retail and service firms, personal selling also involves the day-to-day administration of the selling program, the retail outlet, office, or other selling environment (i.e., telemarketing, door-to-door sales). This includes hiring and managing sales personnel, stocking inventory, and preparing the product for sale, as well as the presentation and maintenance of the facility. For business-to-business and consumer goods firms, personal selling relates to the manufacturers' selling and servicing of its products to the trade and/or intermediate markets (various buyers of the product within the distribution channel from the original product to the ultimate user).

Personal Selling and Service Considerations

For retail and service firms, the overriding issue is determining a realistic and achievable *sales ratio* —the percentage of target persons who will be persuaded to purchase the product or service after walking into the retail outlet or being called up by a sales person. You must also consider customer behavior goals. Are customers more likely to buy if they have been given a demonstration or tried the merchandise? To what degree should a retail store be self-service or full-service? What about after-sale service? What is the cost of a selling as a percent of sales? After you have considered these factors, review the capabilities of your sales staff. If you decide on an aggressive selling philosophy, your company must make the commitment to sales training and ongoing refresher courses.

For manufacturers, the issue is a ratio of *selling effectiveness* —the number of prospects contacted versus the number that actually become customers. Manufacturers must also decide how to sell the product—directly, indirectly, or using a combination of the two. These decisions are based on consideration of factors such as whether the market is horizontal or vertical, the quality of the product and whether it is technical or specialized, market potential, geographic concentration, and the financial strength of the company.

Developing a Personal Selling and Service Plan

A format for developing a personal selling and service plan is provided at the end of this chapter.

<table>
<tr><td>

TASK 1

Establish Selling/Service Objectives

</td><td>

Your sales, operations, and/or service objectives should be as specific as possible and should include the following types of goals:

</td></tr>
</table>

Retail/Service
- Customer contact—the percent of store visitors having contact and the number of contacts with store staff during visit.
- Customer behavior goals such as percentage of customers who are persuaded to try a product or experience a demonstration of merchandise.
- The specific sales ratio—purchaser versus nonpurchaser.

An example of personal selling objectives for a retailer would be:

Establish a minimum of one contact with 90 percent of store visitors and a minimum of two contacts with 60 percent of visitors.

Achieve a 50 percent trial ratio of customers—customers who actually try the merchandise during a hands-on, in-store demonstration.

Achieve a 40 percent sales ratio (40 percent of the people who visit the store make a purchase) over the next year during the holiday selling season and a 30 percent sales ratio during the remainder of the year.

Manufacturers
- The number and type of companies that must be contacted by the sales force.
- The number of sales calls that must be made to each prospect and/or current customer by company type (industry, dollar volume, etc.).
- The sales ratio (number of contacts versus the number of sales).
- The average sales dollar volume and the number of orders per salesperson per year.
- The number of actual product presentations/demonstrations or percentage of product sampling or trial that must be achieved during sales presentations.
- Additional customer behavior goals, such as the percentage of customers who are persuaded to sign up for future sales/product information.

Personal selling objective examples for a manufacturer would be:

Contact each current customer twice and make a sales presentation to the top 50 percent of prospect companies in the newly developed construction and manufacturing SIC target markets.

Make full product demonstrations to 75 percent of the prospects.

Obtain a sales ratio of 85 percent among existing customers and 30 percent among new prospects.

Obtain an average dollar sale of $2,500 and generate an average of two hundred sales per salesperson per year.

<table>
<tr><td>

TASK 2

Establish Selling/Service Strategies

</td><td>

First, review the questions pertaining to selling in the Distribution section of the business review. Answering these questions will help you to form specific selling strategies for your company. The areas to address when you establish specific selling/service/operations strategies to meet your selling/service objectives include the following:

</td></tr>
</table>

- *The type of selling environment/method.* A retailer must decide whether the selling environment will be self-service or whether there will be a full-service sales staff. If there is a full-service sales staff, a decision must be made regarding the selling orientation—hard sell or soft sell. A manufacturer must determine whether to use a direct, indirect, or mixed sales staff.
- *The administration parameters of the sales force.* The selling strategies should outline hiring qualifications, training, and evaluation procedures.
- *Seasonal and geographic requirements.* If staffing is a function of seasonal sales or if there are different staffing requirements by store or by market, there should be a selling strategy developed to address these issues.
- *Demonstration requirements.* The personal selling and service strategy section should also direct service and/or demonstration technique. For retailers, is there a certain technique that should be followed to increase the chance of closing a sale? A shoe retailer may require that its sales force initiate as many trial fittings as possible. This might result from data that shows fitting customers and allowing them to try walking in the shoe leads to a 50 percent higher sales ratio. Similar selling technique decisions should be considered for manufacturers.
- *Timing and priority of the sales presentation.* Manufacturers and brokers/distributors must determine when and in what priority accounts will be given sales presentations. For example, if you are a manufacturer selling to retailers, you might make sales presentations to some retailers before others because you want some retailers to have your product before others.
- *Sales staff selection by presentation.* Depending on the customer or potential customer, the manufacturer or broker/distributor must determine who should make the sales presentation. Should it be the salesperson alone or should a sales management person, technical person, or corporate executive also be involved?
- *Sales force compensation.* Other things being equal, people tend to perform in ways that get them the maximum compensation. In a highly measurable area such as sales (number of contacts, individual sales ratios, and the like are generally easily tracked), employees tend to act in ways in which they are motivated to behave. Therefore, it is critical that the sales compensation approach be in sync with the desired type of selling environment. For example, a retailer that wishes to position itself as a low-pressure, self-service-oriented store would be unwise to structure a large sales commission component into its sales force compensation, as this tends to encourage aggressive closing efforts.
- *Special sales incentives.* If they are going to be used, special sales incentive programs should be developed in this section of the plan. When special incentives are provided for a special event or promotion, for example, make sure the sales staff is made totally aware of the specifics of the special incentive program before, during, and after the event.
- *Store operation guidelines.* Selling and operation strategies should cover
    - Retail staffing requirements in terms of when, where, and what.
    - Stocking/merchandising procedures.
    - Store maintenance considerations.
    - Organization/appearance of the store, office, and shelf display for retailers, service companies, and manufacturers, respectively.
    - In-store product presentation (plan-o-grams), office presentation, and displays of product for retailers, service companies, and manufacturers, respectively.

Examples of Retail Selling and Service Strategies

The following are examples of selling strategies for a ski retailer whose selling objectives were to increase the sale ratio from 30 percent to 45 percent during the next year and to obtain a 35 percent ski equipment demonstration ratio among customers in the store:

> Develop an aggressive selling environment designed to sell customers during an in-store, one-on-one sales presentation.
>
> Develop a program which assures that all customers are greeted upon entry to the store.
>
> Utilize the training hill outside the store as a means of getting customers to actually try the equipment and achieve the demonstration goals established in the selling objectives.
>
> Utilize 2 percent commission plus salary to encourage salespeople to sell.
>
> Establish a bonus system to reward the top producers for each week and each month of the year.
>
> Use mystery shoppers to rate service and selling effectiveness. Rate each salesperson at least once every six months.
>
> Use annual and semiannual reviews of the sales staff to improve performance. Send each salesperson to one selling seminar per year.
>
> Develop quarterly seminars to keep salespeople aware of the latest technology and products in the industry.

Examples of Manufacturer Selling and Service Strategies

The following are examples of selling strategies for a manufacturer of a new plastic patented toy boomerang that has a distribution objective of 50 percent ACV of toy stores and 30 percent ACV of college bookstores in year one. The selling objectives for this manufacturer are 90+ percent contact rates for both targets, sales ratio of 60 percent toy and 40 percent college, and an annual average dollar volume of $500 for toy stores and $200 for college bookstores. The strategies are:

> Employ sales representatives and brokers to call on toy stores.
>
> Employ a national rep organization that calls on college bookstores.
>
> Compensate reps and brokers with 10 percent commission on initial orders and 7 percent on all follow-up orders.
>
> Make Toys "R" Us the number one priority, and follow up with sales calls immediately thereafter to the top tier of toy stores.
>
> Train sales representative groups with a demonstration tape.

FORMAT

Personal Selling and Service

Selling/Service Objectives

Selling/Service Strategies

Rationale

Step 7: Tactical Marketing Mix Tools

MARKETING BACKGROUND

1 THE BUSINESS REVIEW

Scope
Company Strengths & Weaknesses • Core Competencies •
Marketing Capabilities

Product and Market Review
Company & Product Review • Category & Company Sales •
Behavior Trends • Pricing • Distribution • Competitive Review

Target Market Effectors
Consumer/Business-to-Business Targets • Product Awareness &
Attributes • Trial & Retrial Data

2 PROBLEMS/OPPORTUNITIES

MARKETING PLAN

3 SALES OBJECTIVES

4 TARGET MARKETS AND MARKETING OBJECTIVES

5 PLAN STRATEGIES—Positioning & Marketing

6 COMMUNICATION GOALS

7 TACTICAL MARKETING MIX TOOLS

Product	Distribution	Advertising Media
Branding	Personal Selling/Service	Merchandising
Packaging	Promotion/Events	Publicity
Pricing	Advertising Message	

8 MARKETING PLAN BUDGET AND CALENDAR

9 EXECUTION

10 EVALUATION

PROMOTION AND EVENTS

13

IN THIS CHAPTER YOU WILL LEARN

- • HOW TO DEVELOP PROMOTION OBJECTIVES.
- • HOW TO DEVELOP PROMOTION STRATEGIES.
- • HOW TO DETERMINE THE COST OF PROMOTIONS AND ANALYZE PROMOTION PAYBACK.
- • WHAT EVENT MARKETING IS, AND HOW TO SELECT AND PLAN AN EVENT.

I N THE NEXT FOUR CHAPTERS we discuss how the communication elements of the marketing mix—promotion, advertising (message and media) and publicity/public relations—are factored into the marketing plan. Please note that while many people erroneously bunch them together as one and the same, each of these forms of communication is in fact different from the other in terms of what it is capable of doing and what role it plays in the marketing plan. Let's begin with promotion.

Promotion and events are powerful short-term marketing tools. We define *promotion* as an activity offering incentive above and beyond the product's inherent attributes and benefits to stimulate incremental purchase or association with the product over the short run. In other words, promotion provides added incentive, encouraging the target market to perform some incremental behavior, which in turn results in either increased short-term sales and/or an association with the product (e.g., product usage or event-oriented experience).

Developing a promotional plan that may or may not include events requires strategic thinking and creativity. In many instances, marketers begin at the execution stage and randomly consider idea after idea without any thought to the ends they are trying to achieve. The result is usually costly, with time and effort spent on developing promotion ideas that are inappropriate to the target market and the competitive situation and, consequently, do not pay out. The key is to establish promotion objectives and strategies first, then develop innovative, yet targeted, executions. We will address these issues in this chapter.

Five Keys to Successful Promotion Development

As you proceed with this chapter, keep in mind the following five keys to successful promotion development:

1. *Promote what the target market wants.* Don't promote what you can't sell or what is out of fashion. Develop promotions around what will be most appealing to the largest segment of your target market.
2. *Provide the necessary incentive to stimulate behavior.* If you want to get maximum promotion participation, make sure your incentive has the pulling power to get the target market to act. For example, we have found in many retail promotions "10 to 20 percent off" does not move the consumer; it must now be a 20 percent discount or more!
3. *Build the necessary awareness for the offer.* So many marketers do well in promoting what the target market wants with a meaningful incentive, but then they do not make enough of the target market aware of the promotion to garner the

participation required to make the promotion successful. Staging a promotion means very little if you don't tell enough people about it.

4. *Limit the barrier(s) to promotion participation.* To reduce the liability or cost of promotions, many promotions are overly constrained. Review what barriers or requirements you put in front of the target person in terms of amount of purchase, time made available to participate in the promotion, and incremental behavior required to participate in the promotion. Is it too much of a hassle for your target person to participate in your promotion? You can remove many barriers by looking at the promotion from the target person's viewpoint rather than a company viewpoint.

5. *Develop optimum value perception at minimum investment.* Finally, keep in mind that there are two parts to the promotion equation: company cost and target market participation. Accordingly, a promotion should attempt to provide the perception of optimum value to the target market at the minimum of investment to you, the marketer.

Developing Promotion Objectives

Promotion objectives and marketing objectives are similar in that both are designed to affect consumer behavior. The difference is that promotion objectives should be designed to affect *specific incremental* behavior over a *short period of time.* Therefore, promotion objectives must:

- Induce incremental consumer behavior over what was anticipated with no promotion.
- Be specific. The objective should focus on one goal only.
- Be measurable. The results must be quantifiable.
- Relate to a specific time period. However, because promotion objectives are short term in nature, the time period can be from one day to several months.
- Provide direction as to the geographical focus of the promotion.
- Include budget constraints or profit parameters. Promotion is the only marketing mix tool with its own sales objectives.
- Focus on affecting target market behavior to:
  —Retain current users.
  —Increase purchases from target market.
  —Increase trial from new users.
  —Obtain repeat usage after initial trial.
  —Affect attitudes through association with an event.

Promotions should be viewed as one method to help execute marketing strategies. To develop promotion objectives, first review the marketing objective and strategy section of your marketing plan, then restate your marketing strategies in quantifiable promotion objectives. A format for developing your promotion and/or event objectives and strategies is provided at the end of this chapter.

| **TASK 1** *Review Marketing Strategies* | Review your marketing strategies, paying particular attention to those listed under the promotion category and those for which the implementation tool of promotion might be appropriate. For example, a marketing seasonality strategy such as "increase sales during the weaker selling months of |

May through August" could be implemented through promotion. Obviously, a marketing promotion strategy such as "develop in-store promotions during peak selling seasons to encourage purchases of weaker-selling product categories" should be addressed in the promotional plan. Thus, the first task requires isolating those marketing strategies that you feel promotions can help implement.

TASK 2

Review Selected Marketing Strategies and Corresponding Marketing Objectives

Once you have narrowed the list down, look at the corresponding marketing objective for each strategy you chose in Task 1. To form promotion objectives, review the marketing objective to determine *what* needs to be accomplished and *who* is being targeted. Then, rely on your marketing strategy to guide you on *how* to develop a promotion objective. By linking your promotion objective to your marketing objective and strategy(ies), you ensure greater probability of developing promotions that will accomplish your marketing strategies and fulfill the marketing objectives established earlier in the plan. For example, assume the following:

Marketing objective: Increase the number of total users/trial among the current target market by 10 percent.

Seasonality marketing strategy: Increase the purchasing level during the off-season while maintaining purchasing rates during the peak selling seasons.

Other marketing strategies: Note that there typically would be other marketing strategies to achieve the above marketing objective. However, assume that only the seasonality strategy is being implemented through promotion and that the other marketing strategies would be accomplished using other marketing mix executional tools.

In this example, the marketing objective provides *what* the promotion objective should achieve (increase number of users) and to *whom* the promotion should be targeted (current target market). Continuing, the marketing strategy helps determine *how* the promotion objective is developed (increase purchasing during the off-season).

TASK 3

Create Quantifiable Promotion Objective(s)

In combining what, who, and how, the marketing objective and strategy can be restated into a quantifiable promotion objective as follows:

> Increase the number of users from the current target market 25 percent during the off-season of May and June in all markets, with a positive contribution to overhead.

Note that geography and timing considerations and a measurable target market behavior are incorporated into the objective statement to make it as specific as possible. Geography and timing in the promotion objective are consistent with the geography and timing constraints developed in the marketing strategy section of the plan. Also, note that a budget constraint is mentioned. In this case, the objective has to be achieved in a manner that contributes positively to fixed overhead. In a different situation, the objective of new trial might outweigh any short-term profit requirement, because the company would be investing in new customers or trial for future profits; however, a budget constraint would be stated at the end of the promotion objective to limit the amount of the investment in new trial. The promotion objective might be "increase the number of new users 25 percent during the off-season with a promotion budget not to exceed $500,000."

The measurable amount in the promotion objective (in this example, 25 percent) must be realistic. Past experience provides the best assistance in deciding just how much you will affect target market behavior through promotions. Remember that promotion is just one of the marketing tools you will be using to achieve your marketing objectives. If promotions were the only tool, then the measurable goal in the promotion objective would have to equal the measurable goal in the marketing objective. In this example, the goal would have to be to add enough incremental new users during May and June to increase the total new user base for the year 10 percent above last year's results. This is highly unrealistic and points out why there are usually multiple marketing strategies for any given marketing objective. In addition, promotion is most often only partially responsible for the implementation of any given marketing strategy. Other marketing tools, such as advertising, distribution, pricing, and merchandising, might be used in conjunction with promotion to implement a specific marketing strategy.

In going through the above process, you may develop several promotion objectives, as there may be several marketing strategies that can be implemented and accomplished through the use of promotions. Each promotion objective will require one or more promotional strategies.

Promotion Strategy and Execution Considerations

Once the promotional objectives are established, promotion strategies must be formulated. These strategies demonstrate how to accomplish the promotion objectives. Promotion strategies should include:

- The type of promotion device.
- The promotion incentive.
- Whether to implement a closed or open promotion.
- The delivery method.

Type of Promotion Device

Determine which promotional device will best meet the promotion objective. The most common promotion categories are:

1. Price off/sale
2. Couponing
3. Sampling
4. On-pack/in-pack
5. Refunds
6. Premiums
7. Sweepstakes/games
8. Packaging
9. Trade allowances
10. Events

Promotion Incentive

The promotion incentive must include a *basic reward* for the consumer. Since promotions are responsible for affecting target market behavior, the incentive needs to stimulate demand. The promotion incentive must be strong enough to move the market to participate in the promotion and purchase the product. Promotion incentives fall into four major areas:

1. Price incentives
2. Product (sample)
3. Merchandise or gift
4. Experience (special event, prize money, etc.)

Closed versus Open Promotions

A promotion can be open or closed. There are also degrees between these two extremes. An *open promotion* is one where the company offers an added incentive to purchase with no specific behavior required to take advantage of the offer. A good example of this would be a 20 percent off sale at the retail level. To take advantage of this incentive, or offer, consumers merely have to shop at the store. Anyone can participate, with no restrictions.

With a *closed promotion*, an added incentive to purchase is offered to consumers, but they are required to do something in order to take advantage of the offer. An example would be a coupon that must be redeemed at purchase or a refund that requires 10 proof-of-purchase validations.

There are degrees to the extent that a promotion is open or closed. Consider the example of instant coupons: The requirement of the individual consumer, beyond simply shopping, is minimal. The customer has to tear a coupon off the package and present it at the checkout counter. However, a promotion such as a refund requiring multiple proofs-of-purchase may prove to be very restrictive. This type of promotion requires a great deal of consumer purchase commitment before the incentive is received.

Delivery Method

Promotions can be delivered by three basic methods or a combination thereof:
1. *Media*—There are multiple forms of media-delivered promotions. Direct mail, magazines, and newspapers are the most common media delivery methods for package goods and business-to-business firms, while television, newspaper, direct mail, and radio are the most common media delivery methods for retail firms.
2. *On-, in-, or near-package*—For manufacturers, promotions can be delivered on the package itself, in the package, or near the package via a point-of-purchase display. For retailers, the promotions can be delivered in-store through signage and point-of-purchase displays.
3. *Salespeople*—Many companies, especially manufacturers such as package goods or business-to-business firms that sell to intermediate markets, use salespeople to deliver a promotional offer. If the target market is not a major consumer group but a more limited purchasing group, direct personal communication of an offer can be efficient and very effective.

Developing Promotion Strategies and Programs

TASK 1

Review Promotion Objective(s)

Review your promotion objective(s) to make certain you are focused on what you are trying to accomplish. Be particularly cognizant of whom you are targeting and the measurable result that is expected.

TASK 2

Review Problems and Opportunities

Review the listing of your problems and opportunities, as these are your knowledge base and will provide insights and ideas on what direction you should pursue in developing your promotion strategies. As you are reviewing your problems and opportunities, refer to your idea page (discussed in the Introduction of this book) and write down any ideas you may have. Refer to this later when you are actually formulating your strategies.

For example, two purchase rate/buying habit problems might be:

The average shopper is extremely brand loyal.

The Southwest consumes the product category at below average rates on a per capita basis, and your company has poor sales in this region of the country.

These two problems will affect promotional strategies in the area of what incentive to offer. Knowing that the category is extremely brand loyal means that it will be difficult to induce trial, so the incentive will have to be greater. And if the example company is going to target the Southwest, the challenge will be even greater, because it is a low-consumption area where the company has poor sales.

TASK 3

Finalize Promotion Strategies

A promotion strategy should address each of the issues outlined in the section on promotion strategy and execution considerations. These are:
• Type of promotion device.
• Promotion incentive.

- Closed or open promotion.
- Delivery method.

For example, assume the following situation:

Marketing objective: Increase usage rates among the target market nationally over the next year by 20 percent.

Marketing strategy: Expand alternative uses of the product from exclusively a hot drink to include acceptance as a cold-served beverage.

Promotion objective: Obtain initial trial of 100,000 new customers nationally for the product as a cold beverage during the months of April and May. Achieve initial trial with a budget of $2,000,000.

[Note that with this situation there would probably be an alternative promotion objective aimed at stimulating trial from among the existing customer base. This objective would have separate promotion strategies and executions.]

The following promotion strategies could be used to accomplish the promotion objective. Each of four strategy parameters will be addressed. The cost parameter is addressed only indirectly through the choice of an incentive amount. This will be covered in more detail in Task 5.

Utilize sampling of the product in-store to soft drink purchasers.

Provide coupons to potential customers in-store worth 50 cents off the purchase price whenever the product is sampled.

Incorporate a trade program offering price incentives as a way to induce shelf space and merchandising support.

TASK 4

Develop Alternative Promotion Program Executions

The next task is to develop alternative executions for each promotion strategy. Then, choose the most appropriate execution for inclusion in your program. Multiple executions can be developed for each promotion strategy. Be creative and think of as many as you can. Some alternative promotion executions are presented in Exhibit 13.1. These alternatives were developed to meet two of the strategies: "Utilize sampling of the product in-store" and "Provide 50-cent coupons to potential customers in-store." A format to help you channel your thinking and stay consistent from one execution to another is provided at the end of this chapter.

Note that there is a sales objective included within Exhibit 13.1. Since promotions are a short-term marketing tool affecting customer behavior, there will be short-term sales results generated by the promotion. Thus, it is a good idea to establish a sales goal along with the promotion objectives, strategies, and executions. When you analyze your promotion results, you will then have two results against which to gauge your success—the sales goal and the quantitative promotion objective.

TASK 5

Calculate the Cost and Payback Potential of Your Promotions

Expenses must be projected for each promotion in your promotional plan, and all costs associated with communicating and delivering the promotion to the target market should be included. This includes the media costs associated with delivering the promotion; however, it does not include the media costs associated with your normal nonpromotion/image advertising. In addition, you must also estimate the cost of the offer or incentive. If you use 25-cent coupons, you must estimate the redemption number and multiply this by 25 cents plus handling costs to calculate a dollar cost of the coupon incentive.

EXHIBIT 13.1 Alternative Promotion Program Execution

Program Theme

"Have one on us."

Sales Objective

Develop sales of $20,000,000 over a two-month period.

Promotion Objective

Obtain initial trial of 100,000 new customers nationally for the product as a cold beverage during the months of April and May. Achieve the initial trial with a budget of $2,000,000.

Promotion Strategies

Utilize sampling of the product in-store to soft drink purchasers.

Provide coupons to potential customers in-store worth 50 cents off the purchase price wherever the product is sampled.

Description

Display a giant self-serve beverage bottle with product being served hot from one side and cold from the other in grocery stores carrying the product.

Offer free samples in paper cups to all shoppers during four weeks in April and May, effectively leading the summer selling period.

Provide a 50-cent instant coupon to all consumers who sample the product.

Support

In-store signage and display.

Rationale

The promotion will build trial and exposure for the new cold drink. Serving the cold drink with the established hot drink will show customers alternative uses for the product and link the new brand to an established and accepted product. April and May were chosen as the time to sample because the time period effectively bridges cold and warm weather months.

The instant coupon will encourage immediate purchase after trial. The 50-cents incentive will be strong inducement and, along with the sampling, will lower the risk of trying an unknown product.

Note: Alternate executions would be developed for the same objectives and strategies. You could then choose the execution that most effectively and efficiently meets the objectives.

EXHIBIT 13.2 Average Redemption Range

Promotion Technique	Average Redemption Range	
	Low	High
Instant coupon	15.0%	55.0%
In product	7.5	17.5
On product	6.0	15.0
Electronically dispensed in-store	4.0	21.0
On-shelf distributed	4.0	16.0
Cross-ruff or cross-packs	2.0	6.0
Direct mail	1.0	9.5
Free-standing insert	0.7	3.0
Magazine on page	0.5	4.5
Refunds	0.5	4.5
Newspaper (ROP)	0.5	2.5
Newspaper co-op	0.4	1.7
Self-liquidating POS premium	0.3	1.0

Cost Calculation for Closed Promotion

To calculate the cost and potential payback of closed promotions, you need to accurately project redemption rates for your offer.

The participation estimates shown in Exhibit 13.2 are based on a combination of our client experience and redemption averages published by industry sources. These are ballpark estimates for participation or redemption rates using different closed-promotion vehicles. Actual participation rates should be adjusted individually as they are a function of the following:

- *The offer* — Greater incentive and fewer restrictions equal greater participation.
- *The delivery method* — The closer the delivery method is to the product itself, the greater the redemption. For example, on-pack/in-pack will have higher redemption.
- *The timing* — Immediate incentives such as instant coupons will have higher redemptions. Also, promotions run when the target category is purchasing (e.g., bicycles in spring) will have greater participation than those run when category purchasing is at a low level.
- *The product category* — Health and beauty aids, for example, have average redemption rates lower than those of household products or beverages.
- *The price of the product* — The higher the purchase price of the product, the lower the participation. However, a higher promotion incentive can have some positive effect on participation if the high price of the product is not out of the economic reach of the majority of your target market.

Exhibit 13.3 demonstrates how to calculate the cost of a promotion. (A worksheet for calculating your own promotion costs is provided at the end of this chapter.) We used a coupon promotion as an example because it has applications to retail, package good, and business-to-business firms. Three different redemption rates were used in order to provide the marketer with a range of expected responses. The cost of this promotion would be somewhere between $101,250 and $110,000, with a medium estimate of $105,000. This cost will be used, along with incremental sales and profits, when calculating potential payback for a closed promotion.

In addition, if you are a consumer goods firm with coupon redemption in grocery and other stores, there are handling charges to be included. If you are utilizing a clearinghouse, you must pay a charge for each coupon handled. Also, the retailer charges for each coupon handled. At press time of this book, the average total cost was approximately 23–25 cents per coupon redeemed.

Additional promotion administrative costs to consider are:

- *Costs of employing fulfillment houses* — For example, there is an incremental cost for fulfillment regarding refunds, sampling, premiums, and sweepstakes/games. Most companies are not equipped to fulfill promotion programs adequately.
- *Cost of production* — For example, production lines often are slowed to accommodate on-pack/in-pack incentives.
- *Packaging costs* — For example, with bonus packs there will be a cost to reconfigure the package.

Finally, the cost of the promotion must be compared to the incremental sales the promotion is expected to generate. This can be determined through a payback analysis.

Payback Analysis

Before you execute any planned promotion, be sure to review the numbers to determine if the promotion makes sense from a payback analysis standpoint. We recommend calculating

EXHIBIT 13.3 Calculating Cost of a Coupon Promotion

	High	Medium	Low
Redemption Costs			
Value of coupon	50¢	50¢	50¢
Number of coupons distributed	500,000	500,000	500,000
Estimated redemption rate	4.0%	2.0%	0.5%
Number redeemed	20,000	10,000	2,500
Dollar value or offer			
(number redeemed × value of coupon)	$10,000	$5,000	$1,250
Advertising and Media Costs			
Printing of coupons (500,000 × 0.01)	$5,000	$5,000	$5,000
Mailing cost/envelopes (500,000 × 0.19)	$95,000	$95,000	$95,000
Total cost of promotions	$110,000	$105,000	$101,250

EXHIBIT 13.4 Payback Calculation Example for Open Promotion

Situation

Promotion: 20 percent off women's department merchandise
Estimated storewide margin decrease from 50 percent to 45 percent during promotion
Time period: first three weeks of March
Geography: All three stores in Madison, WI

Sales

Estimated sales for period without promotion	$300,000
Estimated gross margin dollars for period without promotion ($300,000 × .50)	150,000
Estimated sales with promotion	360,000
Estimated gross margin dollars with promotion ($360,000 × .45)	162,000
Estimated net margin dollar increase with promotion ($162,000 − $150,000)	12,000

Media and Advertising Cost

Estimated ongoing advertising and media costs with or without promotion*	15,000
Total advertising and media costs with promotion	20,000
Incremental advertising and media costs due to promotion	5,000

Payout

Incremental margin sales	12,000
Incremental advertising and media expenditures	5,000
Contribution to fixed overhead	7,000

*What would have been spent in regular, mainline advertising and media.

the contribution to fixed costs,[1] as this method isolates the promotion and takes into account any incremental variable cost associated with the promotion. In using this method, incremental costs of the promotion (communication of the promotion and incentive costs) are subtracted from incremental sales generated from the promotion.

[1]This method is commonly used by retailers, service firms, and manufacturers. However, manufacturers also utilize a gross margin to net sales method that is detailed in Chapter 18, "Marketing Budget, Payback Analysis, and Marketing Calendar."

Exhibit 13.4 presents an example for a retailer considering a 20 percent off sale as an open promotion. (A payback calculation worksheet is provided at the end of this chapter.) The retailer had experience with similar sales in the past and had a rough estimate on the incremental sales that could be generated by the promotional offer. This method looks at incremental sales and costs to calculate what the promotion will generate in terms of a contribution to fixed overhead. The incremental margin sales are sales above and beyond what would normally be expected for the time period. If you haven't run the promotion before, make a high, medium, and low estimate based upon similar company promotions run in the past and promotion experiences for the product category. This provides best and worst case estimates.

Note that the cost of the promotion (reduction in gross margin dollars) was calculated directly into the projected incremental sales figure. In some cases you may want to break this step out to show what the promotion costs were, particularly if you are a package goods marketer and you wish to show redemption projections.

Remember: The promotion must stand on its own. The only way to determine its potential success or failure is to weigh the projected incremental sales against the expected incremental expenses of the promotion. If the promotion contributes a meaningful positive dollar figure to fixed overhead (expenses that occur no matter what happens—e.g., rent) and meets the promotion sales goals, then the promotion should be executed. If the payback analysis shows that there is a negative contribution to fixed overhead, then you should consider another promotion, or rework the promotion with less incentive or a different product mix. The exception to this is the case in which there is no payback parameter specifying that the promotion must contribute to profits. If the firm is simply trying to gain trial, which it feels will translate into future profits, then the major constraints will be the budget parameter and the amount of desired trial.

<table>
<tr><td>

TASK 6

Select the Most Appropriate Promotion Executions

</td><td>

You have developed promotion objectives and strategies, created promotion execution alternatives, and analyzed costs and paybacks for each execution. Now it is time to select those executions that will best achieve the promotion objectives within the established budget constraints. When choosing your promotion executions, try to make sure the executions complement each other and work together through the year. For instance, two consecutive premium offers would probably be ineffective as compared to other com-

</td></tr>
</table>

binations of promotions. The best method to determine if your promotions properly interface with each other is to list the promotions in calendar form according to when they will be executed. This will allow you to make judgments on whether you have selected promotions that complement each other. It will also be useful when you transfer your marketing tool executions to one master calendar, as is detailed in Chapter 18, "Marketing Budget, Payback Analysis, and Marketing Calendar."

How to Approach Event Marketing

While we have discussed in detail most of the promotion categories, one important category into which we have not delved is events. *Event marketing*, sometimes known as "event sponsorship" or "lifestyle marketing," is a rapidly growing area that personally involves target market persons. Event marketing expenditures by U.S. companies are in the billions annually and are showing double-digit growth each year. The largest portion of these expenditures is devoted specifically to sports sponsorships, although event marketing as a whole certainly encompasses much more than just sports marketing.

What Is the Goal?

Although events can be "leveraged" so that they accomplish several communications objectives, it is best to begin your planning with one central goal. This will keep your planning and execution focused, helping you choose from among the myriad options that are open to you in event marketing.

Events can make a strong element in the marketing mix such as when your goal is to launch a new product, increase product trial, or build personal relationships with the product and people associated with it.

The event you select, and the features you give it, should grow naturally out of your primary goal. As an example, if increasing product trial is a key objective, you should choose an event that reaches the maximum number of people in your target audience and gives them an incentive to try the product via on-site trial or couponing. Also, remember to make every effort to quantify your specific event objective(s) such as providing a specific number of people you want to attract to try the product on-site.

Selecting an Event

Event selection and design is the most critical component in ensuring an event that will meet your marketing objectives. Successful events share the following characteristics:

1. There is a clear and meaningful connection between your product or company and the event itself.
2. Your company or product identity comes through clearly.
3. There is a compelling appeal to the target audience.
4. The event has news value.
5. You can incorporate related communications elements that support the event and further your marketing objectives.

When planning an event, ask yourself the following questions:

- Do you have the resources (time, money, manpower, connections, etc.) to create your own event, or are you better off "piggybacking" onto an existing and already established event?
- Can you establish a tie with a timed event such as an anniversary, sporting event, or designated week or month (e.g., June is Dairy Month)?
- Are there opportunities to localize the event?
- Are there opportunities to affiliate with a suitable charity or cause?
- Can you ally with a media partner who becomes a cosponsor?
- Can you ally with other business partners who can provide resources and add an extra dimension to your event without overshadowing your involvement?
- Is there a theme or creative concept?
- Is a celebrity or expert spokesperson a possible draw?
- How can your company or product identity be reinforced?
- What is the timetable?
- What is the budget?
- How will the success of your event be evaluated?

Types of Events

A wide variety of events is available as marketing communications tools. The following list serves as an idea starter.

Announcement of a new entity or product
News conference
Celebrity appearance
Spokesperson tour
Contest/competition
Professional sporting event
Amateur sporting event

Walkathon/bikeathon
Grand opening/open house
Product couponing/sampling event
Remote broadcast
Dedication/groundbreaking
Commemorative ceremony
Award presentation
Carnival
Parade
Street festival
Vehicle appearance or rides
Community cleanup
Cultural fair
Science fair
Concert
Book release
Telethon
Lecture/demonstration/exhibit
Information display
Seminar
Meeting or convention
Research presentation

FORMAT

Promotion/Events

Promotion Objectives

Promotion Strategies

Rationale

FORMAT

Promotion Program Execution

Program Theme

Sales Objective

Promotion Objective

Promotion Strategies

Description

Support

Rationale

WORKSHEET

Calculating Cost of a Coupon Promotion

	High	Medium	Low

Redemption Costs
Value of coupon
Number of coupons distributed
Estimated redemption rate
Number redeemed
Dollar value or offer
   (number redeemed × value of coupon)

Advertising and Media Costs
Printing of coupons
Mailing cost/envelopes

    Total cost of promotion

WORKSHEET

Payback Calculation for Open Promotion

Situation
Promotion:
Time period:
Geography:

Sales
Estimated sales for period without promotion
Estimated gross margin dollars for period without promotion
Estimated sales with promotion
Estimated gross margin dollars without promotion
Estimated net margin dollar increase with promotion

Media and Advertising Cost
Estimated ongoing advertising and media costs without promotion*
Total advertising and media costs with promotion
Incremental advertising and media costs due to promotion

Payout
Incremental margin sales
Incremental advertising and media expenditures
Contribution to fixed overhead

*What would have been spent in regular mainline advertising and media.

Step 7: Tactical Marketing Mix Tools

MARKETING BACKGROUND

1 THE BUSINESS REVIEW

Scope
> Company Strengths & Weaknesses • Core Competencies • Marketing Capabilities

Product and Market Review
> Company & Product Review • Category & Company Sales • Behavior Trends • Pricing • Distribution • Competitive Review

Target Market Effectors
> Consumer/Business-to-Business Targets • Product Awareness & Attributes • Trial & Retrial Data

2 PROBLEMS/OPPORTUNITIES

MARKETING PLAN

3 SALES OBJECTIVES

4 TARGET MARKETS AND MARKETING OBJECTIVES

5 PLAN STRATEGIES—Positioning & Marketing

6 COMMUNICATION GOALS

7 TACTICAL MARKETING MIX TOOLS

Product	Distribution	Advertising Media
Branding	Personal Selling/Service	Merchandising
Packaging	Promotion/Events	Publicity
Pricing	Advertising Message	

8 MARKETING PLAN BUDGET AND CALENDAR

9 EXECUTION

10 EVALUATION

ADVERTISING MESSAGE 14

- HOW TO DETERMINE WHAT IS EXPECTED OF YOUR ADVERTISING.
- HOW TO DEVELOP ADVERTISING MESSAGE OBJECTIVES AND STRATEGIES.

PLANNING THE ADVERTISING MESSAGE IS A KEY POINT in the marketing planning process because it deals with translating your marketing objectives and strategies into advertising—the most visible communication to your external and internal targets. For purposes of this discussion, we define *advertising* as that which informs and persuades through *paid* media (television, radio, magazine, newspaper, outdoor, and direct mail).

In this chapter we will discuss how to provide the direction for the advertising message. In the following chapter we will discuss how to deliver the message through the appropriate media.[1]

What Is Expected of Your Advertising?

Before you begin developing the advertising section of your marketing plan, you must decide what your advertising can realistically accomplish. We know that advertising can build awareness and positively affect attitude. For your product, advertising can build recognition, help create a positive image, and differentiate it from the competition. Advertising can also build store traffic, assist in introducing new products and line extensions, feature products improvements, and announce promotions. In the business-to-business category, advertising can also generate customer leads ("please send me more information") and open doors for the sales force.

In addition to building awareness and positively affecting attitude, advertising can sometimes also move the target to action and to buy your product through direct response advertising. Direct mail is a good example of this. However, in the majority of situations, advertising cannot make the sale unless the product is on the shelf, there is a conveniently located store to visit, the wholesaler carries your product line, and/or a sales call is made to detail the product and close the sale. Remember: Advertising alone usually cannot initiate behavior; the behavior element is included as a marketing objective elsewhere in the plan (see Chapter 5, "Target Markets and Marketing Objectives").

Developing the Advertising Message

Because of its tremendous attention-getting power and inherent creativity, advertising is continually on stage for everyone to critique. Accordingly, nearly everyone thinks he or she is an expert on advertising, because it is a marketing tool that has much subjectivity associated with it. Therefore, it stands to reason that the more subjective it is as a marketing tool, the more necessary it is to use a process to arrive at advertising that sells. Our disciplined process for developing advertising entails three tasks:

[1]In this book, *advertising* will refer to the message and *media* will refer to the message delivery method.

1. Define your advertising objectives.
2. Write your advertising strategy.
3. Detail what will go into the execution.

By now you have no doubt come up with a number of advertising ideas. However, before proceeding to the actual execution of your creative ideas, go through this disciplined process. Use of this approach will assure that the final advertising is effective or at least more effective than if you had gone with the first ad idea that came to mind. Also, it should be pointed out that, given the choice between nonmarketing-based advertising and advertising based on sound marketing, the latter will win most often. It will win because it is data based and relates to the real marketplace, communicating the meaningful product attributes to the right target market. Accordingly, great advertising is usually based on great marketing. Further, bear in mind that your market positioning is the key to effective advertising. It is, in essence, the bridge from the more objective marketing to the more subjective advertising.

| **TASK 1** | Advertising objectives deal with what you want your advertising to accomplish. The objectives are quantifiable, while the advertising strategy is not. |
| *Define Advertising Objectives* | Your advertising objectives will nearly always define *awareness* and *attitude* goals as they relate to the target market. The strategy deals primarily with describing the message communication needed to fulfill the advertising objectives. |

Refer back to the marketing communication goals and the specific values goals you set for the advertising segment of your plan. Use these value goals as a starting point in setting your advertising objectives. In addition to unaided awareness objectives, you might also want to add first mention or top-of-mind awareness objectives if you did not previously use them as advertising message value goals in the value strategies segment of this plan. Or you might want to include specific advertising awareness goals under advertising objectives. Advertising awareness usually refers to that percentage of the target market that has read, seen, or heard advertising for your product. Unless the respondents who were asked about the advertising can actually identify a portion of the advertising message, they should not be counted as having advertising awareness.

Before you begin, check to see that you did *not* include advertising objectives in your marketing objectives and strategies section. The tendency is to deal with communication issues such as recall and understanding under marketing, but they belong under advertising.

Even if you are not planning, or cannot afford, to implement a research program to measure the effectiveness of the advertising, setting measurable advertising objectives will force you to objectively evaluate the advertising challenge. Further, if your time period to achieve the advertising objectives differs from the time period set for the marketing objectives, indicate the time period with the advertising objectives.

Exhibit 14.1 presents some examples of how to define your advertising objectives. It is easier to set your advertising objectives if you have primary research. However, in many cases you will not have done market research that establishes a benchmark from which to measure awareness and attitude changes. Nevertheless, it is a good learning process to estimate (even if you can only make educated guesses) what percent of unaided awareness is necessary to affect a predisposed attitude to buy that then translates to a specific percent of the target market that will purchase.

| **TASK 2** | The *advertising strategy*, also referred to as the creative strategy, is the catalyst of effective advertising. It provides direction on what should be communicated in the advertising message and how it should be communicated. |
| *Write Advertising Strategy* | It is a big part of the *means* that gets the desired product perception into the mind of the consumer. This strategy is the guide for development of |

creative and communicative advertising; the goals are to gain attention, be remembered, positively affect attitudes, and help move the target market to purchase your product. It becomes a guide for those who will actually create the advertising. Further, the advertising strategy describes the personality of the advertising and the parameters of the creative environment in which the advertising must perform. Without this guide, the final advertising could well be exceptionally entertaining but not necessarily effective. Although we may like the advertising, it might not communicate the benefits of your product that will fulfill the needs and wants of the specified target market.

The advertising strategy is also the basis against which creative work is evaluated to make sure that advertising communicates effectively. Usually, you want to develop alternative creative approaches for the advertising strategy and then identify the approach that best executes the strategy. Also, if you are having an advertising agency execute the creative, both the client and the agency should have input into and mutually agree on the written strategy before it is executed. This strategy agreement is necessary so that, when the advertising work is presented, there is no confusion or disagreement in terms of the description of the product, specific benefits, claims made, and feeling of the advertising. Further, having agreed upon a strategy up front will save time in creative development and help eliminate frustration for all involved.

The advertising strategy should include:

- *Promise:* Define the reward/benefit for the specific target market in solving a problem or taking advantage of an opportunity.
- *Support for this promise:* Substantiate the promise or provide reasons to believe it.
- *Tone:* Describe the feeling of the planned advertising that is consistent with the personality of the product. The tone must be appropriate not only for your product but also for the target market of the advertising.

Look to your positioning statement for direction when writing the advertising strategy, because it will be the key to developing an advertising strategy that differentiates your product from the competition. Make sure your advertising strategy directly conveys the image you want to instill in the minds of the target market.

Don't expect to complete an advertising strategy on the first attempt. Plan to rewrite each segment of the advertising strategy a number of times until you arrive at a strategy that clearly states what you want your final advertising to communicate. Each word in your advertising strategy is critical; therefore, make sure it communicates the intended meaning. Keep the strategy simple, clear, and single-minded in focus. Make sure your strategy conveys the inherent personality of your product, which can come alive in your advertising and play to the needs and emotions of the target person.

The advertising strategy that has been reworked and included in your marketing plan should be the strategy that reflects the positioning and provides the overall direction for a unified advertising campaign. However, it might be that your marketing plan calls for additional, separate advertising strategies, such as for specific products within a company line. For example, an advertising strategy for Green Giant corn would be a modification of the overall campaign strategy for Green Giant canned vegetables. Also, you may need separate strategies for special geographic and demographic markets, promotions, or trade advertising.

Although it is likely that you will need substrategies, it is important that your overall advertising strategy is written to be a campaign strategy to guide all of your advertising. Your primary strategy should lead to an advertising campaign in which all the individual advertisements continually reinforce your positioning. This is very important, because the advertising campaign will create a unified image and will provide a consistency for all of your creative executions. Obviously, there are always exceptions to this, particularly if you are marketing very different products to very different target markets.

An effective strategic advertising campaign will incorporate similarities. The more similarities, the stronger the campaign. The advertising within a campaign should include as many common properties as possible, such as a similar look, sound, and/or feel/tonality, in order to convey a consistent personality. Further, in most cases, each advertisement will include a unified, basic selling idea or theme line.

The rewards of developing a campaign are many. It will become cumulative in scope, with each advertisement reinforcing the others for a multiple effect, making your advertising work harder and maximizing your advertising investment.

Remember: Before moving on to execution, include a brief rationale for the advertising objectives and advertising strategy(ies), defining why the objectives are attainable and why the strategies are appropriate. The rationale should include specific reasons for what is included in the strategy.

Exhibit 14.2 presents two examples of an advertising strategy. The first is a business-to-business example for a national printing company that wants to create an image for itself as the best printer for high-end quality work. The second, a retail example, is for a fabrics and crafts retail chain that wants to create an image of being the do-it-yourself home decorating store for women.

TASK 3
Detail Executional Elements

Most often the execution segment of the advertising section is not included in the marketing plan but is detailed in what is sometimes referred to as an *advertising implementation plan*. This plan includes all of the information needed by those responsible to create the advertising.

In this separate document you might want to include additional copy or product information that is important to know, but that, in order to maintain strategic focus, is not included in the advertising strategy. For example, along with potential legal considerations (in this separate plan), you might include advertising requirements, such as:

• How the company and product name/logo must be used in the advertising.
• How the theme line must be used in all advertising.
• Product line/store location to be included.
• Preproduction copy test requirements, production cost parameters, ad size, etc.

Formats to use for preparing the advertising objectives and advertising strategy and for consideration of executional elements appear on the following pages.

EXHIBIT 14.2   How to Write Advertising Strategies

Strategy Against Users of High-End Printing

Promise

Convince the purchaser of high-end printing that Royle is the high-quality printer for mid-run, high-end jobs because Royle has expert press people and special printing capability to provide sheetfed quality with the economy, efficiency, and versatility of the web presses.

Support for This Promise

1. All major customer segments rated Royle's print quality high relative to the competition.
2. Royle utilizes a Total Quality Program in its pressroom to ensure consistent quality.
3. Royle's Heidelberg Web 8 and Web 16 presses have the capabilities to deliver the best of high-end printing.

Tone

The tone of the advertising should be preemptive and professional, confident (inspiring trust), and project a quality nature that reflects the best of all printing.

Rationale

Results of the survey research, including feedback from the focus groups, indicated that print buyers are involved in the print-buying process not on a personal level but on a purely professional level, particularly given that they often have a wide variety of responsibilities beyond print buying. Further, Royle's efforts to build trial among the target will require establishing a credibility and trust that they truly offer the quality and service they claim.

Strategy Against Women Who Decorate Their Homes

Promise

Convince women 25–54 with children who decorate their homes that Northwest Fabrics & Crafts (NWF&C) is the best store to shop to help decorate their homes because NWF&C is *the* Do-It-Yourself Home Decorating and Activities Center with both fabrics and craft materials for the home.

Support for This Promise

NWF&C has the ideas, the fabrics, and craft materials—from florals to custom framing, along with the experienced help of the store's staff—to make the customer's home-decorating creativity come to life, enabling her to make a more comfortable and beautiful home for her family.

Tone

The tone of the advertising should be warm, helpful, creative (full of ideas), and identify with the unique personality and self-expression of each home decorator.

Rationale

No fabrics or crafts retail chain has positioned itself against the do-it-yourself home decorator, making NWF&C singular in its preemptive claim. Research and experience have shown creativity and self-expression to be important.

—Having both the craft materials and the fabrics is an important point of difference for NWF&C.

—The experience element comes into play both with the in-store help available (at the beginning and throughout a project) as well as in the availability of classes.

Advertising Message

Objectives

Awareness

Attitudes

Rationale for Objectives

Advertising Strategy

Promise

Support for This Promise

Tone of the Advertising

Rationale for Strategy

Advertising Execution (If no separate advertising implementation plan is prepared)

Additional/Key Strategy Information

Specific Legal Consideration

Advertising Requirements

FORMAT

Advertising Implementation Plan

Date: _____

Product: _____

Job Title: _____

Prepared By: _____

Job Description: (including requirements/sizes)

Plan Approval

Name	Approved	Date
1.		
2.		
3.		
4.		

Advertising Strategy:

Due Dates:

Concept _____   Art/photography _____

Copy/layout/boards _____   TV shoot _____

Client OK _____   Mechanical _____

Preproduction (Print/TV/AV) _____   Ship to printer _____

Ship finished job _____

1st air date/insertion/use _____

Budget:

Total Project Cost:

$_____

Estimate needed from:

☐ Art/Photography   ☐ Commercial Production

☐ Multi-image   ☐ Print Production

Estimate needed by: _____

Guidelines for Writing Implementation Plans

Follow general order of subjects listed, selecting those which apply to the current job. If pertinent informtion is not available, indicate date it will be available. Attach additional information to this planning form.

Print	Radio/TV/ Multi-image	Copy	Art	Budget Limitations
Quantity	Storyboards	Product/Service	Layout/	Internal
Stock	Medium (Film,	Objective/Strategy	Storyboard	Time/$
Size	Tape, Slides)	Target Market (Attached	Stage	Outside
Colors	Length	additional information	Art Reference	Suppliers/
Delivery, Mailing List/	Music	to this planning form)	Detail	$ Available
Labels		Benefits—Major	Information	
Proofs		Benefits—Minor		
Printing Process		Exclusives		
Preprints and Reprints		Buying Information		
Publication		Appeal		
Requirements		Emotion		
Releases		Limitations		
Art/Photography		Musts (Incl. Legal Requirements)		
Price Information		Research Info.		
Logo, Sig. Code/Ad #		Competitive Info.		

This copy for:

Name/Department

☐ _____

☐ _____

☐ _____

☐ _____

Step 7: Tactical Marketing Mix Tools

MARKETING BACKGROUND

1 THE BUSINESS REVIEW

Scope
Company Strengths & Weaknesses • Core Competencies • Marketing Capabilities

Product and Market Review
Company & Product Review • Category & Company Sales • Behavior Trends • Pricing • Distribution • Competitive Review

Target Market Effectors
Consumer/Business-to-Business Targets • Product Awareness & Attributes • Trial & Retrial Data

2 PROBLEMS/OPPORTUNITIES

MARKETING PLAN

3 SALES OBJECTIVES

4 TARGET MARKETS AND MARKETING OBJECTIVES

5 PLAN STRATEGIES—Positioning & Marketing

6 COMMUNICATION GOALS

7 TACTICAL MARKETING MIX TOOLS

Product	Distribution	Advertising Media
Branding	Personal Selling/Service	Merchandising
Packaging	Promotion/Events	Publicity
Pricing	Advertising Message	

8 MARKETING PLAN BUDGET AND CALENDAR

9 EXECUTION

10 EVALUATION

ADVERTISING MEDIA

IN THIS CHAPTER YOU WILL LEARN:

- HOW TO DEVELOP MEDIA PLAN OBJECTIVES AND STRATEGIES.
- HOW TO EVALUATE SPECIFIC MEDIA AND MEDIA VEHICLES, AS WELL AS OVERALL MEDIA PLANS.
- HOW TO SUMMARIZE A MEDIA BUDGET.

WITH THE ADVERTISING MESSAGE STRATEGY NOW COMPLETE, the next step is to prepare a media plan that will deliver these messages most effectively and efficiently. From a technical standpoint, media planning is probably the least-understood marketing mix tool. Accordingly, you will find that learning how to plan media is one of the most challenging and complex experiences you will encounter as you write your marketing plan.

Media can be divided into two parts: planning and execution. The overall goal of the two together is to deliver the optimum number of impressions (messages) to the target audience at the lowest cost and within the most suitable environment for the message. *Planning* consists of arranging the various media in combinations and support levels designed to help fulfill the marketing, advertising, and promotion objectives and strategies. In essence, it is the process of refining probabilities in a step-by-step, disciplined manner. *Execution,* on the other hand, encompasses negotiating, purchasing, and placing the media once the media weights, types, and budgets have been determined. Another part of media execution is the evaluation of the purchased media's performance once it has run (the *postbuy*).

The focus of this chapter is media planning—setting media objectives and strategies, evaluating various media, constructing a media plan, and summarizing a media budget. If you intend to purchase your own media, we recommend you consult a text on media buying.

Developing a Media Plan

Just as was the case with developing the advertising message, creating a solid, effective media plan requires the use of a disciplined process. Our approach involves four tasks:

1. Reviewing the background data needed to prepare the media plan.
2. Setting the media objectives.
3. Preparing the media strategy.
4. Developing the final media plan with calendar and budget.

TASK 1 *Review Background Information*	Before you can begin to prepare your media plan, you must first review all of the pertinent marketing and media data. Most of this information should be included in your business review. Below is a list of marketing and media data to be reviewed over a three- to five-year period, with five years of history preferred. Attempt to gather and review all of the items, depending on the data and time available to you.

- Size and growth of the marketplace in dollars and units.
- Competitive market (including your product):

—If available, sales history of each major competitor by size, share, and growth.

—If available, competitive media review of each major competitor:

Level and share of media spending/weight.

Spending and weight levels by medium, seasonality (quarterly if possible), and market.

Media spending as a percentage of sales.

—If available unaided awareness, advertising awareness, and attitudes of the potential users/purchasers, on both a national/system-wide and market-by-market basis.

- Your product(s)'s sales, marketing, and media history:

—Sales history by product, market (CDI & BDI), seasonality, and store/distribution channel.

—Your media target market.

—If available, unaided awareness, advertising awareness, attitudes, and behavior/usage.

—Historical media review of your product:

Overall media weight delivery and spending.

Spending and weight levels by medium (quarterly) and market.

Media spending as percentage of sales.

—Results of media schedules run:

Changes in awareness, attitudes, and behavior.

Impact on overall sales, promotions, events, and media tests.

—Dollars allocated to media versus the other marketing mix tools.

- Problems and opportunities section.
- Marketing plan, from sales objectives to communication goals and tactical tools through advertising message.

This information will provide direction and insight as you develop your media plan.

TASK 2
Set Media Objectives

Your media objectives must provide a clear and definitive direction in the following critical areas:

- To whom is the advertising to be directed (target audience)?
- Where is the advertising to go (geography)?
- When is the advertising to appear (seasonality)?
- What are the weight goals for optimum communication? In other words, how much advertising is deemed sufficient to achieve the advertising objectives?
- Is there an initial set budget allocated for media spending or will a task method approach be applied to arrive at a media budget? If there is a set media budget allocation, it should be included up front in the media plan as a media objective. A task-derived media budget is dependent on the media support necessary to meet the awareness and attitude levels that will stimulate adequate usage to meet the sales objectives. In this case, the media budget is finalized and presented at the end of the media plan.
- Will the marketing plan call for testing of media? If so, you will include media test objectives in this section of the media plan.

Let's look at each of these areas in detail.

TARGET AUDIENCE

To arrive at a target audience, simplify the target market you detailed earlier in the plan by listing the key strategic and segment descriptors.

The *strategic target* relates to purchasing and usage. For example, if mothers purchase powdered soft drinks for their children, while their children who consume powdered soft drinks, are the users, then do you target the purchaser, the user, or both? The *segment target audience* should parallel the segmentation breakouts provided by syndicated media services, which measure audience media habits and media vendors such as direct mail houses, broadcasting stations, and catalog publishers. If you have key submarkets, such as the trade (wholesalers, retailers, etc.) for a package goods product, that cannot be accommodated in one media plan, a separate media plan should be prepared for these target markets. The media target audience should be limited to those descriptors that can be readily and effectively used in the planning, measurement, and evaluation of the various media.

Here are some target audience objective examples.

For a company that sells copiers and fax machines:

> Primary target audience: Decision Makers at small to mid-sized companies—
> 3–5 million dollars (president and general office manager).
> Secondary target audience: Decision Influencers at those same companies
> (senior-level project managers).

For a company selling children's cereals:

> Primary target audience: Kids 6–11.
> Secondary target audience: Mothers (women 25–49).

GEOGRAPHY

Once you have determined your specific media target audience, you must decide where and with what emphasis you want to place your media. Geographic media variation depends on the marketing strategies, potential and profitability differences on a market-by-market basis or within a market, and budget.

Geographic weighting of media levels by market is based on many factors. A few of the geographic factors to be taken into consideration when developing geography media objectives are:

- Sheer geographic size and physical makeup of your trading area.
- Growth potential of the market.
- Competitive media activity.
- Media available to support your product.
- Concentration of potential users of your product.
- Concentration and trending of your product sales.

The last two of these geographic factors can be taken into account by evaluating on a market-by-market basis the sales of the product category and the sales of your product. The market-by-market variations should have been detailed in your business review as a comparison of markets in two ways: category development index (CDI = percent category sales/percent households in a given market) and brand development index (BDI = percent product sales/percent households in a given market). You most likely will place some media weight where you have a set minimum level of sales and even greater weight where there is an above-average concentration of category sales and, more important, an above-average concentration of sales for your product. Accordingly, you will develop a media objective that takes into consideration the CDI, the BDI, and the relationship between the two.

Before finalizing your geographic media objectives, decide, on a market-by-market basis, whether your strategic marketing thrust is *defensive* (spend in markets to protect your business) or *offensive* (spend where there is potential but where sales have not been solidly built). This offensive strategy is also referred to as *investment spending*.

A beginning BDI/CDI guide for a defensive versus offensive approach might be as follows:

	High CDI	Low CDI
High BDI	Defensive—higher media spending to protect share.	Defensive—media maintenance unless competition increases media weight.
Low BDI	Offensive—investment media spending to capitalize on opportunity markets via new advertising, additional promotion, etc.	Limited, if any, media support.

In addition to BDI/CDI considerations, also consider the trending of sales on a market-by-market basis. You might place additional media weight in markets with positive sales trends, while in markets with negative sales trends you might reduce the weight until a non-advertising problem is fixed or add media weight to support promotional advertising to reverse the sales trend.

The remaining factor regarding geography is the budget. If the funds necessary to implement an effective program across all key markets are not available, priorities must be established and the market list pared down. Advertise only where you reasonably believe you can achieve your objectives; otherwise, you risk a diluted, ineffective program across all markets.

Some examples of geography objectives follow.

For a national package goods product:

Provide national media support.

Provide incremental local media weight in high BDI markets that cumulatively account for a minimum of one-third of sales.

	Percent Volume	BDI
Los Angeles	8.3%	119
New York	8.0	123
Chicago	7.7	125
Philadelphia	6.5	121
San Francisco	4.4	118
	34.9%	122

For a business-to-business company:

Provide broad-based media support of the full line of existing equipment.

Provide full introductory media support in addition to base support of the east, north, and central divisions for the new equipment introduction as soon as service commitment has been confirmed.

For a local retailer:

Provide marketwide media coverage.

Provide incremental media weight within one mile of store that accounts for 50 percent of current customers.

SEASONALITY

As important as it is to advertise to the right person in the right place, it is also important to advertise at the right time. Accordingly, to arrive at the right *seasonality media objective(s)*, review the seasonality of your product and category sales to determine when sales for your product and the category are at their highest levels. The general media practice is to plan your greatest media weight support for periods of high sales volume.

Most products have sales skews. When the monthly sales index nears 110 or greater, you would most likely increase your weight levels. Sometimes the seasonality of your product might differ from that of the category, with the category's heavy sales season beginning earlier or later than that of your product. After reviewing the reason(s) for this seasonal sales difference (e.g., special promotion or different competitive weight levels), you will probably want to concentrate your media weight when the target market is most likely to purchase. Where affordable, advertising should lead the natural buying season, placing higher levels of media just prior to heavier sales periods.

Another factor to consider in setting a media seasonality objective is what your competitors have done in the past and what you anticipate they will do in the coming year. You may want not only to lead the peak selling season but also to be the first into the media arena, preempting the competition.

An example of a seasonality objective for a retail fabric chain is:

Provide media continuity support throughout the year, with a concentration of media effort in the heavy selling seasons of August through October and February through April.

MEDIA WEIGHT AND GOALS

Having determined your media objectives of target audience, geography, and seasonality, next determine "how much is enough" in terms of the quantitative media delivery necessary to meet the awareness and attitude goals that will lead to projected sales. This is known as *media weight*.

Basic Media Terms

Before discussing how to arrive at quantitative communication goals to provide media direction, you must have an understanding of some basic media terms: rating point, gross rating points (GRPs), reach, and frequency.

A *rating point* is defined as 1 percent of the universe being measured. A universe could include households, companies, women, men, adults, kids, purchasing agents, or the like in a single market or region or in the total United States. On a total U.S. household basis, a one rating (measured against households) for a commercial or ad means that an impression or exposure is made against approximately 993,920 homes nationally (1 percent of 99,392,000 homes). On a single market basis for Chicago, a one rating equates to approximately 31,642 homes (1 percent of 3,164,150 homes).

Gross rating points (GRPs) provide a common term of measurement to determine how much media weight is going into a defined marketplace and to make comparisons among different media. GRPs are also known as *target rating points (TRPs)* when measured against a universe other than households, such as women 25–49 or children 2–11.

If you buy 100 home GRPs via multiple ad insertions, you are in fact buying a number of household impressions equal to the number of homes in that universe. In Chicago, for example, a schedule of 100 GRPs would generate 3,164,150 household impressions (the total number of homes in Chicago). Please note, however, that these 3,164,150 household impressions will not necessarily be made against 3,164,150 homes in that market. In actuality, when a schedule of ads and/or commercials is run, some homes will be exposed to the ad a number of times and others will not be exposed at all.

This notion leads to two other important media estimate concepts: reach and frequency. *Reach* is the number of different homes/persons exposed at least once to a particular ad/commercial within a given time period. This number is generally expressed as a percentage. *Frequency* measures how often, on average, the different homes/persons have been exposed to one message within a given time period. Reach and frequency are normally estimated on a four-week basis, but figures can also be provided for schedules ranging from one week to a full year.

Reach, frequency, and GRPs are tied together mathematically as follows:

$$\text{Percent Reach} \times \text{Frequency} = \text{Total GRPs}$$

Therefore, to reach 80 percent of a target market with a frequency of 10, you would need a schedule of approximately 800 GRPs of support.

Through research and experience, we have been able to establish standard reach levels for given GRP levels. Using the graph in Exhibit 15.1, you can approximate what each medium would generate in reach at a particular GRP level, as well as the average frequency. If your local market media plan calls for 300 GRPs in radio to support a two-week promotion, it would build an approximate 50 reach and an average frequency of 6 ($300 \div 50 = 6$). Or, if you determined a monthly magazine reach of 50 was required, then your schedule would have to approximate 125 GRPs. At this level, your frequency would be about 2.5 ($125 \div 50 = 2.5$). Exhibit 15.1 provides an overall GRP summary for television, radio, and magazines. For more accurate GRP data specific to your market, check with the appropriate media representatives.

To arrive at a rough approximation of reach and frequency data for each medium (other than television and radio), you can compute your own GRP data for magazines, newspaper, outdoor, and direct mail. For your rough calculations use the following formulas:

Magazine: Use percent coverage for reach (circulation ÷ total market households or target readers ÷ target persons); number of insertions for frequency.

Newspaper: Use percent coverage for reach (circulation ÷ total market households or target readers ÷ target persons); number of insertions for frequency.

Syndicated sources (SMRB or MRI) or magazine readership studies can provide the necessary data to figure coverage of a specific target.

Outdoor: For a standard four-week showing estimate:

50 showing = 85 reach and 15 frequency
100 showing = 88 reach and 29 frequency

Direct mail: Use percent coverage for reach (number mailed ÷ total market target households or target persons); number of mailings for frequency.

Interactive (banner ad): Use exposures to Web sites carrying your banner ad as impressions which, when applied to the target population base can be expressed as a TRP level. You could then directionally buy against a TRP goal. Making the leap from TRPs to actual reach is still very difficult due to the limited base of available data, coupled with the fact that Internet usage continues to change and grow.

For more precise data, contact your specific media representative.

Once you have estimated reach and frequency for a single medium, you may want to combine media weights with another medium. You can use the grid in Exhibit 15.2 to arrive at combined weight levels across media. For example, suppose 300 GRPs of radio and 800 GRPs of magazines are planned (1,100 GRPs total), yielding reaches of 50 and 80, respectively. Using the grid, you can see that the combined reach is approximately 86 (86 is at the intersection of row 50 and column 80); therefore, average frequency for the combined 1,100 GRPs

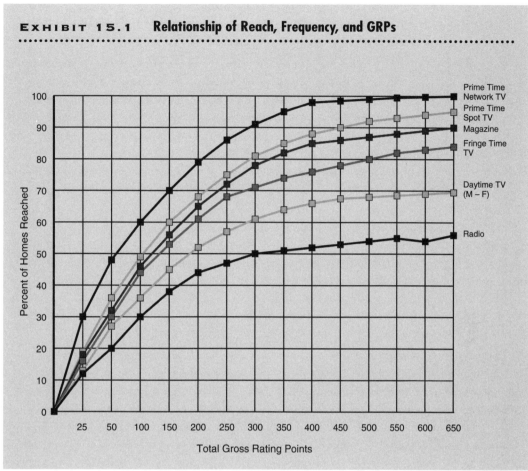

EXHIBIT 15.1   Relationship of Reach, Frequency, and GRPs

Source: Michael L. Rothschild, Advertising, From Fundamentals to Strategies, Lexington, Massachusetts, D.C. Heath and Company, 1987.

must be 12.8 (1,100 ÷ 86 = 12.8). Although neither the graph in Exhibit 15.1 nor the grid in Exhibit 15.2 is perfectly accurate, each gives a good approximation for planning purposes.

Methods of Establishing Media Weight Goals

Determining quantitative communications goals is very difficult even for the most experienced media planner because of the ever-changing marketing environment, in which there is a lack of definitive benchmarks, an uncontrollable competitive marketplace, and the continually changing needs and wants of the potential target market. The problem of accurately determining how much communication is received by the target market and its effectiveness in stimulating action makes this determination even more difficult.

There are three different methods of arriving at a communication weight level goal(s): micro target market method and two macro methods—percentage of sales and share of media versus share of market.

Micro Target Market Method. The micro target method is goal, or task, driven. It is based on moving a specific target market to action. With this approach you attempt to determine what percent of the target market must be reached and how often. You want to reach this target with the frequency necessary to build the product awareness and understanding that will lead to a positive attitude toward the product and eventual purchase. In essence, you are attempting to determine the amount of GRP media weight you will need in order to effectively reach or communicate with a large enough portion of your target market and generate the required sales.

EXHIBIT 15.2 Accumulated Reach Levels Across Media

All Media Combinations (Homes and Individuals)

Reach

	5	10	15	20	25	30	35	40	45	50	55	60	65	70	75	80	85	90
5	10	14	19	24	28	33	38	43	47	52	57	62	66	71	76	81	85	90
10	14	19	23	27	32	36	40	45	50	54	59	63	68	72	77	81	86	91
15	19	23	27	31	35	39	43	48	52	56	61	65	69	73	78	82	86	91
20	24	27	31	35	38	42	46	50	55	59	63	67	71	75	79	83	87	91
25	28	32	35	38	41	44	48	53	57	61	64	68	72	76	79	83	87	92
30	33	36	39	42	44	47	51	55	59	63	66	70	73	77	80	84	88	92
35	38	40	43	46	48	51	53	58	62	65	68	71	75	78	81	84	88	92
40	43	45	48	50	53	55	58	60	64	67	70	73	76	79	82	85	88	92
45	47	50	52	55	57	59	62	64	66	69	72	75	77	80	83	86	89	93
50	52	54	56	59	61	63	65	67	69	71	74	76	79	81	84	86	89	93
55	57	59	61	63	64	66	68	70	72	74	76	78	80	82	85	87	90	93
60	62	63	65	67	68	70	71	73	75	76	78	80	82	84	86	88	90	94
65	66	68	69	71	72	73	75	76	77	79	80	82	83	85	86	88	91	94
70	71	72	73	75	76	77	78	79	80	81	82	84	85	86	87	89	91	94
75	76	77	78	79	79	80	81	82	83	84	85	86	86	87	88	89	91	95
80	81	81	82	83	83	84	84	85	86	86	87	88	88	89	89	90	92	95
85	85	86	86	87	87	88	88	88	89	89	90	90	91	91	91	92	92	95
90	90	91	91	91	92	92	92	92	93	93	93	94	94	94	95	95	95	95
95	95	95	96	96	96	96	96	96	97	97	97	97	97	97	98	98	98	98

Reach

Source: Michael L. Rothschild, *Advertising, from Fundamentals to Strategies* (Lexington, Massachusetts, D.C. Heath & Company, 1987).

A good place to start when determining the desired reach and frequency is to review your marketing objectives and what percentages of the target market you have estimated will try your product, make repeat purchases, and become regular users in order to meet the sales objectives. Then review the overall communication goals and examine the advertising objectives to determine the percent of target market you projected must have specific unaided awareness of your product and a predisposed attitude toward your product.

It is also wise to review the media weight levels supporting your product over the past year, along with the level of media support for any promotions that may have been run. Based on these past supporting media weight levels, attempt to correlate sales results to determine what reach, frequency, and GRP levels are needed for this year's plan to help meet the estimated advertising and promotion objectives.

Every situation is different when setting reach goals, depending on the type of product you are selling and its awareness and acceptance by the target market. As a suggested starting point, based on the authors' experience, you should consider a 60–90+ reach of the target market. For a meaningful impact, it is usually necessary to reach well over one-half of the target market with your message. This is sometimes difficult to accomplish, particularly with short-term promotions, and when the appropriate media vehicles are not readily available.

Once you have estimated your specific reach goal(s) for the year (new product introduction, promotion, event, grand opening, etc.), estimate the frequency needed against the target in order to generate the effective reach necessary to elicit a specific response. In setting frequency goals, the frequency required to move the desired portion of the target market from product recognition to purchase is really a guesstimate. However, a potential range of frequency to make this happen is a 3–10 frequency. To determine whether you need more or less frequency depends upon the following:

More frequency	**Less frequency**
New product	Established product
New campaign	Established campaign
Complex message	Simple message
Nonuser prospects (trial objective)	User prospects (repeat objective)
High competitive advertising levels	Low competitive advertising levels
Nonloyal user category, especially with short purchase cycle	Stable/loyal user base
Promotion/sales event	

In our experience, specifically with retail clients who need immediate results, it is usually more successful to reach a smaller percentage of the target market with greater frequency than to reach a larger percentage of the target market with minimum frequency. Said another way, it is better to have a smaller audience understand and remember your message than to have a large audience that does not thoroughly understand or remember the message.

Once you have determined the required reach and frequency to set a media weight goal, simply multiply your estimated reach by the total needed frequency for your total GRP level. For example:

$$\text{Reach } 80 \times \text{Frequency } 9 = \text{GRPs } 720$$

Keep in mind that, with this methodology, the frequency of message exposure is based on *average* frequency. Some people within the target market will be exposed once and others will be exposed at multiples of the average frequency number.

You probably have surmised from this discussion of setting media weight goals that there is no one hard and fast rule for determining the optimum media weight level for your product; rather, there is a composite of many factors that you must consider. In Exhibit 15.3 we present some guidelines for you to consider and, we hope, modify (possibly dramatically) as you determine the media weight goals for your product. These rough media weight guidelines are based on some quantitative data, but are primarily based on the personal experience of the authors. Therefore, they are subjective in nature and must be used with extreme caution.

Some examples of media weight goals are shown below.

For a nationally marketed package good:

Provide a reach of 90–95 and a minimum of average frequency of 4 over five media flight periods. This will need approximately 2,000 GRPs on a national basis for the fiscal year.

EXHIBIT 15.3 Media Weight Guidelines

Product/Service Type	Target Audience GRP Weight Levels		
	Minimum Weekly	Seasonal/Event 4-Week Period	Annual
Consumer			
Package goods			
Established	75–150	300–600	1,000–3,000
Introductory/Promotional	150–250	600–1,000	1,800–5,000
Retail/Service			
Established	100–200	400–800	2,000–5,000
Introductory/Promotional	175–350	700–1,400	3,000–10,000
Business-to-Business			
Established	25–50	100–200	600–1,600
Introductory/Promotional	50–150	200–600	1,200–3,600

For a package good marketed in the local-opportunity markets of Chicago, Los Angeles, and Philadelphia:

> Provide a reach of 90–95 with a minimum frequency of 6 for the five four-week, heavy-up periods. This will take an additional 1,100 GRPs locally across the year.

For a business-to-business manufacturer:

> Reach a minimum 80 percent of the target market a minimum of eight times annually.

Macro Methods. In the micro method described above, the communication goals were the driving factors. In the macro methods, priorities are established, and the plan reflects the number of objectives that can be accomplished at a predetermined budget level. One macro method establishes the budget as a percent of sales based on industry averages, and the second macro method uses a comparison of share of media to share of market sales. Both are market-based approaches.

Percentage-of-Sales Method. The percentage-of-sales method begins with a review of the percent of sales allocated to advertising by the product category/industry in which you are competing. You could then use a similar percentage of your projected sales for your media budget after reducing this dollar budget by 10–15 percent to cover the cost of production to develop the ads and/or commercials. For example:

Percent advertising of sales for category	3%
Product's projected sales	$100,000,000
Ad budget (3% × $100MM)	$3,000,000
Ad production of 10 percent (10% of $3MM ad budget)	$300,000
Available media budget ($3MM–$300M)	$2,700,000

Once you have established the budget, use this budget to determine a media weight goal.

To arrive at a rough GRP weight level for your product, contact your media representative for an approximate *cost per rating point (CPP)* by medium. For example,

Cost of average insertion or broadcast spot ÷ Average rating = CPP

Or,

Average radio :60 commercial spot cost of $36 ÷ Average rating of 2 = $18 CPP

You can then divide the total media budget by the CPP for each medium to arrive at an approximate idea of how much media weight you can afford by each potential medium. For example,

$27,000 ÷ $18 CPP = 1,500 GRPs

Although the above example is for a consumer medium, you could use a similar approach for business-to-business media using an average cost per point for each medium such as trade publications and direct mail.

The percent-of-sales approach to advertising is not very sophisticated, but it does challenge you to maximize the dollars in your media budget. However, keep in mind that, because this approach is so broad in application, it does not take into consideration your current marketing situation or the competitive marketing environment. Advertising as a percent of sales is only one method of arriving at the optimum media weight goal and should, in most situations, be a means for comparison.

Share-of-Media versus Share-of-Market Method Another method of determining your media weight goal is the share comparison of media activity to sales—the *share-of-media versus share-of-market method*. This method compares your product's *share-of-media voice (SOV)* (in GRP media weight or media dollar expenditures as a percentage of total media advertising in your industry category or marketplace) to your product's *share-of-market sales (SOM)*.

Organization	SOV		SOM	
	$M	Percent	$MM	Percent
A	$370	48%	$94.1	39.1%
B	230	29	70.0	29.1
C	69	9	38.6	16.1
D	105	14	38.0	15.7
Total	$774	100%	$240.7	100.0%

If you are using media dollar expenditures, take the media spending for each competitor, including your own product, from the business review and compare it to the corresponding share of market. Is your share of media spending above or below that of the competition? Is your share of media spending above or below that of your product's share of market? Based on the direction of your marketing strategies and this SOV to SOM comparison, you can determine media weight goals.

As a very rough guide and a starting point in using the SOV to SOM media weight determination, consider the following:

Share of voice should approximate share of market.

Usually the greater the share of market, the greater the share of voice.

If you want to increase your share of market, you most often should increase share of voice.

If your share of voice is below your share of market year after year, your sales share will eventually decease if everything in the competitive market environment and your marketing mix remains constant.

In using this method, keep in mind there is no guarantee that there always will be a direct cause and effect between an increase/decrease of SOV and a similar increase/decrease in SOM. However, while there is not always perfect correlation, there is a direct cause-and-effect relationship between SOV and SOM.

TASK 3	Under media strategy you should include the following:
Prepare Media Strategy	• *A brief summary of the media mix strategy.* This describes the different media to be used—magazines, direct mail, radio, etc.

• *The specific use of each medium.* This is a tactical description of how each of the specific media is to be used, such as magazine types, ad size, broadcast programming/daypart type, and length of commercials.
  • *The scheduling of the media.* A description in terms of when each medium is used and at what levels.

Media Mix Strategy

As you develop your summary of the media mix strategy, several points must be considered, all of which lead to an evaluation of which media will best fulfill your media objectives.

Value Comparison. To begin your evaluation process, do a quick initial screen of the different media, determining which have a possibility of use in a media plan that will meet your objectives. It is a good idea to do this quick screen of all media to ensure that you do not automatically rule out a medium based on your preconceived notions or without determining if it could meet the objectives. In Exhibit 15.4 we review the communication values of each medium. If you require more in-depth background information on each medium, you can review an advertising or media text or check with the appropriate media representatives.

Arriving at the Right Media Mix. In order to arrive at the appropriate mix of media you must screen out the obvious inappropriate media. Do a quantitative and qualitative analysis of the potential media candidates, and consider how your media selection will impact the target market in comparison to the competitive media environment.

Screen Out Inappropriate Media. After reviewing the strengths and weaknesses of each medium in terms of its appropriateness for meeting the media objectives, screen out those media that logically could not meet the objectives. For example, if you are marketing a new product to a broad, general market that requires emotional image advertising, you would not use direct mail; if the product was technical and required detailed explanation, you would not use outdoor; if you were grand opening a single 1,000-square-foot ice cream shop in a suburb of Chicago, you would not use television.

Evaluate Each Medium on a CPM Quantitative Basis. After eliminating those media that will very obviously not meet the objectives, compare the remaining media on a quantitative, *cost-per-thousand (CPM)* basis to determine media efficiency. A CPM is used as a common denominator for media comparison.

To arrive at a CPM for a medium, you can either divide target audience into the medium cost multiplied by 1,000 [Cost ÷ (Audience × 1,000) = CPM] or move the decimal point of the audience three places to the left and divide into the medium cost [Cost ÷ (Audience ÷ 1,000) = CPM]. If a network prime-time television :30 commercial cost is $124,000 and the number of the target persons reached is 6,264,000, then $124,000 ÷ 6,264 = $19.80 CPM.

EXHIBIT 15.4 Communication Values by Medium

Television

Pros: Audiovisual impact, most intrusive, demands less active involvement relative to print, immediate impact, quick reach and good frequency, relatively homoogeneous national coverage, broad homogeneous local coverage that goes beyond metro areas.

Cons: Limited to commercial-length constraints, one exposure per expenditure.

Radio

Pros: Good frequency medium, demands less active involvement, good localized spot coverage for city/metro area.

Cons: Audio impact only, low ratings, limited to commercial-length time constraints, one exposure per expenditure, reach builds slower than television or newspaper.

Local Newspaper

Pros: Immediate impact, high reach potential, coupons get redeemed more quickly, very timely.

Cons: Low readers per copy, very little pass along, very short life span, limited in production quality.

Sunday Supplements

Pros: Immediate impact, high reach potential, good coupon carrier, better production quality than newspaper.

Cons: Low readership per copy, very little pass along, very short life span, not as flexible in timing as newspaper.

Consumer Magazines

Pros: No time constraints per message, potential for multiple exposures per expenditure, in-depth product description potential, generally upscale demography, pass along readership, coupon/promotion delivery vehicle, good productive quality.

Cons: Visual impact only, requires active involvement, less immediate impact, lower reach and local market coverage than television, radio, or newspaper.

Business-to-Business/Trade Publications

Pros: In-depth product description potential, reaches relatively small but targeted audience, ads and editorial area highly read, coupon carrier, low cost per inquiry.

Cons: Visual impact only.

Outdoor/Out-of-Home

Pros: Good for product/package identification, good reach, high frequency, good directional vehicle, local geographic concentration.

Cons: Visual impact only, limited copy development potential, very high total monthly cost for anything approaching national coverage.

Direct Mail

Pros: Extensive copy development potential, very selective, easy to track response, excellent coupon carrier, flexible in terms of timing and types of inclusions per mailing.

Cons: Visual impact only, easy to discard.

Interactive

Pros: Extensive copy development potential, high attention and involvement, direct responsive vehicle closing sale electronically, can quickly reach database of current and potential customers electronically through e-mail.

Cons: Medium is very cluttered, limited control over when someone will visit your site, minimal reach capability.

Evaluate each of the potential appropriate media in your marketplace on a CPM basis. To do your CPM efficiency analysis, you will need both audience and cost information. To more easily compare medium CPMs, you might want to rank each medium from the lowest to highest CPM.

Having reviewed the ranked media CPMs, you can begin to eliminate those media with high CPMs. However, you cannot automatically assume that those with the lowest CPMs should be included in your media mix. You must also consider the most appropriate medium for each product and the competition's use of the media. In the final analysis, it is not always the lowest CPM but the lowest *cost per sale (CPS)* that proves most important. What may appear to be too costly based on a pure CPM evaluation might be the most effective medium in terms of selling goods.

Competitive Media Mix Considerations. Finally, consider the competition's use of the media mix. What is their media mix selection? When do they use each medium? At what levels? How do they use each medium in relation to the others? If a competitor with a considerably larger media budget dominates the medium that would have been your first choice, you might decide to concentrate all of your media dollars in your second choice where you can dominate and where you will not have your media effort diluted.

With or without competition, it is usually better to concentrate your media dollars in a few media rather than to dilute your media dollars over many different media, thereby fragmenting your media effort. Plus, the more competition you have in the media, the more it becomes necessary for you to do a good job in one medium before placing weight in another. Make sure that each additional medium added to the media mix is used with weight levels that will have competitive impact and generate effective reach.

After you've evaluated the media alternatives from quantitative, qualitative, and competitive points of view, write your media mix strategy. Below are some examples of media mix strategies.

For a national package goods client:
> Use a combination of network television for national coverage and spot television in the designated high-opportunity markets of Chicago, Los Angeles, and Philadelphia.
> Use women's service magazines for selective reach against the primary target market and to carry cents-off coupons.

For a business-to-business crafts manufacturer:
> Use national trade publications across a minimum of two top craft magazines to broaden reach potential of both primary and secondary target audiences.
> Use frequency mailings to merchandise new products to large/key accounts.

Specific Usage of Each Medium

Within this media strategy section, define the specific tactical usage of each medium to be employed, based again on the media objectives. Include the following medium specifics where they apply.

> *Television and Radio:* Daypart TV (Day, Fringe, Prime Time, News, Sports), Daypart Radio (AM Drive, Midday, PM Drive, Night), program types, length of commercial.
> *Magazines:* Magazine type (news weeklies, sports, etc.) and/or specific magazines by name; ad size, position; black and white; one-, two-, three-, or four-color.
> *Newspapers:* Daily, weekly, and shopper (nonpaid); ad size; section of paper; black and white; one-, two-, three-, and four-color; day of the week.
> *Outdoor:* Level of showing (25/50/100), special location or directional requirements, size (if not 30 sheet), other specifics (painted, rotary, etc.).
> *Direct Mail:* Size (height/width), number of pages, quantity, black and white/color specifics.
> *Interactive:* Type of message (graphics and copy or banner ad), presence on other advertisers' home page or development of your own, type and placement of messages directing consumers to your home page.

Below are some examples of media vehicle strategy/tactic statements.
For a package goods food client, use full-page, four-color ads in:
  Women's service magazines—*Woman's Day, Family Circle, Ladies' Home Journal,* and *Good Housekeeping.*
  General interest magazines—*People* and *TV Guide.*
  Regional/lifestyle magazines—*Sunset* and *Southern Living.*

For a regional retailer:
  Use a :30 television daypart mix of 30 percent daytime, 30 percent general fringe, 20 percent prime time, and 20 percent late news.
  Use ⅓-page newspaper ads for continuity and ½- to full-page ads to support major promotions on Thursdays in the main news section.
  Use a targeted mailing in the trading area of each store.

For a business-to-business firm:
  Use four-color, full-page ads in *Food Processing,* and use black-and-white, ½-page ads in *Food Engineering.*
  Use black and white plus one-color, 6 × 11-inch postcard for frequency against the 1,000 key accounts.

Media Scheduling

Along with the selection of the optimum medium, media vehicle, and ad size/commercial length, you must also determine how the media should run. While the seasonality media objective provides guidelines for when to advertise throughout the year, the scheduling strategy provides specific direction of how the media is to be run.

There are a number of different strategic approaches to scheduling:
  Continuity schedules are just that, continuous, and run at a relatively fixed, even level to help sustain nonseasonal/nonpromotion programs.
  Heavy-up schedules incorporate incremental media weight to support periods of higher market activity, new product or campaign introductions, grand openings, and promotions.
  Pulsing schedules run in a continuous on/off pattern. For example, the media runs two weeks, then is off two weeks, on two weeks, off two weeks, etc. The on/off pattern is repeated on a regular basis. The pulsing schedule provides more media support when advertising, which helps cut through the media noise level in the market, making the advertising stand out from that of the competition.
  Flighting-in scheduling is generally three to six weeks of continuous advertising followed by hiatus periods, or periods of no advertising. Flighting is used for short-term promotions and events, product introductions, and during periods of high seasonal sales.
  Front loading is the running of heavier weight levels with the commencement of a media schedule when you kick off seasonal advertising, new advertising campaigns, new product introductions/grand openings, promotions, or trade show announcements.

Below are some examples of scheduling strategies.
For a package goods product:
  After the introductory period, schedule support at a minimum of 100 TRPs/week to maintain awareness.
  Schedule support in flights of three weeks on, two weeks off, to maintain continuity across the year.

EXHIBIT 15.5   **Graphic Calendar for a Retail Store Media plan**

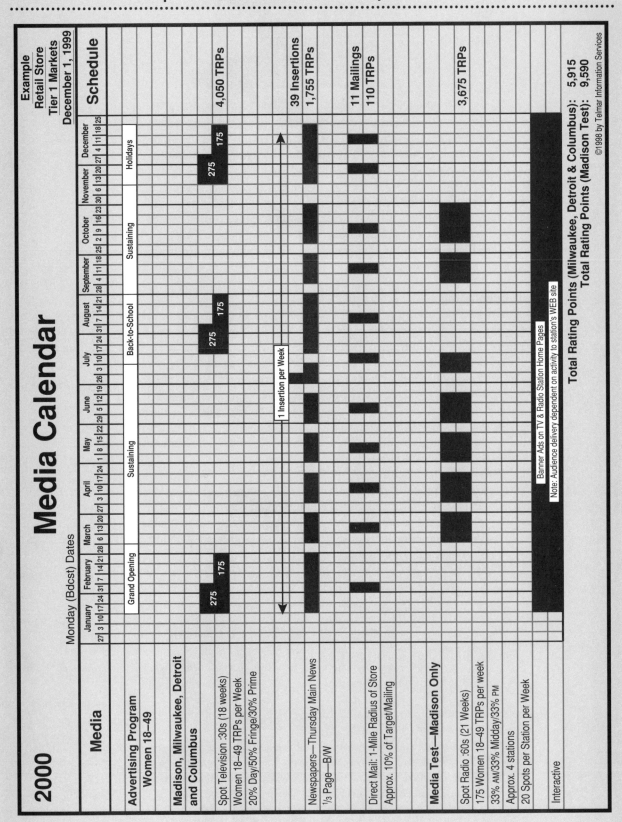

EXHIBIT 15.6 **Media Budget: Spending by Medium and Quarter**

Product: Hot Dogs
Year: 2000
Date: 12/1/99

Medium	1st Quarter ($000)	2nd Quarter ($000)	3rd Quarter ($000)	4th Quarter ($000)	Total ($000)	Percent
1. TV	$5,250.1	$2,361.0	$3,648.1	$4,430.1	$15,699.3	51.4%
2. Newspaper	2,341.0	1,060.7	1,678.0	1,876.4	6,956.1	22.8
3. Magazine	1,960.2	900.2	1,005.8	1,246.7	5,112.9	16.8
4. Direct Mail	1,102.3	534.2	542.7	580.4	2,759.6	9.0
Total	$10,653.6	$4,856.1	$6,874.6	$8,133.6	$30,517.9	
Percent	34.9%	15.9%	22.5%	26.7%		100.0%

EXHIBIT 15.7 **Media Budget: Spending by Market and Media**

Product: Apparel
Year: 2000
Date: 12/1/99

Market	Newspapers $M	Newspapers Percent	Television $M	Television Percent	Yellow Pages $M	Yellow Pages Percent	Spending by Market $M	Spending by Market Percent
Buffalo	$113.4	12.3%	$50.5	14.9%	$1.1	7.0%	$165.0	13.0%
Des Moines	106.6	11.6	19.7	5.8	1.9	12.1	128.2	10.1
Ft. Wayne	49.7	5.4	18.8	5.5	0.9	5.7	69.4	5.5
Grand Rapids	46.6	5.1	36.6	10.8	1.1	7.0	84.3	6.6
Kansas City	114.0	12.5	51.5	15.2	2.9	18.5	168.4	13.2
Lincoln	50.4	5.5	14.9	4.4	1.2	7.7	66.5	5.2
Madison	55.6	6.1	19.8	5.8	0.8	5.1	76.2	6.0
Minneapolis	258.9	28.2	82.8	24.4	2.8	17.8	344.5	27.1
Omaha	62.7	6.8	21.8	6.5	2.2	14.0	86.7	6.8
Spokane	59.9	6.5	22.8	6.7	0.8	5.1	83.5	6.5
Spending by Medium	$917.8	72.1%	$339.2	26.7%	$15.7	1.2%	$1,272.7	100.0%

For a business-to-business product:

Schedule magazine advertising to run alternating months to maintain awareness across a greater portion of the year.

Schedule direct mail drops in months when magazine ads do not run to maintain a higher level of awareness against the primary segments of the target market.

TASK 4

Develop Final Media Plan with Calendar and Budget

At this point, having already set media objectives and strategies, you should have solidified your media thinking. You are now ready to rough out a graphic representation of at least two potential media plans in calendar form. Exhibit 15.5 presents a calendar for a retail store media plan. A blank planning calendar is provided at the end of this chapter. You should prepare alternative plans in terms of different media included, usage of each medium, scheduling, total media weight levels, and budgets. Then compare the alternative plans to each other in terms of total weight placed against the target market (reach, frequency, and GRPs). Also compare corresponding costs to determine which plan meets the media objectives, maximizing the delivery of the message to the target audience at the lowest cost.

Along with a finalized media calendar, also include a media budget that you can exhibit in a number of different ways, depending on the needs of your marketing plan. Two media budget examples are presented. One details spending for each medium by quarter (see Exhibit 15.6). If you want to present more spending detail, you can break out your dollars for each medium by month using a similar budget format. If you want to show both weight levels and spending, you can detail GRPs/TRPs and dollars for each quarter or month using a similar format.

If you have included a number of different products or markets in the marketing plan that require specific media support, you should also include a media budget that details media spending by product/market and medium. This example is shown in Exhibit 15.7. (Formats for each are presented at the end of this chapter.) It is best to show your media budget summary in the media section and then include media totals as part of the total marketing plan budget, which is included at the end of the marketing plan document (discussed in Chapter 18).

Interactive Media

In the 1950s, the new medium was television. In the 1980s, the buzzword was cable TV. In the 1990s, the spotlight is on interactive media.

What differentiates interactive media most from the more traditional forms of advertising is that it is more buyer initiated. The communication process basically begins when the consumer requests some specific information about a product or service. The consumer now plays a direct part in the communication process, choosing both when the message is delivered and, to some extent, the actual content of the message. Instead of an advertiser developing one message, sending it out to the masses, and hoping that it is the right message delivered at the right time, the advertiser can send out a wealth of information, letting consumers select what they feel is most important. Interest and attentiveness are at very high levels, since this is information that has been specifically requested.

There are many advantages and opportunities in the interactive world, some of which are:

- The advertiser is not limited to a page in a magazine or a 30-second time frame in which to communicate the key product benefits to a broad segment of the target market.
- The consumer can potentially find answers to specific questions at a time of his or her own choosing.
- The advertising has the potential to be significantly more effective, due to the higher interest and attentiveness levels.

Much of what was initially viewed as the interactive world of the future had all of this interactivity taking place through the television set. That, however, is still a few years away. The more immediate future (and to some extent, the present) has this taking place through our personal computers. The mechanics of this have already been in place for a number of years. Basically, all you need is a computer and a modem with which to connect to another computer.

Home computers have already become a way of life for many people. Currently, about 34 million homes have computers (approximately 30 percent of all U.S. households). Modems, once an add-on piece of hardware, are now being bundled with most new computer packages and are now in about 14 million homes (40 percent of all homes with computers). The number of homes with computers and modems should continue to increase. In addition, most computer packages also come with access to one or more on-line service, such as Compuserve, Prodigy, or America Online. These services, as well as others, will also provide access to the Internet and the World Wide Web, at which point you really can begin to travel the information superhighway about which so much has been written—all at just the stroke of a key.

Add to all this the fact that we have a society that is becoming increasingly more comfortable with using computers for more than just word processing and balancing checkbooks. The stage has been set, therefore, for the development of more effective ways to communicate with our target consumer.

Currently, there are already well over 30,000 different sites that marketers of various products and services, as well as just information providers, have already set up on the World Wide Web. Most are just experimenting with this new medium, looking for the most effective ways to get even closer to their target consumers.

For advertisers looking to begin experimenting with this new medium, there are basically two ways to get started:

1. *Establish your own site.* Going this route, you would design your site, or contract with someone to do that for you, and then rent space on a computer that is already connected to the high speed networks on the Internet. A listing of several companies in your area that will rent space on their computers, as well as those that can help in the design, can be found on the Internet itself.

   The next step would be to develop a marketing program that would let your customers know:
   - That you are on the Internet.
   - How they can find you.
   - What type of information they can expect to get at your site.

2. *Become part of an existing site.* Under this scenario, you would just pay to be included on someone else's site. You would still have to provide all of the data to be included at your particular site, but you would not have to rent computer space or do nearly as much marketing. You would be at a site that already has people coming to it. For example, a marketer of boating accessories could become part of a site geared to boating, one that has an established user base. An analogy might be the difference between developing, producing, and marketing your own magazine versus running ads in publications that already have a targeted, established readership base. Obviously, the least costly way to find out if print advertising worked would be to run ads in existing publications as opposed to starting your own magazine.

Accountability

As the Internet develops and matures, an element critical to its long-term success will be accountability. There will have to be some form of system in place (just as there is with television, radio, and print) that will measure the extent to which consumers are actually being reached through this form of interactive media. Currently, companies such as A.C. Nielsen and Internet Profiles Corporation (I/PRO) are in the early stages of developing a system to measure how many people are coming to specific sites, who they are, and how much time they spend at that site. That type of information will be important when comparing the actual effectiveness/value of this type of interactive media to other forms of communication.

The next few years should be very exciting years, as more advertisers begin to experiment with this new medium. It will be very interesting to see what direction this new medium takes and to find out if we are both smart enough and creative enough to take advantage of the opportunities this new medium offers.

Media Plan

Media Objectives

Target Audience

Geography

Seasonality

Weighting/Impact Goals
Quantitative

Qualitative

Budget (Optional)

Media Test Objectives (if applicable)

Rationale for Objectives

Media Strategies

Media Mix

Specific Medium Usage

Scheduling

Rationale for Strategies

FORMAT

Media Calendar

YEAR: _____

BROADCAST MONTHS (WEEK BEGINNING MONDAY)

Media	January	February	March	April	May	June	July	August	September	October	November	December

FORMAT

Media Budget

Spending by Medium and Quarter

Company/Product/Service:

Year:

Date:

Medium	1st Quarter ($)	2nd Quarter ($)	3rd Quarter ($)	4th Quarter ($)	Total ($)	Percent %
	_____	_____	_____	_____	_____	_____
Total	$	$	$	$	$	
Percent	%	%	%	%		100%

Spending by Product/Market and Medium

Company/Product/Service:

Year:

Date:

Product/Market	Medium _____						Total Spending by Product/ Market _____
Product/Market	$( ) %	$( ) %	$( ) %	$( ) %	$( ) %	$( ) %	$( ) %
Total Spending by Medium	$ %	$ %	$ %	$ %	$ %	$ %	$ 100%

Step 7: Tactical Marketing Mix Tools

MARKETING BACKGROUND

1 THE BUSINESS REVIEW

<u>Scope</u>
Company Strengths & Weaknesses • Core Competencies • Marketing Capabilities

<u>Product and Market Review</u>
Company & Product Review • Category & Company Sales • Behavior Trends • Pricing • Distribution • Competitive Review

<u>Target Market Effectors</u>
Consumer/Business-to-Business Targets • Product Awareness & Attributes • Trial & Retrial Data

2 PROBLEMS/OPPORTUNITIES

MARKETING PLAN

3 SALES OBJECTIVES

4 TARGET MARKETS AND MARKETING OBJECTIVES

5 PLAN STRATEGIES—Positioning & Marketing

6 COMMUNICATION GOALS

7 TACTICAL MARKETING MIX TOOLS

Product
Branding
Packaging
Pricing

Distribution
Personal Selling/Service
Promotion/Events
Advertising Message

Advertising Media
Merchandising
Publicity

8 MARKETING PLAN BUDGET AND CALENDAR

9 EXECUTION

10 EVALUATION

MERCHANDISING

IN THIS CHAPTER YOU WILL LEARN:

- THE ISSUES AFFECTING A MERCHANDISING PLAN.
- THE VARIOUS NONMEDIA COMMUNICATION VEHICLES USED IN MERCHANDISING.
- HOW TO DEVELOP MERCHANDISING OBJECTIVES AND STRATEGIES.

ONCE YOUR ADVERTISING AND PROMOTION TACTICS ARE DEVELOPED and you have decided how to deliver their message through your media plan, it is time to focus on how merchandising, or nonmedia communication, can enhance the effectiveness of your overall marketing plan. In this chapter we will discuss how to develop a merchandising plan that will deliver the awareness and attitude levels required to fulfill the merchandising communication value goals.

Merchandising is the method used to communicate product information, promotions, and special events, and to reinforce advertising messages through nonmedia communication vehicles. It is a way to make a visual or written statement about your company through a medium other than mass media or without one-on-one personal communication. Such communication methods include brochures, sell sheets, banners, and table tents.

Merchandising Considerations

Four variables should be considered in the merchandising plan: delivery method, geography, timing, and the merchandising's purpose.

Delivery Methods

Like all marketing tools, merchandising vehicles communicate product attributes, positioning, pricing, and promotion information. This communication can be delivered through any of the following methods:

- *Personal sales presentation.* Brochures, sell sheets, catalogs, and other forms of merchandising often are used to enhance a personal sales visit. The material can guide the sales visit, provide visual and factual support, and serve as a reference that can be left behind for the customer or prospect.
- *Point-of-purchase.* In many product categories, over two-thirds of the purchase decisions are made at the point of purchase. For this reason, merchandising displays that enhance the presentation of your product or provide additional information at the point of purchase are useful tools to help affect purchase decisions that are made in-store. Point of purchase merchandising can also include shelf talkers, table tents in restaurants, and banners.
- *Events.* Merchandising is also helpful at special events or company functions where contact with the target market occurs through sales meetings, trade shows, conventions, concerts, and other mass participation events. Banners, product displays, or fliers are commonly used at mass participation events to communicate brand name and product benefits to the target market.

Geography

Your merchandising plan should address where your merchandising programs will be executed. Will they be national, regional, local, or even in selected stores within a market?

Timing

The timing of your merchandising plan is also important. Therefore, the timing of the merchandising execution in relation to the other marketing mix elements must be decided. For example, your plan might require a brochure to be delivered prior to sales visits or after an advertising campaign kick-off. Or, you may want a retail store's featured inventory displayed for the duration of an advertising media blitz.

Merchandising's Purpose

Finally, the merchandising plan must address what the merchandising is being used to accomplish. What marketing tool will the merchandising be assisting? Will you be merchandising product attributes, a new or lower price, a promotion, an advertising message, a personal sell-in presentation?

Developing a Merchandising Plan

Developing a merchandising plan involves two tasks: establishing merchandising objectives and establishing merchandising strategies. A format for you to use in developing the merchandising objectives and strategies is provided at the end of this chapter.

TASK 1

Establish Merchandising Objectives

Your merchandising objectives should include:
- The number of merchandising pieces delivered or displayed at a specific target location(s).
- The geography.
- The timing.
- The merchandising's purpose.

The following are some examples of merchandising objectives:

Achieve placement of the new product display, which communicates the product's benefits, in 40 percent of the grocery stores carrying the product line nationwide in the month of September.

Obtain placement of price promotional tents from June through August in 50 percent of the current accounts in the top 10 markets.

Display four product banners at each event during the concert series in all markets.

TASK 2

Establish Merchandising Strategies

Your merchandising strategies should detail how to achieve your objectives in the following areas:
- The delivery and display method that should be used.
- How to achieve placement of the merchandising elements and what trade incentives are necessary.
- The creative parameters for development of the merchandising materials.

Examples of merchandising strategies include:

Use the personal sales force to deliver the new product brochure during sales presentations.

Obtain placement of the shelf talkers by offering a competitive discount on each case in return for participation in the shelf talker program.

Obtain placement of the brand identification banners by the sales force. Employ a weekly monitoring system to assure that the banners remain in place for the four-week period.

Incorporate visible brand identification in the shelf talkers and highlight the rules of the sweepstakes. An entry pad should be included.

FORMAT

Merchandising

Objectives

Strategies

Rationale

Step 7: Tactical Marketing Mix Tools

1 THE BUSINESS REVIEW

Scope
    Company Strengths & Weaknesses • Core Competencies •
    Marketing Capabilities

Product and Market Review
    Company & Product Review • Category & Company Sales •
    Behavior Trends • Pricing • Distribution • Competitive Review

Target Market Effectors
    Consumer/Business-to-Business Targets • Product Awareness &
    Attributes • Trial & Retrial Data

2 PROBLEMS/OPPORTUNITIES

3 SALES OBJECTIVES

4 TARGET MARKETS AND MARKETING OBJECTIVES

5 PLAN STRATEGIES—Positioning & Marketing

6 COMMUNICATION GOALS

7 TACTICAL MARKETING MIX TOOLS

Product	Distribution	Advertising Media
Branding	Personal Selling/Service	Merchandising
Packaging	Promotion/Events	Publicity
Pricing	Advertising Message	

8 MARKETING PLAN BUDGET AND CALENDAR

9 EXECUTION

10 EVALUATION

MARKETING BACKGROUND

MARKETING PLAN

PUBLICITY *17*

IN THIS CHAPTER YOU WILL LEARN:

- THE VARIOUS COMMUNICATION VEHICLES USED IN PUBLICITY.
- THE ISSUES AFFECTING A PUBLICITY PLAN.
- HOW TO DEVELOP PUBLICITY OBJECTIVES AND STRATEGIES.

THE FINAL TOOL TO CONSIDER IN YOUR MARKETING PLAN is publicity. One facet of public relations, *publicity* is nonpaid media communication that helps build target market awareness and positively affects attitudes toward your product or firm. In a publicity program, your organization provides information to the news media that is used for its news value. Because it uses nonpaid communication through independent news media, it adds a dimension of legitimacy that can't be found in paid advertising.

Obtaining publicity for your firm or product can be difficult, and there are no guarantees regarding placement of your message, if it appears, when it appears, or what is ultimately communicated. But there are some things you can do to help generate positive publicity for your firm. These issues, along with suggestions for developing a publicity plan, are discussed in this chapter.

Publicity can come in many forms, the most common of which are:

- news releases
- feature stories
- exclusives
- opinion pieces
- photos
- public service announcements
- participation in talk shows/local interest programs
- on-line chat rooms
- visibility at conventions, seminars, or public events
- public service announcements

Publicity Considerations

Publicity doesn't just happen. In most instances, positive publicity is the result of a written, well-thought-out plan and a hands-on execution program. As you develop your publicity plan, keep in mind the following considerations:

Publicity is contingent on what is newsworthy. A major task in generating publicity is attracting the attention and interest of the media—the people who decide whether or not your story will be heard or seen by your target market. Be sure your message has a newsworthy element above and beyond the selfish interest of promoting your company or product. A truly successful publicity effort begins with an understanding of each media outlet you are targeting, whom they serve, their editorial style, and what types of publicity materials they consider newsworthy.

Publicity should generate added awareness for your company, product name, and/or key product attributes. Make sure the publicity you receive creates positive awareness. Think carefully about the information you have available for release and how you can enhance its presentation so that the positive attributes come through loud and clear. Ideally, the information should also reinforce the key messages in your marketing communications program.

Always consider and prepare for the potential downside of publicity. One of the disadvantages of publicity is that you lack control over the content. As such, always make an assessment of the potential downside as a part of your planning process and have a contingency plan for responding to negative publicity. If you anticipate problems, try to minimize negative exposure by releasing information in a manner that directly addresses public concerns.

Look for connections between publicity and other tools in your marketing program. Every publicity effort you devise should be examined for its potential value elsewhere in the marketing program. For example, favorable coverage received in an important magazine can be reprinted in quantity (with the publisher's permission) and distributed to salespeople for use as a sales tool, or favorable product reviews from leading media can be cited on packaging or in advertising. Conversely, some companies generate publicity when they create advertising campaigns that are newsworthy because they are controversial or unusual in some way.

Timing is important. Regardless of the type of publicity you are using, the timing of the placement is critical. Does your story rely on a time-sensitive hook, such as reference to a holiday or the start of a certain season? What is the lead time for the various media you are contacting? When are the specific media in need of newsworthy information?

Before incorporating a publicity segment into your marketing plan, ask yourself these questions:

- Do your objectives, marketing strategies, and subject matter lend themselves well to publicity?
- Do you need and want the added dimension of legitimacy to your overall communications effort?
- Do you need the additional media weight without media dollar investment, knowing there is no certainty to the amount (if any) and type of publicity you will receive?
- Knowing its benefits and limitations, are you willing to make the investment in time, either through company staff or an outside agency, to generate publicity? Is there a likelihood that this investment will be worth it?

Developing a Publicity Plan

As with most of the other marketing tools we have discussed, developing a publicity plan involves establishing objectives and strategies. We recommend you conduct a thorough review of the problems and opportunities, pertinent marketing strategies, and communication value goals before you begin. A format for you to use in developing the publicity objectives and strategies is provided at the end of this chapter.

TASK 1

Establish Publicity Objectives

Publicity objectives should be specific, measurable, and relate to a specific time period. However, since publicity is not a paid, controlled message, it does not usually focus on affecting a target market behavior directly; rather, it focuses on making the target market aware of the product or company in a positive light. In this manner, publicity "softens" the market so that prospects are more likely to respond to your advertising or promotional offers. Sometimes publicity does generate inquiries directly from your prospects, though the source of those inquiries may or may not be easy to measure.

Publicity objectives should address the following:
- The specific purpose of the publicity effort (i.e., announce a grand opening, gain additional exposure for a new product, generate PSA support).
- The specific target market (medium and audience).
- The time period and marketplace.
- The expected level of exposure, by medium, to be generated from the publicity effort.

The following are examples of publicity objectives:

> In the next year, achieve maximum exposure among women who sew for the grand opening events through the television, radio, and newspaper media in each of the 20 DMA markets.

> Obtain coverage from a minimum of two television stations and a minimum of three radio stations.

> Obtain coverage from a minimum of one newspaper before and after the event.

| **TASK 2** |
| *Establish Publicity Strategies* |

Publicity strategies describe how to achieve the media coverage delineated in the publicity objectives. Address the following in formulating your strategies:
- What newsworthy material you have and how the material aligns with the interests of both your media targets and your product targets.
- Types of publicity to use.
- Ways to maximize the value of your publicity by incorporating it elsewhere in the marketing program.

Also consider the following:

> *Make sure the news media are thoroughly aware of the event or product's news.* For example, you may write news releases and deliver them in a memorable way. The Coors Downtown Beach Party news releases were delivered by local personnel equipped with flippers, scuba masks, and surfboards.

> *Detail a specific follow-up procedure* to make certain the news releases weren't forgotten or lost and, most importantly, to ensure that they will be used in some manner.

> *Develop ways to tie the media into the publicity event itself,* or obtain a third party to help legitimize your requests for publicity support. For example, provide cosponsorship packages to media and charities in return for publicity. The media and charity cosponsors become cosponsors on all-paid, printed advertising in return for predetermined publicity requirements both prior to and during the event.

> *Provide a unique twist to interest the media in providing publicity.* This can be communicated in a news release or by phone to the media to pique their interest such as informing the media of a national celebrity making a personal appearance at a local store where you are demonstrating your product.

> Where possible, *include memorable but appropriate product identification.*

As an example, assume you are developing publicity strategies for a series of benefit concerts with the following publicity objectives:

> Achieve maximum radio and newspaper exposure in each market among young adults 18–24 for the five concerts to be staged within the next year in five to-be-determined DMA markets.

At a minimum, obtain coverage from two of the top five young-adult radio stations.

At a minimum, obtain coverage from a major daily before and after the event.

Potential publicity strategies would be:

Prepare four different news releases, each with a different newsworthy slant on the event, to be delivered via mail and personally before and after the event.

Stress the various benefits to the charity in the news release, particularly how important the event is in regard to the charity's yearly fundraising.

Have the local press interview the concert performers and the local charity spokesperson, incorporating company identification at the interview site.

FORMAT

Publicity

Objectives

Strategies

Rationale

Step 8: Marketing Plan Budget and Calendar

MARKETING BACKGROUND

1 THE BUSINESS REVIEW

Scope
- Company Strengths & Weaknesses • Core Competencies • Marketing Capabilities

Product and Market Review
- Company & Product Review • Category & Company Sales • Behavior Trends • Pricing • Distribution • Competitive Review

Target Market Effectors
- Consumer/Business-to-Business Targets • Product Awareness & Attributes • Trial & Retrial Data

2 PROBLEMS/OPPORTUNITIES

MARKETING PLAN

3 SALES OBJECTIVES

4 TARGET MARKETS AND MARKETING OBJECTIVES

5 PLAN STRATEGIES—Positioning & Marketing

6 COMMUNICATION GOALS

7 TACTICAL MARKETING MIX TOOLS

Product	Distribution	Advertising Media
Branding	Personal Selling/Service	Merchandising
Packaging	Promotion/Events	Publicity
Pricing	Advertising Message	

8 MARKETING PLAN BUDGET AND CALENDAR

9 EXECUTION

10 EVALUATION

MARKETING BUDGET, PAYBACK ANALYSIS, AND MARKETING CALENDAR

IN THIS CHAPTER YOU WILL LEARN:

- HOW TO SET A MARKETING BUDGET USING THREE BASIC BUDGET METHODS.
- HOW TO DEVELOP A PAYBACK ANALYSIS USING TWO METHODOLOGIES.
- HOW TO DEVELOP AN INTEGRATED MARKETING CALENDAR.

N OW THAT YOU HAVE COMPLETED THE OBJECTIVES AND STRATEGIES for each marketing mix tool, three steps remain before you can call your marketing plan complete. In this chapter we will discuss how to:

1. Develop a *marketing budget*, which provides estimated costs associated with each marketing tool used in the plan.
2. Use a *payback analysis*, which helps you determine if the results of your marketing plan will generate the required revenues to meet sales and profit goals. If the payback indicates that your plan will not allow you to meet sales and profit goals, you may need to revise your budget and/or your marketing plan objectives, strategies, and executions.
3. Develop a *marketing calendar*, which provides a summary of all marketing activities in one visual presentation.

Developing a Marketing Budget

In our experience, it seems there are never enough marketing dollars—there are no unlimited marketing budgets. For this reason, it is important to determine priorities for the plan, along with corresponding executional costs for the various marketing activities. Then, based on the priorities and associated costs, you can pare back the activities to meet the optimum budget level, striking a balance between what needs to be accomplished and what you can realistically afford.

TASK 1

Set Preliminary Budget Using Task Method

We recommend you begin your budgeting process using the *task method* as the first step. With this method, you set a budget (without bias) based not on what the industry category or key competition is spending but on what needs to be accomplished for your product. This method attempts to develop a budget that will adequately support the marketing mix activity in your plan to achieve the sales and marketing objectives. To arrive at the total dollar budget, you must estimate the costs for each marketing tool execution involved in the plan. The assumption is that, through a disciplined planning process, challenging yet realistic sales objectives were established, along with a marketing plan to meet those objectives. Thus, the budget will allow the objectives to be met in an efficient manner. An aggressive marketing plan will result in a more aggressive budget utilizing this method. The caveat is that there is no real test of affordability or profitability; that is why a payout analysis is applied to the marketing budget.

TASK 2

Benchmark Using Percent-of-Sales Method

The second step in developing a budget for your marketing plan is to bench-mark your marketing budget total using the *percent-of-sales method*. Review the amount spent on advertising/media, promotion, and total marketing by other firms in your industry as a percent of sales. Usually, an industry standard exists that will provide the average percent of sales. This standard will account for the advertising/media budget, the promotion budget, and some-times even the total marketing budget.

The major disadvantage with this method is that it creates a situation where sales deter-mine marketing expenditures. However, the whole idea behind a disciplined campaign de-velopment is the belief that marketing affects sales. When sales decline and there are problems to be solved, there is less money available to solve them with the percent-of-sales method.

The percent-of-sales method makes most sense if used as a way to determine whether your task method budget is realistic. Additionally, if your firm has no real history with the effects of marketing and specific tactical tools, then the percent-of-sales method will act as a way to allocate expenditures that should be fairly consistent with industry standards. You can find the industry advertising-to-sales ratios for the standard industrial classifications (SIC) codes within a published report by Schonfeld and Associates. *Advertising Age* also pub-lishes the advertising-to-sales ratio of the top 100 advertisers each year. Another source is *Fairchild Fact Files*, a publication that provides information on individual consumer industries. Annual reports and 10-Ks are another excellent source for this information.

TASK 3

Estimate Competitors' Budgets Using Competitive Method

Next, estimate the sales and marketing budgets of the leading competitive firms and compare those estimates to your sales and marketing budget. This *competitive method* might allow your firm to match or beat specific competi-tive expenditures, helping to assure that you remain competitive in the mar-ketplace. The advantage of this method is that it provides the potential for an immediate response to competitive actions. The disadvantages are that it is difficult to estimate competitors' budgets and it does not take into consid-eration the inherent potential of your firm based upon data developed from the business re-view. Utilizing this method alone, you may be restricting the actual potential of your firm based upon your competitors' lack of insight and marketing ability. However, as with the per-cent-of-sales method, you can use the budget derived from this method as a means of com-parison to the task method to arrive at your final budget.

TASK 4

Finalize Budget Using a Combination of Methods

If the data are available, we recommend using a combination of all three steps in finalizing your marketing budget. First, use the task method to provide you with a budget that will be your best chance to achieve the stated objec-tives in your own marketing plan. As the budget is based solely upon what is required to provide for the success of your individual marketing plan, the task method is not as biased or as limiting as other methods. Product his-tory and industry averages play a lesser role in the budgeting process. However, if the task method budget varies substantially from the percent-of-sales method budget, you need to re-view the reasons why your plan requires either substantially greater or fewer expenditures than the industry average. If, for example, you are introducing a new product, you may be required to spend at greater levels than the industry average to obtain initial trial of the new product and still maintain sales of your existing lines.

Second, use the percent-of-sales method to provide a guideline, or rough, budget figure based upon the historical spending of your product and of the marketplace. Used properly, the percent-of-sales budget will help provide insight into whether your task-generated bud-get is too low or too high based upon the experiences of similar companies in your industry.

Finally, consider using the competitive budgeting method as a device to help you respond to competitive pressures in the marketplace. If your company is consistently spending less

EXHIBIT 18.1   **Heartland 2000 Marketing Plan Budget**

Rationale

The budget for the fiscal year is designed to:

1. Provide support necessary to meet the aggressive sales goal of increasing store-for-store sales 15 percent over the previous year.
2. Provide support necessary to meet the systemwide marketing objectives of:

    Increase existing customer purchasing rates from 1.2 to 2 purchases per year.

    Initiate new trial, increasing the customer base 20 percent above current levels of 5,000 active customers per store.

Marketing Mix Tool (Nov. 5, 1999)	$M	Percent of Total Budget
Media		
Television (6 markets)	$350.0	31.8%
900 TRPs :30s		
900 TRPs :10s		
Newspaper (12 markets)	202.0	18.3
30, ⅓ page insertions		
Direct mail (12 markets/24 stores)	120.0	10.9
10,000 per store per drop		
Postage (4 drops per year)		
Media total	$672.0	61.0%
Production		
Television	$100.0	9.1
2:30 and 3:10 spots (to be used for two years)		
Newspaper	18.0	1.6
Type, photography/illustration for 30 ads		
Direct mail	100.0	9.1
Four direct mail drops, 240M pieces per drop		
Photography, type, printing		
Production total	$218.0	19.8%
Promotion		
Redemption cost	$120.0	10.9
Redemption cost of $5 off coupon in two of the four mailings.		
Estimated response of 5 percent		
5 percent × 480,000 mailing = 24,000		
24,000 × $5 = $120,000		
Media		
Media costs calculated in media section		
Production		
Product costs calculated in production section		
Promotion total	$120.0	10.9%
Merchandising		
Store signage	$30.0	2.7
20 signs per store per month to support planned media promotions and in-store promotions		
Point-of-purchase displays	10.0	0.9
Two p-o-p displays per store to support the April and December promotions		
Merchandising total	$40.0	3.6%
Selling Costs		
Sales incentive programs	$20.0	1.8
Sales total	$20.0	1.8%
Research Costs		
Market research	$32.0	2.9
Marketwide	$20.0	
In-store	$12.0	
Research total	$32.0	2.9%
Total budget estimate	$1,102.0	100.0%
Total sales estimate	$24,000.0	
Marketing budget as a percent of sales	4.6 %	

than a major competitor and is losing market share while this competitor is gaining market share, then you might want to develop a budget that allows you to be more competitive from a spending standpoint. There is not much any marketer can do, no matter how sophisticated, if continually and dramatically outspent by the competition.

TASK 5

Prepare Budget Document

When preparing your final budget, begin with a written rationale that outlines what the budget is designed to accomplish. The rationale covers:
- Restatement of the sales objectives.
- Marketing objectives.
- Geography parameters.
- Plan time frame.

Following the rationale is a breakout of planned expenses by line item under each expense category. The budget line-item categories include all applicable marketing mix tools and any other miscellaneous marketing expense items, such as research. The example shown in Exhibit 18.1 can serve as a prototype for your budgeting process. (A worksheet is provided at the end of this chapter.) The only difference between this budget and one you may develop is that your budget may have more line item expense categories. For example, if you are developing new products, there will be a new product development expense category. If you include publicity in your plan, this marketing tool will also have a budget line item. Exhibit 18.2 shows how you can compare your budget to that of the previous year, industry average, and the competition. A similar worksheet is provided at the end of the chapter.

Developing a Payback Analysis

An important part of any budget is the payback analysis. The *payback analysis* provides you with a projection of whether the marketing plan or specific marketing programs in the plan will generate revenues in excess of expenses. The payback analysis should review both short-run and long-run projected sales and associated costs to estimate the initial program payback in the first year and the projected payback in the second and third years.

If the payout analysis determines that the marketing plan dollar investment cannot be justified, a rethinking and adjustment of sales objectives and marketing plan objectives, strategies, use of the marketing mix tools, and budget expenditures is needed. After this is accomplished, another payout analysis is needed to determine if the new plan will meet payout expectations.

We recommend using one of two payback analysis methodologies: contribution to fixed costs or gross margin to net sales.

Contribution-to-Fixed-Costs Payback Analysis

Retailers, service organizations, and sometimes manufacturers use a *contribution-to-fixed-cost payback analysis method*. It focuses on two sets of figures: sales and revenues and all direct marketing costs associated with the sale of the product to the consumer.

Contribution-to-fixed-costs payback results are determined by first calculating estimated gross sales and then subtracting cost of goods sold to derive a *gross-profit-on-sales* figure. Next, all variable selling expenses directly associated with the sales of the product (selling costs, advertising and media expenditures, etc.) are subtracted from the gross profit figure to provide a *contribution-to-fixed-cost* figure. This method can be used to analyze individual marketing programs or a whole year's plan.

The contribution-to-fixed-costs method is utilized because it accurately demonstrates the results of the marketing executions. Only the revenues and expenses directly attributed to each marketing effort are used in the analysis. By doing this, you can judge each marketing program on its own merits and on the basis of whether it will contribute to help cover the company's fixed costs. The short-term objective is to make sure that the marketing programs

EXHIBIT 18.2 Heartland Marketing Plan Budget Comparison

Marketing Mix Tool	$M	Percent of Sales
Total Budget Compared to Industry Average and Previous Year		
Marketing as a percent of sales per plan	1,102	4.6
Marketing as a percent of sales per industry average		4.0
Index company budget percentage to industry average	115*	
Index company budget to previous year ($1,102M/$1,000M)	110	
Total Planned Budget Compared to Competition†		
Total planned budget for Company	1,102	4.6
Total estimated budget Competitor A	2,000	4.5
Total estimated budget Competitor B	1,000	5.5

*In this example the planned budget would be 15 points above the industry average for marketing as a percent of sales and 10 points above the previous year's plan.

†If the data exists, we recommend that this analysis be accomplished on an individual market basis and a national basis. This will help demonstrate localized geographic spending policies of competitors.

generate enough sales to adequately cover the direct marketing costs necessary to generate the sales. The longer-term objective is to develop programs that cover both direct marketing costs and fixed overhead, resulting in a profit to the firm.

There are few limitations to this methodology for most companies. However, the question of capacity needs to be addressed. If, for example, you brew beer and you are at full capacity, you would need to make sure that the revenues from all of the marketing programs together cover both total variable marketing expenses and total fixed overhead. However, unless there is the issue of full capacity, individual marketing programs should be judged only on their ability to cover variable expenses and contribute to fixed overhead; the overhead will be there whether the program is executed or not. Thus, if there is excess capacity, it is always better to execute an additional program that covers the variable costs associated with the program and contributes some additional revenue toward covering some of the fixed costs.

Exhibit 18.3 provides a contribution-to-fixed-costs payback example for a start-up, direct mail/response program for an existing firm, and Exhibit 18.4 shows an analysis for a retail chain considering the implementation of its yearly marketing plan. The latter analysis determines whether projected sales will cover marketing expenditures and allow for a contribution to fixed costs and overhead. A worksheet for your own contribution-to-fixed-costs analysis is provided at the end of this chapter.

Gross-Margin-to-Net-Sales Payback Analysis

For package goods marketers, payback calculations are sometimes analyzed slightly differently than for retailers. The gross margin is often defined as covering advertising, promotion, and profit, and it is referred to as *gross margin to net sales* or, sometimes, as *advertising, promotion, and profit (AP&P)*. For example, if there is a 40 percent gross margin, 40 percent of all sales would cover advertising and promotion costs (consumer and trade) and provide the profit. Furthermore, 60 percent of the sales would cover all allocated fixed costs (plant, equipment, etc.), as well as the variable selling costs (selling costs, salaries, raw material needed to produce product, etc.).

The example shown in Exhibit 18.5 utilizes the gross-margin-to-net-sales analysis payback methodology. We are assuming a 40 percent margin on a new product. The payback analysis is projected for three years in order to determine both the short-term and the longer-term profitability for the new product. In this example the product is projected to pay back

EXHIBIT 18.3 **Contribution-to-Fixed-Overhead Payback Analysis for a Direct Response Marketing Program**

	Estimated Response		
	Low	Medium	High
Projected Mailing to 10,000 Customers	1 Percent	2.5 Percent	5 Percent
Responses	100	250	500
Gross sales ($26 per order)	$2,600	$6,500	$13,000
Less refunds (5 percent of sales)	130	325	650
Less cancellations (2 percent of sales)	52	130	260
Net sales	2,418	6,045	12,090
Less cost of goods sold (40 percent)	967	2,418	4,836
Gross profit	1,451	3,627	7,254
Less selling expense			
Catalog production mailing (@ 20 cents per piece)	2,000	2,000	2,000
List rental	N/C	N/C	N/C
Photography	N/C	N/C	N/C
Type	N/C	N/C	N/C
Boxes, forms, supplies (2 percent of gross)	52	130	260
Order processing ($3.20/order)	320	800	1,600
Return postage	N/C	N/C	N/C
Telephone	10	10	10
Credit card (30 percent credit card sales with 3 percent charge from store's bank)	23	59	117
Total Expenses	$2,405	$2,999	$3,987
Contribution to Fixed Costs	$ (954)	$ 626	$3,267

EXHIBIT 18.4 **Contribution-to-Fixed-Overhead Payback Analysis for a Retail Marketing Program**

Assumptions

The plan will result in a 10 percent store-for-store increase in sales over last year.
Cost of goods sold will average 50 percent throughout the year.

Nine stores	$M	$M
Sales	$7,920.0	
Less cost of goods sold	3,960.0	
Gross profit		$3,960.0
Less variable costs:		
Media	$316.8	
Production costs	31.7	
Promotion costs	50.0	
Merchandising	30.0	
Selling	25.0	
Research	20.0	
Public relations/miscellaneous	5.0	
Total marketing mix tools		478.5
Contribution to fixed costs		$3,481.5
Fixed costs		3,081.5
Profit before taxes		$ 400.0

EXHIBIT 18.5 **Gross-Margin-to-Net-Sales Payback Analysis for a New Package Goods Product**

Assumptions:
$100MM product category, with growth rate of 10 percent per year.
Three competing brands in the category and miscellaneous private labels.
Introduction of new product at an expected margin of 40 percent.

	Year 1 Projections	Year 2 Projections	Year 3 Projections
Net sales	$10.0MM	$12.0MM	$13.0MM
Gross margin (40%)	4.0	4.8	5.2
Less promotion	3.0	2.5	1.5
Less advertising	2.0	1.5	1.5
Profit/(loss)	(1.0)	0.8	2.2

sometime early in year three. A worksheet for your own gross-margin-to-net-sales analysis is provided at the end of this chapter.

Developing a Marketing Calendar

After the marketing plan budget and payback have been completed, it is time to summarize the plan on a single page. This summary should be in the form of a *marketing calendar*. When completed, the marketing calendar will serve as a visual summary of the marketing plan for the specific designated period or, more likely, for the coming year.

A marketing calendar should contain the following elements:

- Headings, including product/service/store name, time period, date prepared, and a geographic reference (national, regional, group of markets or tier) or individual market name.
- Visual summary of the marketing program week by week, outlining all marketing tool executions and including all other marketing-related activities such as research.
- Visual summary of media weight levels by week.
- Separate marketing calendar for markets with substantial geographic differences and for test markets.

Exhibit 18.6 shows a prototype for you to follow when developing your own marketing calendar. A retail chain plan is used for the example. A blank calendar format is provided at the end of this chapter.

EXHIBIT 18.6   Marketing Calendar for a Retail Chain

2000 National Marketing Calendar

Monday (Bdcst) Dates

December 1, 1999

Media	January	February	March	April	May	June	July	August	September	October	November	December
	27 3 10 17 24	31 7 14 21 28	6 13 20 27	3 10 17 24	1 8 15 22 29	5 12 19 26	3 10 17 24	31 7 14 21 28	4 11 18 25	2 9 16 23 30	6 13 20 27	4 11 18 25

Marketing Programs

On-Going Price/Item

Major Promotions — Clearance Sale — Half-Price Sale — Clearance Sale — Anniversary Sale — Thanksgiving — Holiday

Media Support

Television (50%::10s/50%::30s)
12 Weeks of 200 GRPs

Newspapers—1/3-Page Ads
18 Insertions

Newspapers—1/2-Page Ads
18 Insertions

Direct Mail—4 Mailings
10,000 Per Store Per Mailing

Nonmedia Activities

Point-of-Purchase Displays

In-Store Signage

In-Store Seminars

In-Store Only Price Promotion

In-Store Volume Discount

Other

Research (Market & In-Store) — Market — In-Store

©1999 by Telmar Information Services

Marketing Plan Budget (Date Prepared)

	($M)	Percent of Total Budget
Marketing Mix Tool		
Media		
Television		
Newspaper		
Radio		
Direct mail		
Outdoor		
Other		
Total		
Production		
Television		
Newspaper		
Radio		
Direct mail		
Outdoor		
Other		
Total		
Product/Branding/Packaging		
Total		
Personal Selling/Operations		
Total		
Promotion		
Redemption cost		
Media support		
Production		
Total		
Merchandising		
Production		
Total		
Publicity		
Total		
Research		
Total		
Miscellaneous		
Total		
Grand Total		

WORKSHEET

Marketing Plan Budget Comparison

	$M	Percent of Sales

Total Budget Compared to Industry Average and Previous Year
Marketing as a percent of sales per plan
Marketing as a percent of sales per industry average
Index company budget to industry average
Index company budget to previous year

Total Planned Budget Compared to Competition
Total planned budget for company
Total estimated budget for Competitor A
Total estimated budget for Competitor B
Total estimated budget for Competitor C

WORKSHEET

Contribution to Fixed Overhead

Payback Analysis
Assumptions

Sales
Less cost of goods sold
   Gross profit
Less:
   Media
   Production costs
   Promotion costs
   Merchandising
   Selling
   Research
   Public relations/miscellaneous
     Total marketing mix tools
Contribution to fixed costs
Fixed costs
Profit before taxes

Gross Margin to Net Sales

Payback Analysis
Assumptions

	Year 1 Projections	Year 2 Projections	Year 3 Projections
Net sales			
Gross margin			
Less promotion			
Less advertising			
Profit/loss			

YEAR: _____

MARKETING CALENDAR

Media	January	February	March	April	May	June	July	August	September	October	November	December
MARKETING PROGRAMS:												
MEDIA ACTIVITIES:												
NONMEDIA ACTIVITIES:												

Step 9: Execution

MARKETING BACKGROUND

1 THE BUSINESS REVIEW

Scope
Company Strengths & Weaknesses • Core Competencies •
Marketing Capabilities

Product and Market Review
Company & Product Review • Category & Company Sales •
Behavior Trends • Pricing • Distribution • Competitive Review

Target Market Effectors
Consumer/Business-to-Business Targets • Product Awareness &
Attributes • Trial & Retrial Data

2 PROBLEMS/OPPORTUNITIES

MARKETING PLAN

3 SALES OBJECTIVES

4 TARGET MARKETS AND MARKETING OBJECTIVES

5 PLAN STRATEGIES—Positioning & Marketing

6 COMMUNICATION GOALS

7 TACTICAL MARKETING MIX TOOLS

Product	Distribution	Advertising Media
Branding	Personal Selling/Service	Merchandising
Packaging	Promotion/Events	Publicity
Pricing	Advertising Message	

8 MARKETING PLAN BUDGET AND CALENDAR

9 EXECUTION

10 EVALUATION

PLAN EXECUTION

19

IN THIS CHAPTER YOU WILL LEARN:

- WHAT THOROUGH EXECUTION OF A MARKETING PLAN ENCOMPASSES AND WHY IT IS IMPORTANT.
- THE KEY STEPS TO SUCCESSFUL MARKETING PLAN EXECUTION.

YOU'VE COMPLETED YOUR MARKETING PLAN. From the business review to the objectives, strategies, and tactical tools, all the elements are in place. It's been reviewed and approved, and the budget is authorized. Now you must execute your plan in the marketplace.

Webster's defines *execute* as "to carry out fully; put completely into effect." By its very definition then, *execution* ("the act or process of executing") implies comprehensiveness and thoroughness—attention to details. The genius of successful marketing plan execution is in those details.

A truly integrated marketing plan is greater than the sum of its parts, as the effect of each element is enhanced by the impact of the other elements. A salesperson, for example, has a greater chance of success calling on a prospect who has already heard of the salesperson's company through advertising because part of the selling process has already begun—awareness has already started to build. It is attention to detail in every aspect of implementation that helps assure the synergistic effect of all the marketing plan activities will take place.

Successful marketing plan execution generally requires the coordination of many people and resources. Participation and support are required of many areas, both within and outside the company. Ongoing follow-up with all participants is essential to ensure that they:

- Understand their role and the importance of their contribution to the overall marketing effort.
- Have what they need to do their part in "making things happen."
- Are actually doing what needs to be done.
- Receive feedback on the results of their activities, as well as on the overall marketing effort.

In this chapter we will discuss the keys to successful execution of the marketing plan. These are:

- Reviewing and understanding all elements of the plan.
- Developing activity lists for the first six months of the plan.
- Communicating the plan to key internal and external groups.
- Staying committed to the plan.
- Receiving top management support.

Reviewing and Understanding All Elements of the Plan

No doubt some time will pass between submission of the marketing plan document for review and approval and the point at which you receive the go-ahead and budget authorization. No matter what this interval is, you should review the plan to be sure you:

1. *Have adequate resources in place and committed to carrying out each plan activity.*
   Allocation of supporting resources will have been addressed in the planning and budget approval process. So, as execution begins, the marketing plan activities are not a surprise; rather, they are confirmation of specific tactics designed to respond to the input received. This check is to be sure that those commitments have not been changed and that your need for them remains a high enough priority to accomplish the objectives within the time frame called for by the plan.
2. *Understand the lead time necessary for everyone who needs to participate in each executional element.*
   Generally, more time is better. However, beware the danger (rare though it is) of too much lead time for a project. This can allow other, more pressing assignments to interfere. Also, maintaining energy and enthusiasm for the work over an extended period of time can be difficult and may lead to inefficiencies and "re-starts."
   A good guideline is that you should always begin working at least three to six months in advance of the date on which a program or tactical project must be implemented, six months (or more) in advance for major executional programs and communication campaigns. And the three-month or six-month lead time needs to take into account the time necessary to presell and inform all those who need to participate. A promotion developed for consumers that will be executed by the trade target market or a dealer network needs to be developed in time to allow communication to the dealers, giving them time to plan and stock accordingly.
3. *Understand completely and in detail what each department, vendor, etc., needs in order to execute the element(s) of the plan for which they are responsible and the time they will require.*
   As you review each activity, if you can't answer the executional needs and time requirements with certainty, you must address them immediately. Even if you are confident about the processes and timetables, you will want to confirm these when you communicate with those involved.

Developing Activity Lists
Begin with a summary list of all the major activities covered during the first six months of the marketing plan. You will already have prepared an annual marketing calendar showing these activities. A format like the following can be used to begin to provide more detail:

Major Marketing Activities
January–June 2000
Identification, Responsibility, and Due Date

Activity	Responsibility of	Due Date
1. Develop marketing information system	MIS	01/03
2. Assign marketing services staff	Mktg Dir.	01/03
3. Assign key accounts for phone contact	Mktg Dir.	02/15
4. Develop and implement a survey for customer service and sales staffs regarding customer service	Mktg Mgr.	02/15
5. Develop three inserts for publication advertising	Mktg Mgr./Agency	03/15

For each of the major activities, develop a detailed list of all the tasks that need to be completed to accomplish the given activity, along with due dates. Update this list on a monthly basis so that it always covers at least six months (or longer as projects dictate).

Once these activity lists are completed, you have the structure and outline for the next steps.

Communicating the Plan

Just as you have consumer and end-user target audiences with whom you ultimately need to communicate, you also have a number of important internal and external target groups with whom you must communicate in order to execute the marketing plan. Many of the same considerations that you will give to develop end-user communications should be given to the communications with each of these groups—message content, tone, communication vehicle, and frequency. Your audiences for these communications fall into two general groups: key individuals within your organization (company) and those within the distribution channels (noncompany).

Internal Communication. Everyone within an organization, either directly or indirectly, impacts the company's marketing efforts, since everyone contributes in some way to delivering the products or services being marketed. So, the staff as a whole must understand what the overall marketing program is, what their role is in its execution, and why it is important.

You also need the cooperation of various departments throughout your company to implement the marketing plan, including field sales, telemarketing, and MIS groups. Key personnel will include home office as well as field staff.

Ideally, try to have an initial personal meeting with key individuals, and subsequently with their staff members as needed, to review the activities with which you need their help and involvement and that they have the authority to accomplish. These meetings also give you an opportunity to confirm what information each area will require and the time necessary to complete the tasks being discussed. It is essential that these communications be clear, specific, and concise and that everyone understand and agree to what is expected of them and when.

External Communication. Noncompany staff, such as wholesalers, dealers, brokers, franchisees, and retail trade, are the other group that must be included in marketing plan communications. Without commitment from these channels to participate in the marketing program through carrying product, promoting in-store, etc., effective marketing execution isn't possible.

Because they are not part of your company, these individuals need to be persuaded that what you are asking them to do will enhance their business and will do so better than your competition—and certainly better than doing nothing at all. Communications with this group need to focus on the contribution your product or service will make to the profitability of their enterprise.

Clearly, commitment to carry and promote your product, participate in a given promotion, etc., carries with it the obligation on your part to deliver product and promotional materials, as well as other services like field support, when promised and as needed.

Ongoing Follow-up

A disciplined system of regular, ongoing follow-up with all the individuals involved in implementation is necessary to ensure successful execution of the marketing plan.

In addition to following up, you must also communicate results of the marketing efforts to these individuals. This allows you to show your appreciation for their help and contribution, and to build cooperation in the future.

Staying Committed to the Plan

It is easy to make decisions and do things without regard to the plan. The plan must be looked upon and embraced as a *working document*, guiding all of the marketing decisions you make during the period of the plan. If opportunities or ideas are brought up throughout the year (and they will be), they should be evaluated based on the plan that is being executed, which was designed to achieve very specific objectives. Focus is the key to keeping resources and attention committed to the task at hand: achieving the objectives detailed in the marketing plan. Review the plan, particularly the positioning, frequently.

Receiving Top Management Support

If you have completed a thorough, comprehensive marketing plan, odds are you did so through providing strong, ongoing leadership and the driving energy to complete the task. And, you had the support of your organization's leadership. Top executive involvement, support, and visibility are equally essential in the implementation of the plan.

Top management's support and sponsorship need to be visible when the implementation is kicked off and throughout the year in the form of regular reports on status and evaluation of efforts. As discussed above, execution requires the efforts and contributions of a number of different departments throughout the company. Management's involvement and active endorsement help assure that the cooperation and support needed from these departments will be provided in a timely and effective manner. Without this leadership support, successful execution will be difficult, if not impossible.

Step 10: Evaluation

MARKETING BACKGROUND

1 THE BUSINESS REVIEW

Scope
Company Strengths & Weaknesses • Core Competencies • Marketing Capabilities

Product and Market Review
Company & Product Review • Category & Company Sales • Behavior Trends • Pricing • Distribution • Competitive Review

Target Market Effectors
Consumer/Business-to-Business Targets • Product Awareness & Attributes • Trial & Retrial Data

2 PROBLEMS/OPPORTUNITIES

MARKETING PLAN

3 SALES OBJECTIVES

4 TARGET MARKETS AND MARKETING OBJECTIVES

5 PLAN STRATEGIES—Positioning & Marketing

6 COMMUNICATION GOALS

7 TACTICAL MARKETING MIX TOOLS

Product	Distribution	Advertising Media
Branding	Personal Selling/Service	Merchandising
Packaging	Promotion/Events	Publicity
Pricing	Advertising Message	

8 MARKETING PLAN BUDGET AND CALENDAR

9 EXECUTION

10 EVALUATION

PLAN EVALUATION

20

IN THIS CHAPTER YOU WILL LEARN:

- HOW TO EVALUATE THE OVERALL EFFECTIVENESS OF A MARKETING PLAN.
- HOW TO EVALUATE A MARKETING PLAN USING SALES TREND COMPARISON METHODS.
- HOW TO EVALUATE A MARKETING PLAN USING PRE- AND POSTEXECUTION RESEARCH.
- HOW TO STRUCTURE THE SALES EVALUATION PROCESS.

ONCE YOUR MARKETING PLAN HAS BEEN PUT INTO PRACTICE, you need to evaluate it. The evaluation process allows you to assess the success of the marketing plan, provides feedback with which to make modifications during the execution of the plan, and provides a database from which to make strategic decisions for next year's plan. In this chapter we will discuss evaluation methods that are completed after the plan has been executed. These include evaluating overall effectiveness, comparing sales trends, and comparing pre- and postexecution primary research. Testing, a type of evaluation performed prior to a broad-scale execution of the marketing plan, will be discussed in Chapter 21.

Overall Effectiveness

On an overall basis, a marketing plan's effectiveness can be measured by comparing your original sales and profit objectives, marketing objectives, and communication goals with actual results. A comparison of projected to actual sales and profit is self-explanatory. Marketing objectives can be evaluated via information on customer retention, new customer trial, store visits, dollars per transaction, and the like. You can also conduct surveys to evaluate target market behavior (for the marketing objectives) and target market awareness and attitude (for communication goals). The evaluation of the overall plan will tell you "how well you did."

On a more detailed level, each tactical tool's effectiveness can be evaluated vis-à-vis the measurable objective(s) you established for each. In addition, although more difficult to do, you can also attempt to measure in a directional manner whether each tool fulfilled its individual awareness and attitude communication goals. The tool evaluation will tell you "why" the plan did or did not work—what generated the bulk of the success or caused the plan not to achieve the predetermined sales and profits.

Sales Trend Comparisons

While the previous evaluation was *plan* based, a sales trend comparison compares current sales with the previous year's sales *prior to, during,* and *after* any given marketing execution. Sales are analyzed prior to the promotion period to determine if there was a downward, upward, or flat sales trend as compared to the previous year's sales. Sales are also compared to last year's both during and after the execution period. In analyzing the preperiod, the execution period, and the postperiod separately, added insight is provided on the effect of the individual test or marketing execution. For example, if sales were trending down prior to the marketing execution. Even a small increase during the marketing execution period would mean that the marketing execution might have helped reverse a negative trend. Then, in analyzing sales after the marketing execution period, you can begin to determine if the marketing execution had any long-term effect on sales. If the marketing execution was designed to gain new users or trial of the product, the sales results in the months after the execution will help determine if repeat purchase or continuity of purchase was achieved.

Sales trends can be compared with control markets or without control markets.

Sales Trend Analysis with Control Markets

This methodology utilizes *control markets*—markets with no marketing execution or markets receiving a mainline marketing execution—to compare against test markets receiving a new marketing execution or the marketing execution you want to analyze.

Control markets serve as a benchmark to determine whether the specific marketing execution was responsible for sales increases in the test markets. If the analysis demonstrates that sales and profits in test markets that received advertising were substantially above control markets that received no advertising, then the decision should be made to consider expanding advertising to other markets.

Control and test markets should be similar in terms of sales volume, sales trending, distribution levels, penetration/marketing coverage, size, demographic profile, and other market and media characteristics. Also, there should be a minimum of two test and two control markets to guard against any anomalies.

Sales Trend Analysis Without Control Markets

Whenever possible, we recommend using the sales trend analysis with control markets. However, for many businesses, control markets are not available because the business is located solely in one market, in a minimal number of markets, or there are no control markets comparable in their make-up to the test markets. In other situations, businesses need to analyze results of a marketing execution that was implemented across all markets. In these situations, a sales trend analysis without control markets is used. Sales are analyzed before, during, and after the execution to determine if the period during the marketing execution received greater total sales and greater percentage sales increases or decreases over last year. Without control markets, you can't be sure that the sales results are totally a function of the marketing execution. The results could be the effect of other market factors that caused marketwide sales increases or decreases not only for your company but for the competition as well. However, even without control markets, the analysis of sales trends provides general insight into the success or failure of individual marketing executions.

Sometimes test market performance is compared to national or total company sales. In this case, the national or company total is used as a benchmark. The method is not as accurate as a comparison of test versus control markets but it does provide a basis for evaluation.

Pre- and Postexecution Primary Research

While increased sales is a valuable indicator of the success of a marketing plan execution, it is not the only indicator. Many times, even though sales may remain relatively flat, significant movement can occur in awareness and attitudes. As has been proven time and again, these shifts signal the probability of future sales or a problem with product availability.

To track these shifts, primary research comparing preexecution versus postexecution attitudes, awareness, and behavior can be used. This research method has the ability to provide more in-depth information than sales trend comparisons. For one, pre- and postexecution research can measure specific behavior or tactical objectives, or even the movement of specific plan executions, such as promotions, campaigns, and merchandising programs. It can serve as a diagnostic tool to help explain why sales goals were or were not achieved. It can also identify changes in consumer awareness of your product, attitudes about your product, changing purchase behavior patterns, or competitive strengths and weaknesses as reasons for increases or decreases in sales.

EXHIBIT 20.1 **Advertising Awareness/Attitude Indices**

	No Advertising Control Markets			Advertising Test Markets			
	Pre	Post	Difference	Pre	Post	Difference	Net Gain
Advertising awareness	(100)	(105)	+5	(100)	(152)	+52	+47
Better source of energy information	(100)	(82)	−18	(100)	(135)	+35	+53
More concerned about energy conservation	(100)	(84)	−16	(100)	(127)	+27	+43
More concerned with the environment	(100)	(100)	—	(100)	(115)	+15	+15

The example in Exhibit 20.1 demonstrates the ability of pre- and postexecution research to evaluate the results of an advertising program. In this example, a utility was evaluating the effectiveness of its campaign to persuade consumers that it was a better source of energy information and was more concerned about energy conservation and environmental issues. The numbers have been indexed for confidentiality. The results clearly provided the utility with insights into the effectiveness of the campaign.

Structuring the Sales Evaluation Process

The following method demonstrates how to measure the sales performance for your marketing activities. This method utilizes the *growth rate of improvement (GRI) process*, which is one specific type of sales trend comparison. A retail example is used; however, a similar procedure could be established for any business type.

The only changes needed to make the method applicable to any business would be in the evaluation categories, which would need to be made consistent with the business: a manufacturer would use product sales and units sold; a retailer could use such measurements as visits, transactions, dollars per transaction, units sold, and product sales; a service firm would use sales and people served.

You should plan to use a similar method for your evaluation system. A worksheet is provided at the end of this chapter. However, wherever appropriate, we suggest that the pre- and postexecution research evaluation method also be utilized and that the research be executed by a professional research firm.

In the GRI method, each test market is compared against a control market of similar type and number of stores and per store sales averages. The test markets receive the test activity and the control markets receive the regularly scheduled marketing activity. If you don't have control markets, the test market can be compared against your national system or all other markets.

TASK 1 *Analyze Preperiod*	Analyze a *preperiod* to determine sales trending prior to the test period.
TASK 2 *Analyze Test Period*	For the *test period*, the period during which the marketing program is executed, data are analyzed to determine sales trending.
TASK 3 *Analyze Postperiod*	For the *postperiod*, the period immediately following a test period, data are analyzed to determine sales trending.

TASK 4	Finally, a *growth rate of improvement* is determined by analyzing the dif-
Determine GRI	ference between visits, transactions, and sales dollars per store in the

preperiod, the test period, and the postperiod. The data enables the marketer to determine incremental visits, transactions, and sales during the test period for each market and to evaluate the rate of success.

Whenever feasible you utilize the growth rate improvement method to compare the preperiod to the test period, test period to postperiod, and the preperiod to the postperiod. The preperiod is compared to the test period to determine if the test altered expected behavior. If the preperiod showed that sales were flat and the test period demonstrated a marked increase in sales, a determination would be made that the marketing program executed during the test period was effective. The test period is compared to the postperiod to determine if the marketing execution had a lasting effect and to gain knowledge on how much, if any, sales drop off after the test period. Finally, an important long-term analysis is the comparison of preperiod to postperiod. This comparison shows if the marketing execution had a positive effect on sales after the test as compared to sales trending before the marketing execution or test period.

The following provides retail examples of evaluation objectives and strategies.

Example Evaluation Objective:

> Develop a data feedback methodology to monitor and determine results of marketing test program and executions.

Example Evaluation Strategies:

> Implement a disciplined data feedback system in order to quickly and easily evaluate sales activity for marketing planning and execution.
> Utilize the growth rate of improvement (GRI) method.

The following examples demonstrate a comparison of preperiod to test period. Exhibit 20.2 compares a test market to a control market, and Exhibit 20.3 compares a test market to the national system average.

Exhibit 20.2 Test versus Control Market Dollar Sales Analysis: Test Period 2/24–3/30 (Weekly Per-Store Average)

	Last Year Dollars (000)	This Year Dollars (000)	Percent Change Dollars
Preperiod 1/20–2/23			
Test market—Detroit (2 stores)	$121.0	$185.1	+53%
Control market—Indianapolis (2 stores)	$118.0	$159.3	+35%
Test Period 2/24–2/30			
Test market—Detroit (2 stores)	$29.0	$53.4	+84%
Control market—Indianapolis (2 stores)	$26.0	$25.7	−1%

	Preperiod Percent Change	Test Period Percent Change	Percent Point Gain/Loss
Growth Rate Improvement (GRI)			
Test market—Detroit (2 stores)	+53%	+84%	+31%
Control market—Indianapolis (2 stores)	+35%	−1%	−36%
Net percent point difference	+18%	+85%	+67%

Incremental Sales: GRI: +67 percent × Test Period Sales $53,400 = Net Weekly Gain $35,778.

Note: The same method would be used for visits and/or transactions if the data are available.

Exhibit 20.3 Test versus National Dollar Sales Analysis: Test Period 2/24–3/30 (Weekly Per-Store Average)

	Last Year Dollars (000)	This Year Dollars (000)	Percent Change Dollars
Preperiod: 1/20–2/23			
Test market—Detroit (2 stores)	$121.0	$185.1	+53%
National system average	$120.0	$144.0	+20%
Test Period: 2/24–3/30			
Test market—Detroit (2 stores)	$39.0	$53.4	+84%
National system average	$27.0	$31.6	+17%

	Preperiod Percent Change	Test Period Percent Change	Percent Point Gain/Loss
Growth Rate Improvement (GRI)			
Test market—Detroit (2 stores)	+53%	+84%	+31%
National system average	+20%	+17%	−3%
Net Percent Point Difference	+33%	+67%	+34%

Incremental Sales: GRI: +34 percent × Test Period Sales $53,400 = Net Weekly Gain $18,156.

Note: The same method would be used for visits and/or transactions if the data are available.

WORKSHEET

Growth Rate of Improvement Sales Trending Method

Evaluation Objective

Evaluation Strategies

Evaluation Execution

Test Market versus Control Market Dollar Sales Analysis

Test Period_____

		Last Year	This Year	Percent Change
Postperiod versus	Preperiod			
Preperiod _____	Test market			
	Control market			
	Test period			
	Test market			
	Control market			

Growth Rate Improvement	Preperiod Percent Change	Test Period Percent Change	Point Gain/Loss
Test market			
Control market			
Net percent point difference			

Incremental sales: GRI _____ × Test Period Sales $_____ = Net Weekly Gain $_____

		Last Year	This Year	Percent Change
Test Period versus	Test period			
Postperiod _____	Test market			
	Control market			
	Postperiod			
	Test market			
	Control market			

Growth Rate Improvement	Test Period Percent Change	Postperiod Percent Change	Point Gain/Loss
Test market			
Control market			
Net percent point difference			

Incremental sales: GRI _____ × Test Period Sales $_____ = Net Weekly Gain $_____

Growth Rate of Improvement Sales Trending Method—continued

		Last Year	This Year	Percent Change
Postperiod versus Preperiod _____	**Postperiod**			
	Test market			
	Control market			
	Preperiod			
	Test market			
	Control market			

Growth Rate Improvement	**Postperiod Percent Change**	**Preperiod Percent Change**	**Point Gain/Loss**
Test market			
Control market			
Net percent point difference			

Incremental sales: GRI _____ × Test Period Sales $_____ = Net Weekly Gain $_____

Test Market versus National System Average Dollar Sales Analysis

Test Period _____

		Last Year	This Year	Percent Change
Preperiod versus Test Period _____	**Preperiod**			
	Test market			
	National system average			
	Test Period			
	Test market			
	National system average			

Growth Rate Improvement	**Preperiod Percent Change**	**Test Period Percent Change**	**Point Gain/Loss**
Test market			
National system average			
Net percent point difference			

Incremental sales: GRI _____ × Test Period Sales $_____ = Net Weekly Gain $_____

		Last Year	This Year	Percent Change
Test Period versus Postperiod _____	**Test Period**			
	Test market			
	National system average			
	Postperiod			
	Test market			
	National system average			

Growth Rate Improvement	**Test Period Percent Change**	**Postperiod Percent Change**	**Point Gain/Loss**
Test market			
National system average			
Net percent point difference			

Incremental sales: GRI _____ × Test Period Sales $_____ = Net Weekly Gain $_____

Growth Rate of Improvement Sales Trending Method—continued

	Last Year	This Year	Percent Change
Postperiod versus			
Preperiod _____			

Postperiod
    Test market
    National system average
Preperiod
    Test market
    National system average

Growth Rate Improvement	**Postperiod Percent Change**	**Preperiod Percent Change**	**Point Gain/Loss**
Test market			
National system average			
Net percent point difference			

Incremental sales: GRI _____ × Test Period Sales $_____ = Net Weekly Gain $_____

Step 10: Evaluation

MARKETING BACKGROUND

1 THE BUSINESS REVIEW

Scope
Company Strengths & Weaknesses • Core Competencies • Marketing Capabilities

Product and Market Review
Company & Product Review • Category & Company Sales • Behavior Trends • Pricing • Distribution • Competitive Review

Target Market Effectors
Consumer/Business-to-Business Targets • Product Awareness & Attributes • Trial & Retrial Data

2 PROBLEMS/OPPORTUNITIES

MARKETING PLAN

3 SALES OBJECTIVES

4 TARGET MARKETS AND MARKETING OBJECTIVES

5 PLAN STRATEGIES

6 COMMUNICATION GOALS—Positioning & Marketing

7 TACTICAL MARKETING MIX TOOLS

Product	Distribution	Advertising Media
Branding	Personal Selling/Service	Merchandising
Packaging	Promotion/Events	Publicity
Pricing	Advertising Message	Interactive Communication

8 MARKETING PLAN BUDGET AND CALENDAR

9 EXECUTION

10 EVALUATION

MARKETING RESEARCH AND TESTING

21

IN THIS CHAPTER YOU WILL LEARN:

- WHY AND WHEN TO RESEARCH AND TEST.
- HOW TO TEST WITHIN THREE TYPES OF EXPERIMENTAL ENVIRONMENTS.
- THE BASIC PARAMETERS FOR RESEARCH AND TESTING VARIOUS MARKETING PLAN ELEMENTS.

MARKETING IS DEEMED TO BE AS MUCH ART AS SCIENCE, and as such, there is much chance for failure, especially when you use new strategy approaches, go against new target markets, or implement new tactical tools. Evaluating these new elements through research and testing (R&T) *before* they are put into broad-scale practice can help enhance their success. Both testing and research are a means of staying ahead of the competition and avoiding costly errors.

In this chapter we will discuss the rudiments of research and testing. Because they are challenging and complex disciplines, we recommend you seek professional assistance to help with their implementation.

Why and When to Research and Test

Every business situation can be thought of as a test. Many small entrepreneurs do not spend any money on a formalized research and testing program. But they do "test" the market by posting a sign and setting up shop. Accordingly, the vast majority of them do not make it through their third year in business. With a research and testing program, you can significantly reduce the odds of failure. A testing program can be thought of as a form of risk management. You would not think about running your business without insurance. Why run your marketing plan without research and testing?

Not every marketing tool or tactical execution needs to be, or should be, tested. Testing every alternative would not be feasible from a cost or time standpoint. Thus, a prioritization approach should be considered. Some questions to consider when determining what to test include the following:

- *What is the risk of not having this information?* This is probably the most critical question. If you are sinking millions of dollars on a positioning strategy, then spending a few thousand dollars on research makes sense. However, to take the time and money to test a one-week, single-market media flight may not be worth the investment in research.
- *What is the cost of obtaining reliable information?* This would appear to be somewhat obvious. For example, in order to test the effectiveness of an advertising campaign, you need to conduct an in-market test, matching several markets with different advertising messages. It may cost almost as much to develop and test the campaign as it would to implement the campaign without testing, in which case the decision may be to not test.
- *What are the time constraints?* If test results cannot be obtained in time to impact the decision-making process, then one must question the value of testing.

- *How valid and translatable is the testing environment?* You must be able to take the research results and apply them to your marketing situation.

Types of Research and Testing Environments

For the purposes of this book, we can categorize marketing research and testing environments into three types: exploratory, experimental, and in-market.

Exploratory

Marketers should always base their marketing objectives and strategies on what their consumers need. Marketing tools should relate to how the consumers think, what their attitudes are, and how they behave. In many instances, *exploratory research* can provide help in the development process of marketing tool alternatives and in preliminary evaluation of alternatives. Focus groups are probably the most prevalent form of exploratory research.

A focus group is a discussion among target group respondents. Typically, group sizes range from eight to 10 participants, although groups of four to six participants are also common. The group discussion is led by a moderator who follows an outline of topics to cover. Focus groups are an excellent way to generate ideas and obtain feedback from target respondents on complex attitudinal issues such as positioning, product concepts, and advertising messages; and increase understanding of the buying dynamics of a product or service category. When utilized early in the planning process, focus groups can help develop alternatives and provide initial qualitative feedback on alternatives. Focus groups are very qualitative in nature, although when done in numbers (six or more preferably), marketers can gain an enlightened, but not quantifiable, insight into the target market.

Experimental

When focus groups are used extensively for exploring the dynamics of the consumer attitudes and behavior, they are really a form of experimental research. *Experimental research* is any kind of research that is not conducted under "real" conditions. Evaluating advertising copy via mall intercepts, testing pricing strategies via telephone interviews, and testing positioning concepts through a mail survey are all forms of experimental research.

In-Market Testing

In-market testing is really a small-scale implementation of a specific marketing approach. The key to effective in-market tests is to match markets as much as possible, so that you are controlling for all variables except the one you are testing. The ability to accurately read test results relies heavily on the ability to match test markets as closely as possible.

Developing Testing Programs for Various Plan Elements

You can literally test anything related to your marketing plan. Also, there is no one absolute right way to test marketing alternatives. The following examples outline some parameters for research and testing of various marketing plan elements.

Positioning Concepts

Positioning is the heart of the marketing plan. All marketing mix tools are developed to support the product's or service's positioning, which in turn is the link to the consumer's relationship with the product or service. Positioning concepts generally consist of complex attitude structures, which require a sensitive means of testing.

The objective of testing positioning alternatives is to evaluate the connection between the target market relative to the product and competition. Important issues include identifying the relevance of the positioning to the target, the importance of the positioning to the target, and the likelihood that the positioning would encourage trial. Positioning can be tested through many forms, including focus groups, mall intercepts, or mail surveys. Generally a "positioning concept board" is created. The concept board has a visual element and copy points to convey the benefits and positioning elements. Targeted consumers can be shown the concept board and then be asked to respond to a short survey covering attitudinal and intention-type questions.

One limitation to the concept board approach is that consumers tend to be literal in research settings; they begin to be copywriters rather than focusing on the positioning "idea." An approach developed to counteract this tendency is the audio concept "board." Here, the positioning is stated on an audio tape that is played to respondents. Because they cannot read the concept, respondents are less likely to be quite so literal; they must take away the key positioning from what they heard. This method is effective for positioning with a strong emotional appeal, as the tone of the audio can impart the desired emotion more easily than the writing on a concept board.

Product Testing

Probably the greatest amount of testing dollars is associated with research for new product development. Product concepts are explored and formulated through numerous focus groups. Concepts are refined through more consumer testing using all of the methods discussed above. There are also simulated test models that produce expected market shares when fed with market and benefit criteria. Much of the research on new product development is conducted to determine the ideal bundle of benefits, both rational and emotional, that a product should contain. The ultimate test of a new product is putting it into a real market situation.

Brand Testing

The target market will recognize your offering through the brand name of your product. But what is the best brand name? And how do you determine the best brand name? The process for brand testing is to first develop alternative names for testing (see Chapter 9). As a rule, the number of names for consumer testing should not be more than seven names. A number beyond seven creates respondent fatigue and results in a lack of name discrimination.

The objectives of branding research are to narrow the list of alternative names and to identify the strengths and weaknesses of each name alternative. There are factors other than target market preferences to be considered in branding. Creative consideration is one example. If some names can be eliminated through branding research, then other factors can be considered in the final decision-making process. When evaluating brand alternatives, three areas of questioning are used to achieve the above objectives:

1. *Word association.* What connotations does the name elicit? Are they positive or negative? For example, when our agency tested name alternatives for a merged pair of hospitals, one of the test names generated for our client was Meriter. Through word associations, two common themes were Merit cigarettes and the word *merit* (to be worthy). The word association was done out of context of a hospital name. Thus, when put in context of a hospital, the cigarette association would be expected to disappear, while the *merit*—"to be worthy"—definition could be used in an advantageous way.

2. *Ratings on product/service benefits.* Each name is rated against various product/service benefits to ascertain strengths and weaknesses. In the hospital example, the names were rated on leadership, caring, professional, state-of-the-art, and quality.

3. *Preference scores.* Respondents are asked for their name preferences, given a concept statement read to them. Reasons for their preferences are also obtained.

All three types of measurement—association, ratings, and preferences—are analyzed to determine viable names. This type of testing can be conducted through telephone interviews or mall intercepts.

Promotion Testing

Promotion testing can be performed at the idea development stage or at the execution stage. The key objective in evaluating promotions is to determine the effectiveness of the promotion in generating incremental sales, new trial, or brand loyalty. At the idea generation stage, focus groups can be a useful tool for obtaining ideas and feedback. Mall intercepts can also be used to evaluate the stopping power and selling power of alternative promotions in an advertising context. At the execution stage, in-store exit surveys can be used to determine consumers' buying habits and profiles. For example, this type of survey can determine if the promotion was a specific reason that consumers shopped at a store. The profile of the customers can also be checked to determine first-time shoppers, improved purchase ratios, or higher average-transaction amounts.

Advertising Message Testing

Advertising is probably one of the most difficult marketing tools to measure. This is due, in part, to the long-term and cumulative effects of advertising and to the difficulty of isolating advertising effects. The closest one can come to truly measuring the "effectiveness" of advertising is through in-market testing. However, controlling for all other variables is difficult with in-market testing, and the necessary time and budget are seldom available for this type of measurement. Nonetheless, assessing the communication value of advertising can be done more readily and efficiently.

Copy testing is a means of measuring the communication value of advertising. As a diagnostic tool rather than an evaluative tool, copy testing can be instrumental to the creative development process. There are two key objectives in a copy-testing framework. One objective is to determine whether the advertising can cut through the clutter and make people notice the ad. The second is to assess whether the ad communicates the intended message.

Media Testing

Which medium or media mix is the right one? How much media weight do you need? How many media dollars do you need to spend? Media testing can help answer these questions.

In testing media there are two key variables to evaluate: media mix and media weight. Testing the impact of alternative media or weight levels is difficult to accomplish in a forced-exposure experimental design. In-market tests typically are used for media mix and weight tests. Market tiers are derived, which receive different weight levels of similar messages. Or, the variable may be different types of media such as TV versus newspaper. There may be many combinations to consider, with markets and dollars available for testing being the limiting factor. The key is to control for all variables except for the media weight or mix. The typical measurement tool would be sales analysis. Survey research can also be utilized to determine awareness levels affected by the alternative media plans. Telephone research generally is used for this purpose.

Index

monday morning®

LITERATURE TEACHES ABOUT THE U.S.A.

by Tanya M. Lieberman & Annalisa Suid

illustrated by Marilynn G. Barr

This book is dedicated to:
Larisa, Julie, Bart, & my class—T.L.
Kimberly, Michael, & Lacey—A.S.

Publisher: Roberta Suid
Copy Editor: Carol Whiteley
Production: Santa Monica Press

For a complete catalog of our products,
please write to the address below:
P.O. Box 1680, Palo Alto, CA 94302

Monday Morning is a registered trademark of
Monday Morning Books, Inc.

ISBN 1-878279-92-0

Printed in the United States of America

987654321

❖ CONTENTS ❖

❖ INTRODUCTION ❖

From Native American settlements to the Gold Rush of '48, from covered wagon trains to a rocket to the moon, the United States boasts a colorful history. A trip to your local library or bookstore will open up a wealth of knowledge about this fascinating subject, as rich and diverse as the stories behind the patches in your grandmother's quilt.

Each chapter in *Literature Teaches About the U.S.A.* includes:
* *Story Summaries* that allow you to sample in advance chapter books (which can be read aloud to younger children), storybooks, and nonfiction resources (these are listed as C, S, and N);
* *Discovery/Exploration* activities related to the featured resources;
* *Literature Links* presenting language activities based on the resources; and
* *Class Projects* to tie the units together.

Class Projects

Class projects are culminating activities ranging from creating a classroom museum to building a covered wagon; they provide a focal point for each unit's activities. The projects will inspire excitement for learning while allowing students to demonstrate their new knowledge and to develop cooperative skills.

Teaching Objectives

Learning about the history of their country can be a fascinating process of discovery for children. While students focus on the past, they will develop their understanding of the present, and look forward to their role in the future. The activities in this book encourage growth in students':

* knowledge of U.S. culture and history;
* understanding of democracy and civic values;
* skills for living in a diverse society, such as communication, tolerance, problem solving, and cooperation; and
* understanding of their role in their nation's history.

Teaching Strategies

To make your activities and projects successful:
* Introduce the class project at the beginning of each unit, and emphasize the project throughout.
* Develop student "ownership" of the projects. When children discuss their projects, they should talk about "our museum" or "our covered wagon."
* Allow for student input and modifications in class projects.
* Use small groups to develop different parts of a project at the same time.
* Let students present what they have learned to each other, parents, or other classrooms.

PART I

The Beginnings

Native American communities thrived long before Christopher Columbus "discovered" America in 1492. These peoples had a unique relationship to the land, the animal world, nature, and each other that changed drastically when the newcomers arrived.

What was it like to live in a Native American community? Through exploration and study, you can give students a taste of the cultural strengths, as well as some of the daily challenges, of Native American life. Students will also be interested to learn about the European explorers who felt as if they had found a new world. Encourage your students to discover more about the early history of our country by reading the selected books noted in this chapter.

The activities in this chapter will give depth to the class project, a three-dimensional mural contrasting the Europeans' viewpoints with the Native American perspective of the Europeans' arrival. The activities will also deepen students' understanding of both cultures' feelings, and how the world changed as a result of their meeting.

Objectives:
Through the activities in this chapter, students will:
• develop an understanding of Native American daily life;
• consider the Native Americans' relationship to their environment;
• understand the two cultures' perspectives upon the arrival of the Europeans;
• learn about different forms of communication.

NATIVE AMERICAN DAILY LIFE

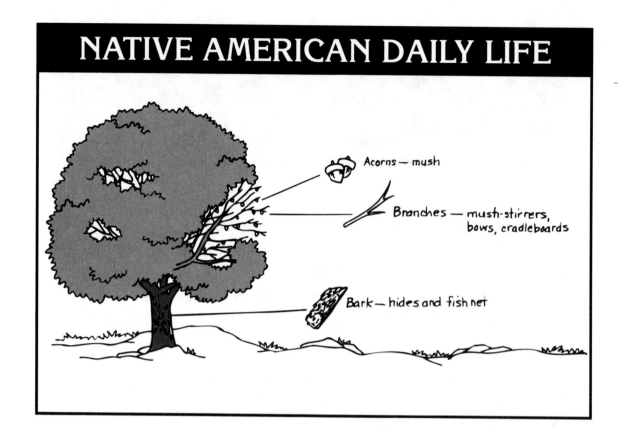

Acorns — mush

Branches — mush-stirrers, bows, cradleboards

Bark — hides and fish net

The First Americans.

Stories about Native American daily life will help children understand the fascinating culture of the peoples who lived in this country before the Europeans arrived. The books described in this chapter focus on different tribes from different parts of the country.

As they listen to the stories, students can compare their own lives to the lives of the people in the books. They can imagine what it was like to live alone like Karana in *Island of the Blue Dolphins*. Would they have been as resourceful as Karana? Could they have taken care of themselves if left alone? *People of the Breaking Day* provides further information about the housing, clothing, food, and traditions of a Native American tribe. Children can compare their own family units, styles of dress, types of housing, food sources, roles of family members, and community life with the lives of the Wampanoag people.

The books for this unit are:

C: *Island of the Blue Dolphins* by Scott O'Dell (Houghton Mifflin, 1960).
S: *The Friendly Wolf* by Paul and Dorothy Doble (Bradbury Press, 1974).
N: *People of the Breaking Day* by Marcia Sewall (Atheneum, 1990).

❖ ACTIVITIES ❖

STORY SUMMARIES

The Friendly Wolf follows a tribe to the valley where the berry bushes grow. Here, the women and children gather berries to mash and make into cakes for winter. The illustrations in this book show the tribe at work, their style of dress, and their type of shelter. The tale also tells of the "wolf-people," and of their possible future extinction.

Island of the Blue Dolphins tells the story of Karana, a young Native American girl, who lives happily until the rest of her tribe is taken from their island to the mainland. Left alone on the island for 18 years, Karana works to find her place among wild dogs, devil fish, and sea elephants. Based on a true story, this book depicts the daily life of her tribe.

The *People of the Breaking Day*, or Wampanoag, were a tribe from south-eastern Massachusetts. This book presents both their traditions and family life. Roles of men, women, and children are illustrated. A glossary of Native American words is included.

EXPLORATION: USE IT OR LOSE IT

Can your students be as resourceful as Karana? Native American people knew many uses for the natural materials in their environments. For example:

PLANT	PART USED	USES
Oak Tree	Acorns	Cooked into mush
	Bark	Dye for hides and fish nets
	Branches	Mush-stirrers, bows, cradleboards
Willow	Wood	Poles for house frameworks
	Shoots	Baskets, seed beaters
	Bark	Skirts, medicinal tea for fever

For this activity, divide the children into small, cooperative "tribes." Give each group assorted materials and challenge them to transform the materials into items necessary for their daily life. For example, paper clips can be bent into fishing hooks, halved milk cartons form bowls, an old shoelace (or length of yarn) tied to the end of a yardstick creates a fishing pole, paper grocery bags can be cut for clothing. Have on hand egg cartons, cardboard tubes and boxes, and plastic tubs, and provide glue, scissors, paints, brushes, and crayons for children to use to decorate their finished products.

THE AGE OF EXPLORATION

We're in India!

When Europeans arrived in North America, they claimed to have "discovered" the Native Americans. But since the Native Americans were already living here, an important question is: "Who discovered whom?"

Stories about the European arrival and exploration of North America will help children develop perspectives for both participants of the event. Have your students imagine what it would be like to travel aboard Columbus' ship. Would they get cabin fever from being on the ocean that long? How would they feel at the first sight of land? Then ask your students to imagine that they were the Native Americans, ready to greet the Europeans as their guests but not prepared to lose the land that they felt they were "borrowing" from nature. Let the children design "pictographs" depicting Columbus' arrival from the Native American point of view.

The books for this unit are:

C: *The Boy Who Sailed with Columbus* by Michael Foreman (Little, 1991).
S: *My Name Is Pocahontas* by William Accorsi (Holiday House, 1992).
N: *This Land Is My Land* by George Littlechild (Children's Book Press, 1993).

❖ ACTIVITIES ❖

 **STORY SUMMARIES**

The Boy Who Sailed with Columbus is about 12-year-old Leif's voyage to the Americas, where he learns the ways of the tribes as well as the greediness of his fellow voyagers. This book provides personal insights into the Native American and European worlds, both forever altered by the age of exploration.

My Name Is Pocahontas recounts the famous story of the Algonquin princess caught between the worlds of her tribe and the white settlers. In reading the story of her rescue of John Smith, her marriage to John Rolfe, and life in England, we see both clashes between and common themes in the two cultures.

This Land Is My Land relates the arrival of the Europeans to the lives of present-day Native Americans. One two-page spread, "Columbus First Saw," describes the "discovery" concept from a Native American's point of view: How could Columbus have discovered America when Littlechild's people were already here?

LANGUAGE LINK: TWO PERSPECTIVES

The Europeans captured their arrival in logs, recording their experiences landing, meeting the Native Americans, and attempts to communicate with them. The Native Americans recorded this meeting in entirely different ways: through stories that were passed down from generation to generation, and through their art.

- Provide children with drawing paper and crayons to use in recreating Columbus' arrival. Have children develop icons: zig-zags for water, triangles for ships, and so on. These will be used later in the class project.
- Christopher Columbus kept a running log of his journey from Europe to the New Land. Because his men were nervous about traveling a great distance from home, Columbus "fiddled" with the mileage. Give each child note paper (singe the paper ahead of time for an added worn look, or use thick manila paper cut in a scroll shape). Have children imagine that they are traveling on Columbus' ship. They can record the day of their arrival in the New World, noting the weather, their first sight of land, and their meeting with the Native Americans. Bind these entries together in a book to use in the class project.

RELATED BOOKS

The Explorers and Settlers: A Sourcebook on Colonial America edited by Carter Smith (The Millbrook Press, 1991).
Eyewitness Books: Explorers by Rupert Matthews (Knopf, 1991).

❖ CLASS PROJECT ❖

THREE-DIMENSIONAL MURAL

Your classroom walls can tell the story of Native American life before and during the age of exploration. Prior to beginning this mural, discuss with students which elements of Native American daily life and the arrival of Europeans they would like to represent in their mural.

Materials:

Products from prior activities, butcher paper, tempera paint, paintbrushes, pencils, glue, tape, scissors, silver glitter, construction paper, additional craft materials

Directions:

1. Cover one wall (or chalkboard) of your classroom with white butcher or bulletin board paper.

2. Have students draw figures and objects in pencil. Or trace outlines of students' bodies directly onto the mural before mounting.

3. Have students paint the outlines and fill in the features.

4. Add the craft projects made in previous activities. (Use tape, glue, or tacks to secure the crafts, or display heavier projects on a table directly beneath the mural.)

5. Fasten the book of journal entries from the "Two Perspectives" activity to the hands of one "explorer."

6. Post the pictographs from the "Two Perspectives" project as a border for the mural.

Using Your Project:

Once your project is done, consider:
- bringing in students from other classes to view your mural (you may have students act as docents for the exhibit);
- making an audiotaped recording of the two perspectives to play when visitors arrive;
- presenting the mural to parents at open house night;
- videotaping a tour of the mural to show to future classes;
- posting the mural in the school library for all to see (it can be used as a backdrop for books on this subject);
- using the mural to inspire journal entries, poems, raps, and other writing projects.

Option:

Stories are passed down not only through books but through spoken language from generation to generation. To emphasize the Native American's oral tradition, have children tell family stories to the class. (This could be done in teams of two or three.)

10

❖ PART 2 ❖

Colonial Times

Colonists who came to the New World had fought for their right to religious freedom. They came with high hopes, but establishing a life on the continent wasn't easy. Their new lives were very different from the ones they'd left in England, and their challenges were great.

What was it like to be a child in Colonial America? You can give students a taste of children's roles in their family and community at that time through exploration and study. Students will also be interested to learn about the War of Independence (which they probably know a bit about through "Yankee Doodle Dandy"), the signing of the Declaration of Independence, and the drafting of the Constitution. Encourage your students to discover more about the early history of our country by reading the books noted in this chapter.

The activities in this chapter lead to a final project: a live drama of a Classroom Constitutional Convention, based on the 1786 convention that established the democratic order of our country.

Objectives:
Through the activities in this chapter, students will:
• gain an understanding of daily Colonial life;
• learn about major events of the War of Independence;
• comprehend the process of creating a new nation.

COLONIAL LIFE

We're here!

Once the colonists arrived in America, they had a lot of work to do to establish their communities. The stories in this unit will help children compare their lives to those of the children in the colonies. Children will learn about the jobs of men and women, the roles of children, the style of schooling, community activities (such as barn raising), types of food eaten (the many uses for corn), and other aspects of the daily life.

While students work with the featured books and activities, encourage them to consider how the lives of the characters would be affected by the War of Independence and the development of the new nation. What would change in their lives, the lives of their children, and the lives of their grandchildren?

The books for this unit are:

C: *Constance: A Story of Early Plymouth* by Patricia Clapp (Lothrop, 1968).
S: *Three Young Pilgrims* by Cheryl Harness (Bradbury Press, 1992).
N: *Samuel Eaton's Day: A Day in the Life of a Pilgrim Boy* by Kate Waters, photographs by Russ Kendall (Scholastic, 1993).

❖ ACTIVITIES ❖

STORY SUMMARIES

Samuel Eaton's Day: A Day in the Life of a Pilgrim Boy shows young Sam getting ready for his first chance to help his father harvest the wheat. Sam dresses himself, does his morning chores, then serves his stepmother and his father breakfast before helping himself to the gruel. The story is told in simple text and photographs (taken at Plymouth Plantation, a 17th-century living museum). *Sarah Morton's Day: A Day in the Life of a Pilgrim Girl* is in the same series.

Constance: A Story of Early Plymouth is the imagined diary of a real girl, Constance Hopkins, written by one of her descendants. In the New World, Constance becomes a young adult, falls in love, and eventually weds.

Three Young Pilgrims tells the story of a family, the Allertons, and their adventures during the year between the autumns of 1620 and 1621. The book is an illustrated primer that focuses on the ways of the Pilgrims. In the book, the characters are taught how to plant corn by a Native American named Somoset.

EXPLORATION: COLONIAL CLOTHING

Although the styles are a bit different, Sam Eaton does wear some of the same types of clothing that young boys do today: pants, jackets, and socks. Students can create Colonial styles that are not around today. For example, a boy's collar can be made from the corrugated rim of a paper plate. A girl's bonnet can be created from a white paper napkin, hole-punched at two diagonal corners, and strung with a length of yarn. Garters (for both girls and boys) were thin pieces of fabric that held up socks. (Children can wear them now for fun, even though today's socks stay up by themselves.) Pockets were cloth bags tied with string and fastened to the waistband (not sewed on). Children can make a simple pocket by tying a length of yarn or ribbon around the neck of a small paper bag, then fastening the bag to their waistband with a safety pin.

LANGUAGE LINK: TWO "TO DO" LISTS

Have children imagine what it would be like to live in the Colonial era. At dawn, when they get up, what would they have to do? How are those tasks different from what they do in their modern lives?

Give each child a sheet of paper to fold lengthwise. Have children write their own average daily "To Do" list on the left-hand side, and a Colonial child's "To Do" list on the right-hand side. Writing prompts could include: feeding farm animals versus feeding pets, lighting fires versus turning on the thermostat, "points" (sewing themselves into their clothes) versus pulling on a sweatshirt, eating gruel versus eating oatmeal. Post completed lists on a bulletin board for all to see.

WAR OF INDEPENDENCE

Enough is enough!

When the colonists' lives became increasingly constrained by the "mother country," they prepared for war. Their leaders in independence included working men, such as silversmith Paul Revere, as well as some of the world's great minds, such as Benjamin Franklin. These men, along with numerous others, worked hard to set the struggling colonies on their feet. Children can imagine people in their local community fighting strongly for something they believe in. What do your students feel is worth fighting for?

The War of Independence featured some of the most memorable moments in our country's early history: Revere's ride ("One if by land, two if by sea"), Patrick Henry's famous speech, as well as the event behind the song "Yankee Doodle" (after the British insulted some Americans, the Americans replied, "We'll be Yankee Doodles and proud of it!"). The information that the children learn will help them prepare for the class project.

The books for this unit are:

C: *Mr. Revere and I* by Robert Lawson (Little, Brown, 1953).
S: *Where Was Patrick Henry on the 29th of May?* by Jean Fritz, illustrated by Margot Tomes (Coward-McCann, 1975).
N: *Yankee Doodle* by Gary Chalk (Dorling Kindersley, 1993).

❖ ACTIVITIES ❖

 ## STORY SUMMARIES

Where Was Patrick Henry on the 29th of May? The Revolutionary hero was delivering his "Give me liberty or give me death" speech on that very day. This book chronicles Patrick Henry's rise from a lazy, bare-foot farm child to one of our nation's most famous orators.

In *Mr. Revere and I*, the "I" is Paul's horse Scheherazade, or "Sherry." Previously a loyal member of the king's army, Sherry becomes a true patriot when she carries the silversmith on his famous ride and helps the Sons of Liberty to victory over the British.

Yankee Doodle is a favorite tune of young children, and this book provides much additional information about the song, such as the fact that "macaroni" was another word for a dandy or fashionable gentleman. The many verses to the song are included.

 ## EXPLORATION: DESIGNING THE CLASSROOM FLAG

The person who actually created the American flag is up for debate. Legend has it that it was Betsy Ross. Some believe that Caroline Pickersgill and her family made the flag. Still others say that Francis Hopkinson helped with the design. Children can create flags symbolizing their classroom that they can use in the class project. Provide construction paper, crayons or markers, glue, and glitter. As an option, show children flags from different states and countries for inspiration, such as those in *Eyewitness Books: Flag* by William Crampton (Knopf, 1989).

 ## LANGUAGE LINK: A DECLARATION OF INDEPENDENCE

When the delegates of the Second Continental Congress issued the Declaration of Independence, they took the risk of being called "traitors." The Declaration did three things: it described the delegates' beliefs about good government, listed what the king did wrong, and announced that the colonies were free and independent states. Students can write a Class-room Declaration describing their ideal school. Have all students sign at the bottom. Tell them the story of John Hancock, who wrote his name in large letters so that King George would be able to see it without his glasses!

 ## RELATED BOOKS

The Biggest (and Best) Flag That Ever Flew by Rebecca C. Jones (Tidewater, 1988).

Black Heroes of the American Revolution by Burke Davis (HBJ, 1976).

THE NEW NATION

Now what?

Once the War of Independence was won, the colonists had to decide how the new nation would run. The stories in this chapter give students a view into the lives and achievements of the founding mothers and fathers whose ideas and commitments govern us to this day. What was it like to live in freedom for the first time? Who would have the power to make the rules?

Challenge students to imagine that they are responsible for creating and enforcing laws. Do they have any such responsibility in their own lives? Do they take care of younger brothers and sisters, setting limitations and enforcing rules?

The activities in this chapter set the stage for the Classroom Constitutional Convention.

The books for this unit are:

C: *A Gathering of Days: A New England Girl's Journal* (1830-32) by Joan W. Blos (Scribner's Sons, 1979). A Newbery Award winner.
N: *Shh! We're Writing the Constitution* by Jean Fritz, pictures by Tomie de Paola (G.P. Putnam's Sons, 1987).

❖ ACTIVITIES ❖

STORY SUMMARIES

Thirteen-year-old Catherine Cabot Hall tells of the events in her life in New Hampshire in 1830. *A Gathering of Days* is filled with information about her daily activities, her friend Cassie, and her family.

Shh! We're Writing the Constitution describes how the Constitution came to be written and ratified. This resource also includes the full text of the document produced by the Constitutional Convention of 1787. *Will You Sign Here, John Hancock?* is by the same author.

LANGUAGE LINK: CLASSROOM CONSTITUTION

To introduce the project, define a constitution as the highest law of the land, and explain that your Classroom Constitution will equal the highest law of your classroom. Students will determine how the classroom government should be run.

Divide your students into cooperative groups, giving one of the topics below to each. Assign each group the task of taking a position on their topic. Students will be responsible for presenting and trying to persuade others to agree with their position at the convention. Remind students that when taking a position, they must be able to provide support or reasons for their position. (From the list, choose topics that are age-appropriate to your students. Younger children may also be given the sentence starter: We think _____ because _____.) Note: Be sure to give students time to rehearse their presentation.

Possible Topics:
- Who makes the laws in the classroom?
- Who carries out the laws?
- Who decides what is fair?
- Who can vote?
- How do we select a classroom leader?
- After we agree on it, how can we change the constitution?

RELATED BOOKS

Give Me Liberty by Franklin Folsom (Rand McNally, 1974).

The Joke's on George by Michael O. Tunnell (Tambourine, 1993).

Men of the Constitution by Pamela Bradbury (Julian Messner, 1987).

If You Were There When They Signed the Constitution by Elizabeth Levy (Scholastic, 1987).

❖ CLASS PROJECT ❖

CLASSROOM CONSTITUTIONAL CONVENTION

Let your students take over (for a morning) and create a Classroom Constitution!

Setting the Stage:

Arrange desks in a circle so that the delegates can face each other, and line up chairs for a visitors gallery in back. If possible, find a podium (or teacher's desk) for the president. Have children make name tags, desk tags, and press passes (for reporters). Discuss rules of order (e.g., one person speaks at a time, children must raise their hand to be recognized). Set a speech time limit of one minute.

Assign roles for the convention: clerk (opens/closes the door, provides delegates with proper materials), reporters (interview delegates), time keeper (holds speeches to one minute), vice president (calls for/counts votes), secretary (records proceedings), delegates. The president (oversees the meeting, calls on people to speak) should be elected by the delegates.

Materials:

Period costume materials, butcher paper, markers, delegate name tags, desk tags, gavel (or other tool for calling meeting to order), period music, flags from "Designing the Classroom Flag" activity

Directions:

1. The door is opened by the convention clerk.

2. Students enter in costume, wearing name tags to identify their constituency, and take their seats in their delegation (marked by desk tags).

3. The meeting is called to order by the teacher, who leads delegates in the selection of the convention president.

4. Group by group, delegates present their issues and proposals. The convention president leads them in an election on each issue, calling for "yea" or "nay" votes. Once the students vote on a flag, it should be posted.

5. When all issues have been resolved, articles of declaration should be written on a large sheet of butcher paper, and all delegates should sign the constitution.

6. The convention is called to a close by the convention president.

Using Your Project:

- Videotape your convention and play it back for the class to review.
- Invite other classes to fill the visitors gallery.
- Produce a newspaper chronicling the historic meeting. Use notes from reporters.
- Design convention buttons, posters, and t-shirts.

PART 3

Westward Expansion

Once the War of Independence had been won, settlers like the Wilder family, whose experiences are recounted in *Little House on the Prairie*, began to move west. As they traveled across previously uncharted territories, their lives changed drastically. They were excited by the prospect of their new lives, but establishing communities wasn't easy, and the troubles that assailed them were numerous.

What was it like to travel in a covered wagon or live in a log cabin? How did the first miner feel when he struck gold? What did the Native Americans think about the growing numbers of European settlers? How did the settlers get along with the Native Americans, whose land they claimed as their own? Through exploration and study, you can give students a taste of the daily challenges that faced those courageous people. Students will also be interested to learn about the get-rich-quick philosophy of the miners in the California Gold Rush.

The activities in this chapter will be reinforced through the class project, creating a replica of a covered wagon, the type of transportation most often used to move West.

Objectives:
Through the activities in this chapter, students will:
- develop an understanding of the daily life and hardships of the pioneers;
- comprehend the relationships between settlers and Native Americans;
- learn about the Gold Rush and the communities that grew as a result.

GOLD RUSH

Eureka!

Gold, and the promise of a quick fortune, brought prospectors, merchants, and adventurers to the newly discovered fields. One of the most famous of these gold rushes was the California Gold Rush of 1848, when the discovery of gold at Sutter's Mill brought tens of thousands of prospectors to the site. Although few prospectors struck it rich, their presence stimulated rapid economic growth in the area.

Your students can imagine that they are prospectors, sifting through silty riverbeds in hopes of discovering gold nuggets. How would they feel if they struck it rich? They can also learn about inventions that came into being during this period; some, like Levi's, are still used today.

The books for this unit are:

C: *Chang's Paper Pony* by Eleanor Coerr (Harper and Row, 1988).
N: *The Great American Gold Rush* (Bradbury Press, 1989).

❖ ACTIVITIES ❖

STORY SUMMARIES

Chang's Paper Pony is the story of a young Chinese American boy, Chang, and his dream of owning his own pony in the gold-mining camps of California. When Big Pete agrees to teach Chang how to dig for his own gold, Chang finds enough gold to buy a pony!

The Great American Gold Rush discusses "The Age of Gold" and the results of the discovery as gold fever spreads to many parts of the country. People clamored to join the rush, all with the idea of getting rich quickly.

EXPLORATION: GOLD!

Turn your children into prospectors by giving each plastic or paper containers (bowls, plates with rounded edges). Ahead of time, spray-paint small pebbles or rocks gold. Mix the "gold" with a quantity of sand. Let children scoop a bit of the mixture into their mining pans and shake it until the "gold" rises to the top. Miners would hunt through pan after pan without success, so don't put too many nuggets into the mixture. (Colanders or sifters can be used outdoors.)

LANGUAGE LINK: SONGS OF THE TIME

Students may know two Gold Rush songs without realizing it. "Clementine," which became prominent after the Civil War, is about a "miner, forty-niner" and his daughter. "Oh, Susanna" became the theme song of the Gold Rush in 1849. Teach the songs to children who don't know the words. Just for fun, children can also try to create their own songs by writing new lyrics to the famous tunes. For example, they can substitute their own names for Susanna, or change the location of the miner in "Clementine." Instead of "In a cavern, in a canyon," they could write:

In a town in California, working hard to find some gold,
Lived a miner, forty-niner, and his daughter, I am told.

"Home on the Range" is also fun to rewrite:

I wish I were home,
I do not like to roam,
I am sick of the pioneer way.
I don't mean to bawl,
But the wagon is small,
And there just aren't spaces to play.

Range life's not for me,
Though I know others might not agree.
But we're moving so slow,
And we're bored, don't you know,
I sure miss my old life by the sea.

PIONEERS

Are we there yet?

In the 19th century, thousands of families decided to try their luck out west, moving steadily toward the Pacific coast. These brave families loaded their belongings into covered wagons and traveled great distances to reach their new homes. As they traveled, they often lightened their loads, getting rid of jars, wooden buckets, even pickles. "Too unhandy to carry," said pioneer woman Amelia Stewart Knight in *The Way West*.

Your students can imagine they are pioneers, traveling with their families across the vast prairies through all types of weather, in sickness and health. Wagon trains often traveled together in groups of 15 to 20. Do your students know 15 families they would want to travel with for six months? How would they feel eating the same food over and over again? Or trying brand-new foods such as buffalo meat? These exercises will help prepare students for the class project.

The books for this unit are:

C: *Sarah, Plain and Tall* by Patricia McLachlan (HarperCollins, 1985).
C: *Little House on the Prairie* by Laura Ingalls Wilder, pictures by Garth Williams (HarperCollins, 1935).
N: *The Way West* by Amelia Stewart Knight (Simon & Schuster, 1993).

❖ ACTIVITIES ❖

STORY SUMMARIES

Little House on the Prairie is the story of Laura Ingalls, who traveled with her family across the prairie. This book tells of the family's journey in a covered wagon, their daily life during their travels, and the building of their little house. This is the second book in the series that chronicles the life of Laura, her future husband, and her family. The *Little House Cookbook* by Barbara M. Walker (Harper & Row, 1979) contains recipes for some of the foods eaten by prairie families.

When Sarah, in *Sarah, Plain and Tall*, sends word that she will be coming to the frontier, the children wonder what their new mother will be like. Will she snore? Can she braid hair and make stew? Can she sing? In this pioneer tale we learn of the creation of a new family and one woman's struggle to adjust to life on the frontier.

The Way West follows Amelia Stewart Knight as she, her husband, and their seven children set out from Iowa for the Oregon Territory in 1853. They travel in wagons pulled by six or eight oxen, which go only 10-15 miles per day; it sometimes took four to six months for a family to reach the Pacific. During rough times, families lightened their loads by throwing away things they loved: rocking chairs, cradles, even pianos.

DISCOVERY/EXPLORATION: LIGHTENING THE LOAD

If your students were settlers traveling in covered wagons, they would be allowed to bring only a certain amount of belongings with them. Have your children imagine that their families are moving to a new place, where nothing is available: no manufactured items, clothing, or packaged foods to be bought at any price. What necessities would their families need? What items would they want to bring with them (for comfort, sentimental value, etc.)? Students can work individually or in small groups to compile their lists. Set a limit, such as 15 items, at the beginning. Then take students on an imaginary journey across the plains. As they reach rough roads they must "lighten their loads" by crossing off an item. As their oxen tire, they must get rid of more items. Discuss the staples that children end up with (perhaps 10 of the 15). Have students or groups compare their lists. Save these lists for use in the class project.

RELATED BOOKS

Grandma Essie's Covered Wagon by David Williams, illustrated by Wiktor Sadowski (Knopf, 1993).

The Cowboy Trade by Glen Rounds (Holiday House, 1972).

Caddie Woodland by Carol Ryrie Brink (Alladin, 1935). Newbery Award winner.

WHOSE LAND IS IT?

Whose land?

As pioneer families and miners moved westward, tensions over rights to "unclaimed" territories developed. Who had the right to claim land? How would disputes be resolved? Who had the right to the animals of the territories?

This chapter introduces students to the battle over territory, which ensued as a result of the westward expansion. Through writing and negotiating a treaty between native peoples and the new residents of the west, students can feel the tensions of the time. These exercises will also help prepare students for the class project.

How would your students feel if people moved into their homes and claimed them? Do your students believe that no one should "own" the earth, that we are only borrowing it from nature? Or do they think that each person has a right to own territory, no matter who was using it previously (animals, plants, or other people)?

The books for this unit are:

S: *Red Hawk's Account of Custer's Last Battle* by Paul Goble
(University of Nebraska, 1969).
N: *Buffalo Hunt* by Russell Freedman (Holiday House, 1988).

❖ ACTIVITIES ❖

STORY SUMMARIES

Red Hawk's Account of Custer's Last Battle recounts the story of one of the Native Americans' greatest and last battles against the invading white men's armies. The story of this famous battle presents what might have been the Native Americans' perspective on the struggles and tragedies over territory that characterized the western expansion.

Buffalo Hunt tells of the two ways a buffalo hunt was considered: by the Plains Indians as a time to pay respect to this sacred animal; and by the white traders, who sought buffalo hides to make robes for the elite of the east coast. Within decades of the white man's arrival, the buffalo became endangered. The story of the endangerment of the buffalo is a lesson in the ways that the westward expansion indelibly affected the landscape of Native American life.

EXPLORATION: USING THE BUFFALO

To the Plains Indians tribes, the buffalo was a sacred animal, one which gave them everything they needed to survive. Tribesmen and women praised the spirit of the animal before and after every hunt, and used every part of the buffalo whenever one was slain. White settlers and traders did not share these beliefs, and reduced the buffalo population from tens of millions to a few hundred by the early 1880s. Pioneers often shot buffalo for food during their trek. Allow your students to try to be as resourceful as the Native Americans were with this animal. Divide students into cooperative groups. Have each group think of an object that the pioneers could have made from a part of a buffalo (e.g., the skin turned into a blanket, the meat used for food). Give students paper grocery bags and other art supplies to construct these items for use in their covered wagon class project. They can crease and smooth the bag a few times to create the feel of a hide.

LANGUAGE LINK: CREATING A TREATY

Divide your class into two sections. One should "live" in the classroom. The other should arrive in the classroom and claim it as their own. What is the problem here? There are two separate factions, both wanting the same land. How can your children solve the problem? They can develop a treaty, listing the rights possessed by each party. Have children take turns saying what they want for their side. Point out that if both groups claim total right to the land, they will never reach a solution. The concept is to compromise. A "scribe" can keep notes during the proceedings, and an "overseer" can call on children as they raise their hands. Once a simple treaty (no more than a couple of lines) has been drafted, both parties should sign it.

Although treaties between the Native Americans and the settlers were signed, many were never actually honored by the white people.

❖ CLASS PROJECT ❖

A COVERED WAGON

Set your students on the road to a new frontier with this covered wagon class project!

Materials:

Products from previous activities, craft knife, two Hula-Hoops, white bed sheet, refrigerator or other large box, cardboard pieces, ropes, masking tape, glue, brown and other colors of tempera paint, paintbrushes, grocery bags, newsprint, cardboard boxes, buckets and pans, miscellaneous items

Directions:

1. Place the refrigerator box on the floor on its side.
2. Cut out a front opening.
3. Use masking tape to attach one Hula-Hoop to each end of the refrigerator box.
4. Spread the sheet over the Hula-Hoops and secure with tape to make a large "canvas" wagon top.
5. Help students cut four large half-circles from cardboard for wagon wheels. (Students can paint spokes on the wheels with brown tempera paint.)
6. Wheels can be glued or taped to the sides of the wagon.
7. Inside the finished wagon, students can place materials made from "buffalo hides," plus assorted buckets, pans, and food props (paper grocery bags stuffed with crumpled newspapers and taped closed make good sacks of flour or other dry goods). Cardboard boxes make good crates to hold blankets and other miscellaneous items.

Using Your Project:

- Act out a scene from *Little House on the Prairie* with the wagon.
- Bring other classes in for a tour of the wagon.
- Have students use their lists from "Lightening the Load" as they travel. They can remove the sacks of "food," extra pots or pans, and so on as their oxen team grows weary.

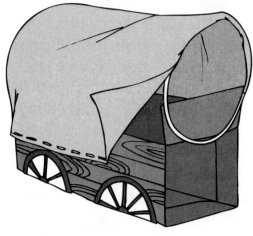

PART 4

Civil War

Many factors contributed to the Civil War. These included rivalry between the states, anti-slavery statements made by the abolitionists, and the question of whether to extend slavery into the new territories. The Union victory on April 9, 1865, was followed by the assassination of President Lincoln (on April 14th) and by the deaths of many Americans. But the Union was saved, slavery was abolished, and the seceded states were readmitted to the Union.

The issue of slavery was an important one in the Civil War. The abolitionists regarded it as an unmitigated evil while the South considered it necessary to their economy. The formation of the Republican Party with its anti-slavery platform and the election of Lincoln led to the secession of southern states and the Civil War.

Through exploration and study, you can give students a taste of the challenges that faced President Lincoln, the generals in the war, and the abolitionists. Encourage your students to discover more about the early history of our country by reading the books noted in this chapter.

Objectives:
Through the activities in this chapter, students will:
- understand the life of Abraham Lincoln and his contributions to the country;
- gain knowledge of the events of the Civil War;
- comprehend the institution of slavery and the Underground Railroad;
- demonstrate their understanding of the Civil War through the class project, a Civil War newsstand.

ABRAHAM LINCOLN

A penny for your thoughts . . .

Abraham Lincoln, the 16th president of the United States, was born in a log cabin in the backwoods and was almost entirely self-educated. In 1834 he was elected to the Illinois state legislature and in 1836 became a lawyer. He was not an abolitionist, but regarded slavery as an evil and opposed its extension.

In 1863, he moved to free the slaves by issuing the Emancipation Proclamation, but preserving the Union remained his primary objective. He was shot by John Wilkes Booth while attending a play in mid-April, 1865, and died the next morning. Your students can imagine living in a log cabin and educating themselves like Lincoln.

The activities in this section (imagining interviewing Lincoln and drawing his likeness) will prepare students for the creation of a classroom newsstand filled with news and information relating to the Civil War.

The books for this unit are:

C: *Citizen of New Salem* by Paul Horgan (Farrar, 1961).
S: *Honest Abe* by Edith Kunhardt, paintings by Malcah Zeldis (Greenwillow, 1993).
N: *Lincoln: In His Own Words* edited by Milton Meltzer, illustrated by Stephen Alcorn (Harcourt, 1993).

❖ ACTIVITIES ❖

 ## STORY SUMMARIES

Citizen of New Salem is a historical work covering the years Lincoln spent in the frontier village of New Salem, Illinois. Lincoln was 21 when he arrived, working on a boat he had navigated down the Sangamon and the Mississippi to New Orleans. He left when he was 28. This book presents a background on the frontier society from which the president-to-be drew his vision of humanity.

Lincoln: In His Own Words is a compilation of our 16th president's speeches, letters, and writings. This resource reveals the man behind the words and his unfailing dedication to the ideals upon which America was founded.

Honest Abe is a biography in storybook form told in simple words and folk art-style paintings. It relates the story of Lincoln, from his birth in a log cabin through his childhood through the many jobs that prepared him for the presidency. The Gettysburg Address appears at the end of the book.

 ## EXPLORATION: LOOKING AT LINCOLN

Give each child a penny to look at. Ask if the children know who is on the penny, and then tell them if they don't know. After children interview "Lincoln" (see below), they can draw a portrait of our 16th president by sketching his face as it appears on a shiny penny.

 ## LANGUAGE LINK: INTERVIEWING LINCOLN

After they read the different selected books, students can prepare a sheet of questions regarding Lincoln's life that they can answer. Then have them prepare to be interviewed by their classmates. Children can take turns being interviewed while the rest of the class act as reporters and take notes. Then children can prepare brief write-ups of the interview to appear in their newspaper class project. Children can accompany the interview with their "Looking at Lincoln" portraits.

Children (as Lincoln) can appear in costume. A simple hat can be made by taping a rolled and taped piece of construction paper to a construction-paper brim. Fabric or construction-paper beards are optional.

 ## RELATED BOOKS

Lincoln and the Emancipation Proclamation by Frank B. Latham (Franklin Watts, 1969).

SLAVERY

The Freedom Train.

For hundreds of years, a trade in slaves flourished between Africa and North America. Kept uneducated and without basic human rights, slaves worked under horrible conditions for generations.

By the early 19th century, slavery had disappeared in the northern United States, but it had become critical to the South's plantation system. The "Underground Railroad" developed to transfer slaves to freedom in the North.

Northern victory ended the Civil War and U.S. slavery, and Lincoln's Emancipation Proclamation, freeing the slaves in secessionist states, was followed by the 13th amendment to the Constitution.

The books for this unit are:

C: *The Slave Dancer* by Paula Fox (Bradbury Press, 1973).
N: *The Freedom Ship of Robert Smalls* by Louise Meriwether
(Prentice-Hall, 1971).
N: *Freedom Train* by Dorothy Sterling (Scholastic, 1954).
N: *Many Thousand Gone: African Americans from Slavery to Freedom* by
Virginia Hamilton, illustrated by Leo and Diane Dillon (Knopf, 1993).

❖ ACTIVITIES ❖

STORY SUMMARIES

The Slave Dancer tells the story of 13-year-old fife-playing Jessie Boiler, who is kidnapped from New Orleans and carried across the ocean to the coast of Africa. Jessie is forced to play the fife while the slaves "dance" on board to keep their bodies strong, and this tale relates his life and near death on board the "Moonlight."

The Freedom Ship of Robert Smalls is the true story of a slave who brought his family, along with 15 other runaway slaves, to freedom on a captured Confederate gunboat. Smalls became captain of the captured boat in the North's Navy, and after the war he served in Congress for five terms.

Many Thousand Gone traces the history of slavery in America, from the earliest slave trading through the growth of the Underground Railroad to the Emancipation Proclamation. Included are individual profiles of Harriet Tubman, Sojourner Truth, and Frederick Douglass.

Freedom Train is the biography of Harriet Tubman, the freed slave who transported slaves to freedom on the Underground Railroad. This book highlights the conditions of life under slavery as well as the growing differences between North and South that eventually led to the Civil War.

LANGUAGE LINK: TAKE A POSITION

Explain to your children what an editorial in a newspaper is, making sure that they understand the differences between fact and opinion. (You can start this activity by having them choose between fact and opinion on simple statements. For example: Our class has 31 students. Our class is the best class in the whole school.) Bring in some examples of editorials from your local paper. Read them together or in small groups, and have students write one sentence stating the opinion of the author.

Then have the children take a position on the issue of slavery. They can answer one of these questions: Do you think slavery should have continued in America? Would you have been willing to fight in a war to stop slavery? Why do you think the idea of slavery is good/bad? If you were a plantation owner, how would you feel about slavery? Could you think of another way for your plantation to be run? If you were a slave, would you have tried to escape on the Underground Railroad?

Have students think of supporting statements for their opinion and then write up a one-paragraph editorial answering their chosen question. They can draw a picture to illustrate their topic. These articles will be featured on the editorial page of their Civil War newspaper.

RELATED BOOKS

Rosa Parks: My Story by Rosa Parks with Jim Haskins (Dial, 1992).

THE CIVIL WAR

The night they drove Old Dixie down.

The Civil War took place between the northern states (the Union) and southern seceded states (the Confederacy) between 1861 and 1865. The election of Abraham Lincoln as president and the secession of South Carolina, soon followed by six other southern states, precipitated war. Eventually, four more states seceded, making an 11-state Confederacy. The ensuing war was the bloodiest in U.S. history.

In the war-torn society, some families were so divided on the issues that fathers were pitted against sons and brothers against brothers. What was it like to live in a nation divided? Can your students imagine believing so strongly in an issue that they would be willing to fight their own family over it?

The activities in this unit will prepare students for the class project, a classroom newsstand filled with information relating to the Civil War.

The books for this unit are:

C: *The Red Badge of Courage* by Stephen Crane (Macmillan, 1965).
S: *Tin Heart* by Karen Ackerman, (Atheneum, 1990).
N: *Civil War! America Becomes One Nation: An Illustrated History for Young Readers* by James I. Robertson, Jr. (Knopf, 1992).

❖ ACTIVITIES ❖

STORY SUMMARIES

Tin Heart is the story of two friends who live on either side of the Ohio River. Each girl wears half of a tin heart to symbolize the friendship. When the war breaks out, the girls' fathers find themselves on opposite sides, and the girls are separated. This story shows how lives and friendships were torn apart in the Civil War.

The Red Badge of Courage is the classic tale of Henry Fleming, a young man sent to fight in the Civil War. As Henry fights on the side of the Union in the Battle of Chancellorsville, readers gain insights into his internal struggles over fear, shame, indecision, and courage.

Civil War! We're going to war! the American newspapers screamed in the spring of 1861. Although both sides expected a short conflict, the war lasted for four years and resulted in a devastating slaughter. The book chronicles the story of the Blue against the Gray, brother against brother. This resource is illustrated with maps, drawings, vintage photos, and prints.

LANGUAGE LINK: NEWS FROM THE FRONT LINES

Bring in a copy of the local newspaper and let your students observe the front page. See if they can find the most important news stories. Point out the large headlines that feature the biggest breaking stories.

Once students have read (or listened to) the selected books on the Civil War, have them imagine that they are reporters on the front line, trying to relate the news of the war to the civilians at home. Have the students choose one topic to focus on, for example, a particular battle, the arrival of a famous general, the feelings of the African American troops, battles at sea, burning plantations, the way of life on the front lines, a strategy used by one side in a battle, predictions for how long the war will last, the number of casualties on a particular day, the final battle, the signing of the surrender document, the feelings of victory/defeat, hopes and fears about life after the war.

Younger students can write brief (one-paragraph) articles on their chosen topic, and illustrate the piece. Older students can write longer features, including a lead (a catchy topic sentence) and a first paragraph that includes the who, what, when, where, and how of their story.

RELATED BOOKS

The Story of Ulysses S. Grant by Jeannette Covert Nolan (Grosset & Dunlap, 1952).

A Picture Book of Robert E. Lee by David A. Adler, illustrated by John & Alexandra Wallner (Holiday House, 1994).

The Civil War by Fletcher Pratt, illustrated by Lee Ames (Doubleday, 1955).

❖ CLASS PROJECT ❖

CIVIL WAR NEWSSTAND

Extra! Extra! Read all about it! Or, *write* all about it, in the case of this group project. Turn your students into Civil War reporters. Each group of four to six students will produce their own newspaper, which can be displayed in a Classroom Civil War Newsstand at a table in the front of the classroom.

Materials:

Paper (construction and lined), products from previous exercises (Lincoln interviews, slavery editorials, and Civil War articles), black markers (for headlines), glue or tape, scissors, crayons or colored markers, rulers

Directions:

1. Have your students work in cooperative groups to plan the organization of the paper (where the articles should go, how many illustrations per page, and so on).

2. Students can vote on a name or "logo" for their newspaper, and the motto (the *New York Times* motto is "All the news that's fit to print"). If they like, they may also include on the front page the price (make sure it reflects the time of publication), the weather, the date of the issue, and the volume number.

3. Children can vote on which story to feature and write a banner (large) headline for it using a thick black marker.

4. Assembly can be as easy as cutting the hand-written articles out and gluing or taping them to the appropriate pages. Or, for fancier layouts, students can type the articles to fit specific box or line lengths. Children should make sure that their by-lines appear with their stories.

5. Illustrations from the activities should accompany the stories. If there is extra space, students can draw additional pictures. Actual photos from books such as *Civil War!* can be traced or copied to lend authenticity to the paper.

6. Additional inserts could include advertisements for products of the time (elixirs, bayonets, tooth powders). Obituaries and wedding and birth announcements could appear, along with sports features and news from England.

7. Don't forget a staff box listing all of the contributors and their jobs on the paper!

Using Your Project:

- Photocopy the papers and distribute to parents, other classes, and teachers.
- Allow each group to read and compare all the newspapers.
- Send a copy of the papers to the local newspaper office.

PART 5

American Mosaic

What makes the United States truly unique in the world? Our diversity of cultures, races, and religions forms the American "mosaic." While our differences can be a source of conflict, they also enrich nearly every part of our lives. And when we appreciate and respect all of the many cultures living in the U.S., the results can be magnificent.

In this unit, you can build on the diversity of your own classroom. Many of your students' families will have stories of immigration to share. Others will have traditional recipes to delight your class' palate. And everyone can share a bit of his or her heritage with the class.

What better way to demonstrate our ethnic pride than by putting it on display! The class project for this chapter is a Living Museum, in which students lead other students, parents, and teachers through exhibits they've created.

Objectives:
Through the activities in this chapter, students will:
- understand the process of immigration in the late 19th century;
- appreciate the diversity of communities represented in their classroom;
- learn about the challenges of living in a diverse society.

IMMIGRATION

Give me your huddled masses . . .

Immigration is a unifying experience for families of many ethnic backgrounds. Fleeing persecution or searching for a more prosperous life, millions upon millions of immigrants have arrived in the United States.

The process of entry has never been an easy one. Whether stuck at sea with meager rations, subjected to months of detention in the barracks at Angel Island, or ostracized in their new home, immigrants have endured many hardships while trying to claim their rightful place in this land.

The stories and activities in this unit will allow students to share the immigration experiences of some families as well as simulate that difficult process themselves.

The books for this unit are:

C: *Dragonwings* by Laurence Yep (HarperCollins, 1975).
A Newbery Honor Book.
S: *Soon, Annala* by Riki Levinson (Orchard Books, 1993).
N: *Ellis Island* by Leonard Everett Fisher (Holiday House, 1986).

❖ ACTIVITIES ❖

STORY SUMMARIES

In *Ellis Island*, the famous New York port of entry during the large wave of immigration between 1860 and 1880 stands as a monument to the sacrifices new Americans made for freedom and economic opportunity. From 1892 to 1943 the island also served as America's busiest immigrant port of entry. With its photographs and drawings, this book will give students an insider's look into the Ellis Island station.

Dragonwings is the story of Moon Shadow, an eight-year-old boy who moves from China to San Francisco at the turn of the century. When his dream, to create a flying machine, is realized, he names the machine Dragonwings. This book provides excellent insight into the Chinese American immigrant experience.

In *Soon, Annala*, Annala's father repeats the title words as the two stand on the docks waiting for Annala's two younger brothers to arrive from Ellis Island. Anna, a native Yiddish speaker, has been learning English in her new home, and cannot wait to teach her brothers her new language.

EXPLORATION: IMMIGRATION STATIONS

Ellis and Angel Islands are signposts of America's most dramatic era of immigration. Using *Ellis Island* and other resource books, draw a floor plan for a model station. Using art supplies, children can make number tags to put on applicants waiting for inspection. They can assist you in making a medical inspection table, a baggage area, a banner reading "Immigration Station," and tags for marking those with health problems (H= heart problem, T= tuberculosis).

Set aside rows of chairs to be a waiting area, and designate an interview table. At this table, a student (or pair of students) can ask fellow students the following battery of questions: What is your name? Can you read and write? Are you married? Do you have children, and if so, where are they? Have you ever been in jail? Have you ever been sick? How do you feel now? How did you earn a living in the old country? How will you earn a living here? Do you have a job in America? Is someone coming to meet you? How much money do you have? Can I see it?

Those who "pass" the interview should be given a "landing card." Those who do not will be told that they will be "sent back to their old country." Be sure to have your students occasionally misspell an applicant's name, or change it, as immigration officials actually did!

RELATED BOOKS

The Story of the Statue of Liberty by Betsy & Giulio Maestro (Lothrop, 1986).

COMMUNITIES

Chinatown. Little Italy. The Barrio.

Ethnic enclaves such as these form the heart of the American ethnic mosaic. Sometimes pushed into communities by a hostile larger society, sometimes settling together out of familiarity with Old World ways, ethnic communities give our country a remarkable richness.

In this chapter, students get a window on the world of several ethnic communities. By contributing to their project they will get to sample the cuisines of their neighbors as well as share in each other's family history. Both activities will contribute to the Living Museum class project.

The books for this unit are:

C: . . . *and now Miguel* by Joseph Krumgold (Harper Collins, 1953).
A Newbery Award winner.
S: *Everybody Cooks Rice* by Norah Dooley (Carolrhoda Books, 1991).
S: *Tar Beach* by Faith Ringgold (Crown Publishers, 1991).

❖ ACTIVITIES ❖

STORY SUMMARIES

In *Tar Beach*, the roof of Cassie's apartment building in New York, which she has dubbed "Tar Beach," is where she spends hot summer nights. When her wish to fly comes true, we are treated to a bird's-eye-view tour of her community.

Everybody Cooks Rice is both the title of the book and what the narrator discovers when he is sent out into his neighborhood to bring his brother home for dinner. Each family he visits is of a different ethnicity and each cooks rice in their own unique way. This book includes recipes for the rice dishes it highlights.

. . . and now Miguel is the story of 12-year-old Miguel Chavez, a Mexican American boy living in New Mexico. His dream, to go on a long sheep drive with the adults in his family, comes true, but not without many adventures. This story provides a personal window on a community of the southwest.

EXPLORATION: FAMILY MOBILE

Make mobiles to show each student's family history! Have students research the names, dates of birth (and death, as appropriate), and place of origin of each of their grandparents, parents, and siblings, as well as themselves. Have them write the information on index cards and punch holes in the tops and bottoms of each. Using paper clips, hook the earliest generation to a clothes hanger, and hang the others in place.

LITERATURE LINK: RECIPE ROUND-UP

Everybody cooks . . . differently! You can show off the delicious variety of foods from your students' communities by featuring ethnic foods. Have students record a favorite family recipe at home. (Use any cookbook to provide students with a model of a recipe.) Compile the recipes into a cookbook, and have students bring in samples of these dishes to make a buffet. If students' families don't have a recipe to share, they can use one from *Everybody Cooks Rice*.

GETTING ALONG

Can't we all just get along?

The diversity of the American people has led to great achievement as well as many problems. Despite attempts to establish equality among all citizens, prejudice and discrimination are a mainstay of American history.

What has this meant for people who live in the U.S.? The books featured in this chapter all demonstrate the effects of intolerance on our lives. Some of the stories have happy endings. Others do not. They all remind us that while we cannot rewrite our history, we always have the chance to create a better future—one that tomorrow's students will read about with pride.

The books for this unit are:

C: *A Jar of Dreams* by Yoshiko Uchida (Atheneum, 1981).
S: *Baseball Saved Us* by Ken Mochizuki (Lee and Low Books, 1993).
Parents' Choice Award winner.
S: *Leagues Apart* by Lawrence S. Ritter (William Morrow, 1995).

❖ ACTIVITIES ❖

STORY SUMMARIES

In *Baseball Saved Us*, Shorty and his family are Japanese Americans forced into internment camps during World War II. To combat the humiliation and boredom of their imprisonment, Shorty and his friends organize a Little League inside the camp. Once out of the camps, Shorty again finds baseball to be a savior in his relations in a prejudiced society.

Leagues Apart tells of the time before 1947, when African American baseball players were excluded from mainstream baseball leagues. The "Negro Leagues" gave great African American baseball players a chance to compete. Without them, professional baseball would not be what it is today.

A Jar of Dreams is the story of 11-year-old Rinko, who has a lot to dream about. Growing up a Japanese American during the Depression is difficult, especially when people in your town won't stop bothering you because you are different. When Rinko's aunt comes from Japan, Rinko begins to take pride in her heritage.

EXPLORATION: POSTER/ESSAY CONTEST

Provide writing materials and art materials for students to use to design posters and write accompanying essays to answer the question "Can we get along? If so, how? If not, why not?" Children could look at society as a whole, at their local environment, or at smaller, more easily accessible areas in their own lives. For example, they could focus on whether children of different nationalities get along on the playground, or on the bus, or in the classroom. Display the posters and essays at your museum. Confer an award on each entry, for example, Most Colorful, Most Imaginative, Most Practical, Most Serious, and so on.

LANGUAGE LINK: MUSEUM BROCHURE

Provide children with paper and crayons or markers to use to design brochures for the class project museum. The brochures should show the history of American ethnic relations that your students have studied. Children can introduce the museum exhibits in the brochure by charting immigration history, discussing ethnic communities, and highlighting points of tension and cooperation between communities. The brochures might also include the names of the children who work on the museum, as well as a thank you to parents or friends who assist (by cooking, donating their time, and so on).

41

❖ CLASS PROJECT ❖

A LIVING MUSEUM OF AMERICAN HERITAGE

Your students can show off both their knowledge and their ethnic pride in a living museum!

Materials:

All products from past lessons, name tags, schedule of classes coming to view museum, rope, masking tape

Directions:

Several days before:

- Have students make and post posters around the school that promote your museum.
- Invite other teachers to visit with their classes.
- Have students make and distribute invitations for parents and other family members.
- Have students make and distribute invitations for school administrators.
- Designate museum-visit roles: greeters, docents, museum security, ushers.
- Have students design a floor plan for the museum.

The day before or the day of the museum opening:

- Assemble the museum exhibits: immigration station, ethnic foods buffet, mobiles.
- Rope off areas that shouldn't be touched.
- Put a masking tape dotted path on the floor.
- Put out the museum brochure for visitors' information.

The day of the museum opening:

- Bring classes and other visitors through your museum.
- Have fun!

Using Your Project:

- Videotape your museum to show at other gatherings.
- Have students write a review of the museum exhibits.

PART 6

American Ingenuity

The past 150 years have brought us many advancements, from the days of the Pony Express to the days of *overnight* express. Because of such great minds as Alexander Graham Bell, we are able to talk to people easily in almost every part of the world. In a matter of minutes (or seconds) we can send messages via fax or e-mail.

Because of inventors such as Wilbur and Orville Wright, who refused to believe naysayers who stated that air travel was still 1,000 years in the future, not only can we send information quickly, we can send *ourselves* quickly. These advancements are all results of American ingenuity.

Through exploration and study, you can give students a chance to fly on a plane with the Wright brothers, drive a car with Henry Ford, and zoom to the moon with the astronauts. And, when children use their imaginations, they can travel beyond the planets, beyond the solar system, and into the future! Who knows what awaits us in the next century!

Encourage your students to discover more about American ingenuity by reading the books noted in this chapter. The activities will give depth to the class project, a time machine.

Objectives:
Through the activities in this chapter, students will:
- develop an understanding of the technological advancements of our time;
- learn about the present state of American ingenuity;
- stretch the imagination to encompass the future!

TRANSPORTATION

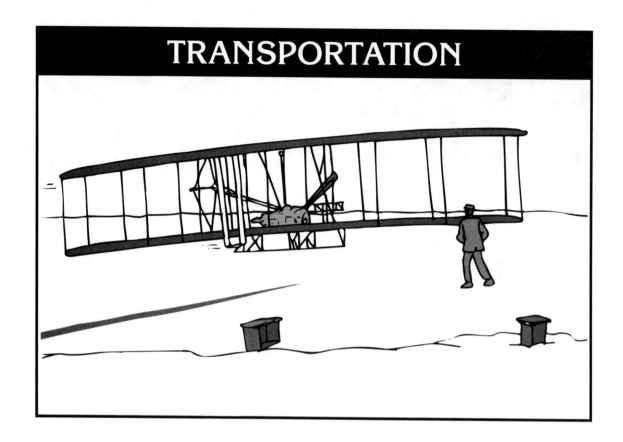

Row, row, row your boat . . .

. . . to your job working on the railroad! Or ride to school on a bus with wheels that go 'round and 'round. Children know many songs about transportation, and the songs refer to the many different types of vehicles that exist.

Have students brainstorm the types of vehicles that they (and their families) use to get around: bikes, buses, cars, trains, trolleys, trucks, planes, boats, and so on (American ingenuity has made many of these vehicles possible). Now have the children imagine that none of these devices exists. What would they do if they wanted to get from one place to another? They could ride on an animal. (But what type?) They could walk.

Some of the books in this unit describe the vehicles that take people places, and how these vehicles came to be. Other books are more fanciful, describing the types of creations we may someday see in the future. All will help students prepare to make a time machine for the class project.

The books for this unit are:

N: *One Giant Leap* written and illustrated by Mary Ann Fraser (Holt, 1993).
N: *The Wright Brothers: How They Invented the Airplane*
by Russell Freedman (Holiday House, 1991).
N: *We'll Race You, Henry: A Story About Henry Ford* by Barbara Mitchell
(Carolrhoda, 1986).

❖ ACTIVITIES ❖

STORY SUMMARIES

The Wright Brothers tells the story of two brothers from Ohio who created and flew the world's first powered, sustained, and controlled airplane near Kitty Hawk, North Carolina, in 1903. This book has photographs taken by the brothers of their planes, the flights, and themselves.

We'll Race You, Henry is about Henry Ford's fascination with "horseless" riding machines, a fascination that began in 1876 and lasted his entire life. This book features the origins of the Model T, as well as the daring side of its inventor and the early days of automobile racing.

One Giant Leap has a running clock of the 1969 moon landing, featuring the astronauts, the ground crew at NASA, and the *Columbia* and *Eagle* ships.

EXPLORATION: CREATE A CAR (OR BOAT, OR PLANE, OR . . .)

Have your students imagine that there are no transportational devices (aside from walking). How would they get around? What type of transportation would they want? Give each child a piece of paper and crayons or markers to design the ultimate traveling machine. The creations should list all of the features. For example, a child could make a car that flies, a bike that does chores, or a rocket that can go to the moon in an afternoon. What would each invention need to be brought to completion? Who could the children contact to help them with information for their project? (The Wright brothers wrote to the Smithsonian Institution in 1899 and requested "all that is already known" about flight experiments.)

LANGUAGE LINK: INTERVIEW A TRAVELER

Ask your students to list the transportation vehicles that they have traveled in. Then have them find another person (in the class or school, a parent at home, etc.) who has traveled in a vehicle that they have not. For example, a child could interview someone who has ridden in an airplane, a train, a hovercraft, a trolley car, a motorcycle, and so on. Have children write up the interview and present it to the class. Ask the writer if he or she would like to someday ride on the same vehicle. Children can also read biographies of famous inventors or travelers and write fictionalized interviews with them.

RELATED BOOKS

Young Orville and Wilbur Wright by Andrew Woods (Troll, 1992).
Wilbur and Orville Wright by Louis Sabin (Troll, 1983).
Workin' on the Railroad by Richard Reinhardt (American West, 1970).
Hello, Alexander Graham Bell Speaking by Cynthia Copeland Lewis (Dillon, 1991).

INTO THE FUTURE

R is for rocket . . .

What will life be like in the 21st century. . . or beyond? Children can imagine a future filled with flying machines and super-speed trains. Or perhaps they'll visualize a time when people can transmit themselves by thoughts alone.

The books noted in this unit give examples of how some authors envision the future. After reading them, the students can decide whether they would like to live in these future worlds or create their own futures. Do they think that the types of inventions they read about are possible? Remind your students of the fact that in the past 100 years, many inventions have been created that their great-grandparents would not have been able to comprehend (a craft that could fly to and land on the moon, a device that sends video-pictures during phone calls, and so on).

The books for this unit are:

C: *The Time Machine* by H.G. Wells, adapted by Les Martin
(Random House, 1990).
C: *2095* by Jon Scieszka, illustrated by Lane Smith (Viking, 1995).
S: *The Magic Rocket* by Steven Kroll, illustrated by Will Hillenbrand
(Holiday House, 1992).

❖ ACTIVITIES ❖

STORY SUMMARIES

2095 tells of the adventures of the "Time Warp Trio" when they arrive in a futuristic New York City.

The Time Machine tells of the Time Traveler who finds himself in the year 802,700—with everything changed. The Time Traveler plans to study the creatures who seem to dwell together in perfect harmony, unearth their secret, and then return to his own time—until he discovers that the Time Machine has been stolen.

The Magic Rocket is the story of a little boy named Felix who is thrilled when he gets a toy rocket for his birthday. It's long and thin and gold, it has three booster engines and a shiny cockpit, and it glows mysteriously when Felix looks at it. But even more wonderful—Felix can fly! His space journey takes him into contact with aliens when he rescues his pet dog Atom.

LANGUAGE LINK: LETTER FROM THE FUTURE

Have your students imagine that they are Time Travelers, beamed to some future time—perhaps the year 802,700—but with the ability to write to their friends back home. What would they want to say? What would the future look like? Give each child a large (8"x 5") index card, crayons, and writing materials. Have them draw a picture of a future city (perhaps with glowing silver buildings), future school, future environment (red sun, no trees?) as they see it. Then have them turn the card over (so that the picture is upside-down), and write on the lined side their impression of the future. Are they happy in their new environment, or would they like to return to their old life? What would they change about the future? What do they miss about the past? Post the completed cards on a bulletin board using "hinges," so that observers can look at the pictures, then lift the cards and read the backs.

RELATED BOOKS:

R Is for Rocket by Ray Bradbury (Doubleday, 1962).

Robert Goddard: Trail Blazer to the Stars by Charles Michael Daugherty (Macmillan, 1964).

Women in Space: Reaching the Last Frontier by Carole S. Briggs (Lerner, 1988).

Transportation in the World of the Future by Hal Hellman (M. Evans, 1974).

Chuck Yeager: The Man Who Broke the Sound Barrier by Nancy Smiler Levinson (Walker, 1988).

❖ CLASS PROJECT ❖

TIME MACHINE

Materials:

Refrigerator box (or other very large cardboard box), tempera paints, paintbrushes, assorted lids (from juice bottles, jelly jars, etc.), glue, aluminum foil, scissors, tape, battery-operated pocket calculator, masking tape, craft knife (for teacher use only)

Directions:

1. Explain to the children that they will be making a time machine to take them to any place and any time (using their imaginations).

2. Provide materials for children to use to decorate the machine. Assist them by cutting out windows or doors where they would like.

3. Children can make dials and control panels by gluing assorted lids and juice tops to the inside of the machine. Aluminum foil adds to the sci-fi look.

4. When the machine is completed, use masking tape to fasten a lightweight pocket calculator to one of the time machine's walls. Children can enter the date of the year they wish to travel to by pressing the appropriate numbers.

Using Your Project:

- Invite other classes to see the time machine.
- Have children choose a year that you have already studied, for example, 1776. When they "arrive" back in time, they can use their previously learned knowledge to act like the people in this time. (They could travel back in time to the Civil War, the Explorer age, the Colonial period, and so on.)

Options:

- Play music while children work on the project, such as the theme from "2001."
- Use this opportunity to teach about the planets. Children can cut out replicas of the planets to hang from clothesline strung across the classroom. "Time Travelers" can look out the windows in the time machine to see the planets.